Justice Kennedy's Jurisprudence

Justice Kennedy's Jurisprudence

THE FULL AND NECESSARY MEANING OF LIBERTY

Frank J. Colucci

 University Press of Kansas

© 2009 by the University Press of Kansas
All rights reserved

Published by the University Press of Kansas (Lawrence, Kansas 66045),
which was organized by the Kansas Board of Regents and is operated
and funded by Emporia State University, Fort Hays State University,
Kansas State University, Pittsburg State University, the University of
Kansas, and Wichita State University

Library of Congress Cataloging-in-Publication Data
Colucci, Frank J.
Justice Kennedy's jurisprudence : the full and necessary meaning of
liberty / Frank J. Colucci.
    p. cm.
Includes bibliographical references and index.
ISBN 978-0-7006-1662-6 (cloth : alk. paper)
1. Kennedy, Anthony M., 1936– 2. Civil rights—United States. I. Title.
KF4749.C6425   2009
342.7308'5—dc22
2009011964

British Library Cataloguing-in-Publication Data is available.

Printed in the United States of America

10 9 8 7 6 5 4 3 2 1

The paper used in this publication is recycled and contains 30 percent
postconsumer waste. It is acid free and meets the minimum
requirements of the American National Standard for Permanence of
Paper for Printed Library Materials z39.48-1992.

To my parents

Contents

Preface

Like most observers of the U.S. Supreme Court over the past two decades, I have been struck by the formation of two four-justice blocs with opposing approaches to constitutional interpretation and the increasing number of cases decided by a 5–4 vote. Justice Anthony M. Kennedy has often cast the pivotal vote across a wide range of areas in constitutional law—from abortion to religion to federalism to executive power to free speech and affirmative action. Although appointed by President Ronald Reagan in 1987 after Robert Bork's rejection by the U.S. Senate and Douglas Ginsburg's withdrawal, in many high-profile cases Kennedy has departed from ideologically conservative positions. Understanding his approach is thus critical to understanding the current, closely divided Court.

Given Kennedy's apparent ideological flexibility, it is not surprising that he has been the object of criticism in both the popular press and academic literature. Journalists have variously characterized him as an agonizer, a flip-flopper, an instrument of his clerks, a sphinx, and an arrogant judge bent on maximizing his power. Kennedy's own actions have helped to fuel these negative perceptions. He has disclaimed any larger approach to constitutional interpretation, changed his votes on several high-profile issues, repudiated past votes without sufficient explanation, and attempted to court the media. Scholars fault his opinions as (at best) incompletely theorized, characterizing his approach to judicial decision-making as inconsistent, unprincipled, undefined, or confused.

In this book I challenge these prevailing popular and scholarly interpretations of Kennedy. Although my focus is on the body of the Supreme Court opinions he has written over the past twenty terms across several areas of constitutional law, I also examine the opinions he wrote during his prior service on the Ninth Circuit U.S. Court of Appeals and review transcripts of public speeches that he delivered before his nomination to the Supreme Court, as well as his confirmation proceedings. I gained further insight from information drawn from the papers of Harry A. Blackmun.

I argue that Kennedy employs a consistent jurisprudence based on what he considers the "full and necessary meaning" of liberty. In method, Kennedy's approach shares much with the moral reading of the Constitution championed by theorist Ronald Dworkin and former justice William J. Brennan as well as with the "presumption of liberty" advocated, more recently, by libertarian law professor Randy Barnett. Kennedy's expansive conception of liberty and his willingness to use judicial power to enforce it make him the justice most likely to strike actions of federal and state governments on constitutional grounds. In substance, Kennedy seeks to reconcile his conception of personal liberty and human dignity with the social, political, economic, and jurisprudential legacies of a post-Warren Court and a post–New Deal America.

While generally sympathetic to Kennedy's record, I criticize his decisions in some areas of law. In others—even when I agree with his result—I either disagree with his reasoning or regret his grandiose rhetoric. Overall, however, I find Kennedy to be someone who struggles to separate his personal beliefs from his official duty to enforce the limitations established by the Constitution. More fundamentally, his jurisprudence seeks to bring considerations of personal liberty to the forefront of constitutional interpretation. I hope this study contributes to a more informed understanding of Kennedy's arguments about the nature of human liberty and the proper role of courts in defining and enforcing it.

In writing this book, I have incurred many debts. I must begin by thanking Donald Kommers, Walter Nicgorski, Sotirios Barber, and Michael Zuckert at the University of Notre Dame for their support in the early stages of this project. Professors Kommers and Zuckert have given especially valuable continued advice and support.

I have many to thank for their assistance during the research and writing process. I acquired transcripts of Kennedy's public addresses from the National Archives; Bill Davis's assistance was critical. I appreciate the access to the Blackmun and Marshall Papers at the Manuscript Room of the Library of Congress in Washington and the assistance that I received from the staff there. I greatly benefited from participation in a Summer Institute sponsored by the Supreme Court Historical Society and the Institute of Constitutional Studies led by Larry Kramer and Gordon Wood. Purdue University Calumet, my home institution, has also provided generous support, including a summer research grant that helped me complete the first draft of the book manuscript and release time that allowed me to make final revisions.

I greatly appreciate the close reading of reviewers Thomas Keck and Kenneth Kersch. Their detailed comments helped me to produce a more concise and focused manuscript. The staff at the University Press of Kansas—especially Susan Schott and Jennifer Dropkin—saved me from many embarrassing mistakes. Fred Woodward provided substantial assistance, advice, and patience.

I also have many more personal acknowledgments of gratitude. I'd like to thank Ryan Strode, Brenda Cheeks, Laura Lee, Angelo Cicco, Vincent Stark, and Kasey Swanke for their assistance during the preparation of this book. I appreciate the support of my colleagues at Purdue Calumet, especially Craig Hammond, Mita Choudhury, Tanya Stabler, Richard Rupp, Meg Rincker, Miriam Joyce, Joe Bigott, and Susan VanTil. I must also thank Brendan Dunn, Jarrett Carty, Kevin Cherry, and Geoff Bowden for the numerous helpful e-mails.

Most important, I would like to acknowledge the support of my family, including my grandparents Jean and Pat, my brother Michael, and my sisters Karen and Sue. Finally, I dedicate this book to my parents, Frank and Linda, who have been wondering what I have been doing for all of these years.

Introduction

I do not have an over-arching theory, a unitary theory of
interpretation. I am searching, as I think many judges are,
for the correct balance in constitutional interpretation.
  —CONFIRMATION TESTIMONY (1987)

Justice Anthony M. Kennedy has assumed a critical yet underexamined role on the current U.S. Supreme Court. Since arriving in 1988, he has been in the majority more than any other justice.[1] His votes in areas across constitutional law can be categorized as uniformly neither liberal nor conservative. He has written more than his share of important majority opinions—often for a closely divided Court[2]—and his separate concurring opinions limit and re-fine doctrine announced by the majority.[3] During the 2006–2007 term, Kennedy was in the majority in all twenty-four cases decided by a 5–4 vote.[4] Journalists and scholars have long recognized his key role.[5] Some say his influence is so profound that the current Court should be considered the Kennedy Court.[6]

Understanding Kennedy's approach to judicial decision-making is essential to understanding the current Court. Yet commentary on Kennedy tends to focus more on the votes he casts than on the opinions he writes. In contrast to scholarship that explores the interpretive approaches of other justices, studies of Kennedy primarily investigate his voting record to determine the extent to which he forms part of a centrist bloc on the Court[7] or whether he has voted consistently in specific areas such as federalism, homosexual rights, abortion, or the First Amendment.[8] Some try to extrapolate Kennedy's broader constitutional vision from one or a handful of opinions.[9]

No one, however, has yet surveyed the larger body of Kennedy's writings to determine whether he applies a consistent approach to constitutional interpretation. The general consensus—usually offered in the course of discussing other topics—is that Kennedy "does not have a consistent judicial philosophy to guide his decision making,"[10] or that he has, "to say the least, an undeveloped mushy legal philosophy."[11] Others argue that he applies competing interpretive strategies,[12] is "a legal pragmatist" who "goes case by case,"[13] or is "content simply to advance policy preferences through advocacy of conservative outcomes."[14] Some say Kennedy occasionally displays "an un-predictable streak of libertarianism";[15] while others find his jurisprudence an example of moderate libertarianism.[16] Kennedy has been called a profile in caprice,[17] someone who "trims his jurisprudential sails to what he perceives to be the prevailing political winds," and a "sphinx."[18] Although one recent empirical study finds Kennedy to be among the most ideologically consistent justices,[19] another asserts that "the more closely one examines Kennedy's Supreme Court jurisprudence, the more confused one becomes."[20]

Kennedy himself initially disclaimed any larger theory of constitutional interpretation. At his Supreme Court confirmation hearings, he testified:

> It is somewhat difficult for me to offer myself as someone with a complete cosmology of the Constitution. I do not have an over-arching theory, a unitary theory of interpretation. I am searching, as I think many judges are, for the correct balance in constitutional interpretation. So many of the things we are discussing here are, for me, in the nature of exploration and not the enunciation of some fixed or immutable ideas.[21]

Kennedy asserted that constitutional interpretation should move beyond all-encompassing theories. "The imperatives of judicial restraint," he said in a speech prior to his nomination, "spring from the Constitution itself, not from a particular judicial theory."[22] "I am not sure how you can be satisfied that a judge will not overstep the constitutional bounds," Kennedy testified. "What you must do is, number one, examine the judge's record—document his or her qualifications and commitment to constitutional rule."[23]

Kennedy's disavowal of interpretive theory included rejecting an original-ist jurisprudence based on text, history, and specific tradition professed by, among others, Justice Antonin Scalia.[24] Kennedy stated that a judicial duty exists to find the true meaning of the "spacious phrases" of the Constitution and Bill of Rights. Original intent thus "is best conceived of as an objective rather than a methodology." Previewing a later move in legal scholarship from original intent to original public meaning, Kennedy stated in 1987 that the relevant study involves investigation of the Founders' public words, "the legal consequence of what they did . . . not their subjective motivations." Though "it is highly relevant what the framers thought," Kennedy said, "the general inquiry, the principal inquiry, should be on the official purpose, the official intent"—the "institutional intent" indicated in the text eventually ratified. As he stated elsewhere, "the framers of the Constitution would not have used such spacious phrases as due process, cruel and unusual punishment or equal protection of the laws, if they had thought otherwise."[25]

Given Kennedy's initial self-portrayal, Cass Sunstein's concept of judicial minimalism suggests one explanatory framework. Sunstein describes minimalists as judges who "seek to avoid broad rules and abstract theory, in an attempt to focus their attention only on what is necessary to resolve particular disputes." Minimalists "operate against an agreed-upon background," begin with "a 'core' of agreement about constitutional essentials," and "tend to use abstractions only to the extent necessary to resolve a controversy." [26] According to Sunstein, Sandra Day O'Connor embraced judicial minimalism,[27] and at times he includes Kennedy in this category. Yet Sunstein has difficulty classifying Kennedy's jurisprudence as consistently minimalist.[28]

Prior to coming to the Court, however, Kennedy did express the core of an alternate interpretive approach, one based on the broad moral value of individual liberty. "The framers had . . . a very important idea when they used the word 'person' and when they used the word 'liberty,'" Kennedy testified. "And these words have content in the history of Western thought and in the history of our law and in the history of our Constitution, and I think judges can give that content." Judges thus have the responsibility "to insure that the word liberty in the Constitution is given its full and necessary meaning, consistent with the purposes of the document as we understand it."[29]

Kennedy criticized judges who "often make a quick bow to the words and text and then go off into this mass of precedents in which we have normative rules of vast dimension, and begin announcing the law." The self-aware judge must determine whether the moral principles embodied in the Constitution "extend . . . to situations not previously addressed by the courts, to protections not previously announced by the courts."[30] That duty may not always be clearly marked by text, history, or precedent, but "uncertainty over precise standards of interpretation does not justify failing in the attempt to construct them, and still less does it justify flagrant departures."[31]

In outlining the judicial role to enforce liberty, Kennedy transcends history, text, and tradition by appealing to extraconstitutional moral ideals. "Essentially," he testified, "we look to the concept of individuality and liberty and dignity that those who drafted the Constitution understood."[32] Kennedy engages in a substantive consideration of whether the government action challenged in the case violates "the essentials of the right to human dignity, the injury to person," or whether such action results in "the inability of the person to manifest his or her own personality, the inability of a person to obtain his or her self-fulfillment, the inability of a person to reach his or her own potential" (180).

Kennedy also reads history differently than originalists do. Popular acceptance of Supreme Court decisions depends "on the perception by the people that the Court is being faithful to a compact that was made 200 years ago." Without "some historical link to the ideas of the framers," then the legitimacy of the ruling "is in some doubt" (86, 141). Historical study alone, however, cannot provide answers. The Constitution, he wrote, "cannot be divorced from its logic and language, the intention of its framers, the precedents of the law, and the shared traditions and historic values of our people."[33] Kennedy further suggested that present-day Americans can gain a better understanding of what the Constitution means than the Framers themselves had. "I think 200 years of history gives a magnificent perspective on what the framers did intend," Kennedy testified. "Over time the intentions of the Framers are more remote from their particular political concerns and so they have a certain purity and a certain generality now that they did not have previously" (183–184).

According to Kennedy, the "ultimate objective" of constitutional interpretation does not require strict adherence to precedent or to the most specific level of tradition. Rather, it requires judges to exercise their own independent judgment about how best to enforce the principles and structure of the Constitution. "The object of our inquiry," he testified, "is to use history, the case law and our understanding of the American constitutional tradition in order to determine the intention of the document broadly expressed" (192, 86). Judges have the choice to describe "what was" or "what is," Kennedy wrote, but they "must never fail to ask what the law ought to be." And no formalistic approach to constitutional interpretation can define this effort. "While it is unlikely that we will devise a conclusive formula for reasoning in constitutional cases," Kennedy stated, "we have the obligation to confront the consequences of our interpretation, or the lack of it."[34] As he later put it after several years on the Court, judges must "continue to ask whether the results they achieve are yielding real and substantial justice."[35]

Kennedy thus rejects originalism and accepts a judicial role to discover the true nature of the substantive moral ideals stated in the text of the Constitution.[36] According to Kennedy, "the whole lesson of our constitutional experience has been that a people can rise above its own injustices, that a people can rise above the inequities that prevail at a particular time" (149). The Fourteenth Amendment—and the Constitution as a whole—"has far more validity and far more breadth than simply what someone thought they were doing at the time." Although "it sometimes takes humans generations to become aware of the moral consequences, or the immoral consequences, of their own conduct," Kennedy testified, "that does not mean that moral principles have not remained the same" (153).

In this book I argue that Kennedy, properly understood, is neither a profile in caprice nor a judicial minimalist. Rather, his opinions exhibit consistent, distinctive assumptions about how judges should interpret the Constitution and about the substantive values of liberty and human dignity its provisions protect. He rejects originalism and employs a moral reading of the Constitution similar in approach to that taken by liberals like Ronald Dworkin or Justice William Brennan. Kennedy, however, uses that interpretive method to enforce individual liberty, not equality, as the moral idea he finds central to the Constitution. His approach in rhetoric and substance shares many similarities with the presumption of liberty recently advocated by Randy Barnett, including a judicial duty to "protect all the rights retained by the people equally whether enumerated or unenumerated." In practice, however, Kennedy accepts more of the social, economic, and legal changes brought about after the New Deal than Barnett does.[37]

I follow the methodology of other recent studies of sitting justices.[38] Following Sue Davis, who wrote about Chief Justice William H. Rehnquist, I seek to move beyond studies of voting behavior to analyze a justice's "legal philosophy by utilizing his judicial opinions or papers with the goal of understanding his methods and values and the way they translate into judicial decisions."[39] During his confirmation testimony, Kennedy professed to hold no unitary theory of constitutional interpretation and disavowed theoretical and philosophical thought. Nevertheless, his jurisprudence rests on basic understandings of the nature of personal liberty and the scope of judicial power. Those understandings may appear "incompletely theorized"[40] in one or another of his opinions, but they have visible roots in opinions, speeches, and testimony he delivered before coming to the Court.[41] In this judicial study[42] I focus on Kennedy's record on the Supreme Court, his previous service on the Ninth Circuit, and his off-the-bench statements and confirmation testimony.[43] I also employ the contemporary confirmation of his behavior and motivations documented in the papers of his colleagues, particularly Justice Harry A. Blackmun.[44] I examine whether Kennedy's opinions are shaped by a consistent vision of personal liberty—his larger idea of "real and substantial justice"—and compare that vision of judicial power to those of other current justices.[45]

This study of Kennedy's jurisprudence proposes an alternate explanation of the vote that determines the direction of the current, divided Court. Kennedy's individualistic conception of liberty often leads him to vote the same way as originalist justices, but for different reasons. In many high-profile cases, this ideal has led him to depart from them to expand judicial power. In 1984, Kennedy described himself as a judge "unlikely to accept doctrines which substantially expand the role of courts."[46] Yet on a Supreme Court considered by some the most activist in history, Kennedy has been the justice most likely to strike state and congressional actions for violating the Constitution.[47] Similar tensions within the Court and within conservative constitutional thought have recently received a great deal of scrutiny. For both political and theoretical reasons, Kennedy's jurisprudential approach deserves further scholarly attention.

I explore Kennedy's moral vision of constitutional liberty and his argument for expanding judicial power to enforce it. In Chapter 1 I examine the ideals of individual liberty and dignity that have driven his opinions in cases involving school prayer, homosexual rights, and the death penalty. I use these cases to outline the basis of Kennedy's vision of judicial power and trace similarities between his interpretive approach and those advocated by Dworkin and Barnett. In addition, I probe Kennedy's substantive ideal of human personality; his citations of international law, political consensus, and social science research; and some likely roots of his rhetoric in Catholic thought.

In Chapter 2 I focus on Kennedy's abortion jurisprudence. Despite expressing unease about *Roe v. Wade* during his early tenure, Kennedy voted to reaffirm its core holding in *Planned Parenthood v. Casey*. He has since attempted to offer a "reasoned, careful balance" to reconcile his broad constitutional commitment to liberty with a government interest in promoting profound respect for fetal life. As the rhetoric of his 2007 opinion upholding a federal ban on partial-birth abortion illustrates, nearly twenty years after his admission in chambers to Harry Blackmun, Kennedy is "still struggling" to articulate this balance.

Chapter 3 explores how Kennedy's ideals of personal and political liberty explain his expansive conception of free speech. On the Court, Kennedy has voted most often to strike government action for violating free speech in a variety of contexts—from political speech to commercial speech to sexually themed speech. He protects speech claims based on an ideal that individuals have the right to determine for themselves the ideas worthy of consideration, expression, and allegiance. At the same time, Kennedy seeks to expand First Amendment speech and association to justify judicial involvement into other areas of constitutional law often considered political questions.

In chapters 4 and 5 I consider how Kennedy recasts other questions of constitutional law in terms of liberty in order to justify a broad judicial role. In Chapter 4, I analyze Kennedy's substantive ideal of equality as neutral individualism. Consistent with his core approach to judicial power, Kennedy rephrases questions of equality in the language of personal liberty and human dignity. Although his substantive conception of personality often leads him to vote with justices who espouse the color-blind Constitution, Kennedy applies individualistic principles more consistently to government actions in other contexts that classify citizens by race, religion, sex, and sexual orientation.

In Chapter 5, I investigate Kennedy's approach in cases involving government structure. Kennedy also recasts these constitutional questions in terms of political morality and personal liberty. Founding principles of federalism, he states, should be revived not out of tradition, but because they "reflect an underlying, fundamental, essential, ethical, moral value" of the liberty of citizens to control their government's actions.[48] He relies on metaphors of a split atom of sovereignty and state dignity to justify judicial enforcement of separation of powers and federalism in a post–New Deal society.

In the conclusion I evaluate the larger visions of personal liberty and judicial power that form the foundation of Kennedy's jurisprudence. I use two of Kennedy's most recent majority opinions—*Kennedy v. Louisiana* and *Boumediene v. Bush*—as well as the *per curiam* opinion in *Bush v. Gore* to exemplify the main characteristics and criticisms of his approach. Kennedy's votes may appear ideologically inconsistent or seem to be merely strategic maneuvers to increase his personal power within the Court.[49] Seen as a whole, however, his opinions articulate a distinctive approach to constitutional interpretation based on coherent moral conceptions of personal liberty and human dignity, the limits of government power, and the role of courts in enforcing both. I conclude by situating Kennedy's jurisprudence as a departure from a twentieth-century consensus preoccupied with limiting judicial power in a democratic system, assess criticisms of his argument for an expansive role for the Court, and evaluate the promises and perils of his particular moral reading of the Constitution.

1. Liberty, Dignity, and Personality

*The enforcement power of the judiciary is to insure that
the word* liberty *in the Constitution is given its full and
necessary meaning.*

—CONFIRMATION TESTIMONY (1987)

Anthony Kennedy has written several controversial opinions for the Court
that outline his conception of individual liberty. His majority opinions have
invalidated clergy-led prayer at a public school graduation as a violation of
the First Amendment's Establishment Clause,[1] struck state laws criminalizing
sodomy as a violation of liberty protected by the Fourteenth Amendment,[2]
and ruled that the execution of persons who commit capital crimes before
turning eighteen constitutes cruel and unusual punishment under the Eighth
Amendment.[3] Most prominently, the plurality opinion in *Planned Parenthood
v. Casey* that he coauthored upheld the core of *Roe v. Wade*[4] and reaffirmed a
woman's right to have an abortion.[5] In each case, Kennedy retreated—or appeared to retreat—from an earlier position. Each of these cases provoked
dissent from Justice Antonin Scalia accusing Kennedy of betraying the Constitution with his decisions and his citation of sources such as social science
research, political consensus, and the constitutional decisions of other nations. Kennedy's behavior in *Lee v. Weisman, Planned Parenthood v. Casey,
Lawrence v. Texas,* and *Roper v. Simmons* has fueled charges that his jurisprudence is confused.[6]

In this chapter I examine Kennedy's conception of the judicial role in enforcing liberty. I begin by surveying statements he made about his interpretive
approach before he came to the Court, when he articulated a view that not
only rejected originalism but also had many parallels to the moral reading of
the Constitution advocated by Ronald Dworkin and the presumption of liberty later championed by Randy Barnett. I then analyze Kennedy's conception
of personal liberty in *Lee, Lawrence,* and *Roper.* (I consider *Casey* and his
abortion opinions in Chapter 2.)

Kennedy's ideal of liberty transcends constitutional text and tradition. It
independently considers whether government actions have the effect of pre-

venting an individual from developing his or her distinctive personality or acting according to conscience, demean a person's standing in the community, or violate essential elements of human dignity. His citations of psychological and sociological research, political consensus, and comparative constitutional law attempt to provide "objective referents" for his interpretations of Western concepts of liberty and human dignity. Kennedy's particular moral conceptions of liberty and human dignity have clear rhetorical roots in post–Vatican II Catholic social thought. In the conclusion, I assess Kennedy's moral conception of liberty and his defense of the judicial role to enforce it.

DISCOVERING THE FULL AND NECESSARY MEANING OF LIBERTY

Before coming to the Court, Kennedy rejected the originalism of text and specific tradition and embraced a moral reading of the Constitution. In his confirmation testimony, he stated that "the enforcement power of the judiciary is to insure that the word 'liberty' in the Constitution is given its full and necessary meaning, consistent with the purposes of the document as we understand it."[7] For Kennedy, rights claims do not imply larger interpretive debates about the existence of unenumerated rights but instead deal with "whether or not liberty extends to situations not previously addressed by courts, to protections not previously announced by courts" (87).

To resolve these disputes, Kennedy believes, "essentially, we look to the concept of individuality and liberty and dignity that those who drafted the Constitution understood." Although judges need to determine "whether or not the right has been accepted as part of the rights of a free people in the historical interpretation of the Constitution and the intentions of the framers," Kennedy said, he suggested that Americans today can have a better understanding of those rights than the Framers did (170–171). "Over time," he testified, "the intentions of the framers are more remote from their particular political concerns, and so they have a certain purity and a certain generality now that they did not have previously" (183–184). Put another way, "it sometimes takes humans generations to become aware of the moral consequences of their own conduct. That does not mean that moral principles have not remained the same" (153). Kennedy admitted the moral idea of liberty is "spacious"; its boundaries are "wavering," "amorphous," and "uncertain" (86). Yet judges have a constitutional duty to define and enforce those uncertain lines.

Asked what factors judges should consider when determining what the Constitution protects under liberty, Kennedy replied:

> A very abbreviated list of the considerations are the essentials of the right to human dignity, the injury to the person, the harm to the person, the anguish to the person, the inability of the person to manifest his or her own personality, the inability of a person to obtain his or her own self-fulfillment, the inability of a person to reach his or her own potential. (180)

He admits the state may have "strong" interests on the other side, including "the deference that the Court owes to the democratic process . . . and the respect that must be given to the legislature because it knows the values of the people." When Senator Gordon Humphrey (R-N.H.) objected that some of these considerations "sound like very subjective judgments," Kennedy replied, "The task of the judge is to try to find objective referents for each of those categories" (180).[8]

The interpretive method Kennedy expresses prior to coming to the Court shares similarities with the moral reading of the Constitution advanced by Ronald Dworkin.[9] Kennedy did criticize the substance of Dworkin's approach before coming to the Court.[10] Nevertheless, Kennedy's description of the spacious phrases and moral concepts contained in the Constitution and his distinction between "what the framers thought"—their "subjective motivations"—and the moral concepts embodied in the words they ratified echo Dworkin's distinction between concepts and conceptions.[11] To Kennedy, the term *liberty* embodies a moral concept that judges must independently enforce to its full and necessary meaning; Dworkin claims judges can enforce the text of the Constitution only by coming to their own best interpretation about what the moral concepts mean (136). The list of considerations Kennedy would consider in determining the content of liberty accords with Dworkin's formulation that "a claim of right presupposes a moral argument and can be established in no other way" (147).

Kennedy's insistence on a demonstrable historical link to the Framers may appear to represent a commitment to text and specific tradition. And from precedent, he admits, "you get a sense of what the Constitution really means" (171). But past practices and original expectations do not eliminate the need for judges to make moral judgments. Kennedy criticized judges who "often make a quick bow to the words and text and then go off into this mass of precedents in which we have normative rules of vast dimension, and begin announcing the law."[12] Kennedy compares judges—not, as Dworkin does, to chain novelists[13]—to architects who "seek to preserve the best elements of our past and to create structures that meet the demands of a dynamic present and an uncertain future."[14]

Important differences between the two do exist. Kennedy admits that the considerations he would use to evaluate a claim of constitutional liberty must be balanced "against the rights asserted by the State, of which there are many."[15] Conversely, in Dworkin's view rights imply that "an individual is entitled to protection against the majority even at the cost of the general interest."[16] Kennedy's substantive theory of personality also emphasizes individual liberty, while Dworkin takes as his central focus equal concern and respect.

Despite these substantive differences, both advocate a similar interpretive approach. Like Dworkin, Kennedy considers the constitutional text to contain general concepts, such as liberty, that contain moral content. This content may be illuminated by history, tradition, original intent, and precedent, but its full and necessary meaning extends beyond those sources. Judges obligated to interpret the Constitution must resort to moral argument about the nature of liberty, the human personality, and human dignity as well as the use of judicial power to enforce them. Prior to coming to the Court, Kennedy expressed a commitment to the fusion of constitutional law and moral theory that Dworkin recommends.[17] Tradition and history are important, but the moral concepts embodied by the text of the Constitution—and not prior understandings or interpretations of those concepts—provide the basis of determining the extent of individual liberty. "History and tradition are the starting point," Kennedy wrote in a later case, "but not in all cases the ending point."[18]

Kennedy's approach shares premises with the "presumption of liberty" more recently advocated by libertarian law professor Randy Barnett.[19] Barnett argues that courts should "protect all the rights retained by the people equally whether enumerated or unenumerated" (254). This ideal does not defer to Congress, the executive, or state governments. Barnett rejects the presumption of constitutionality, which "rested, in part, on a belief that legislatures would consider carefully, accurately, and in good faith the constitutional protections of liberty before infringing it" (260). Instead, he "places the burden on the government to establish the necessity and propriety of any infringement on individual freedom" (267, 259–260). Despite differences in application, Kennedy—like Barnett—requires government to "acknowledge its constitutional responsibility and begin to articulate its legislative judgments in constitutional terms." As early as 1982, Kennedy stated that if Congress fails to fulfill this responsibility, "I would contend that courts should rescind the rule that legislative act is presumed to be constitutional. A presumption should not exist if it does not mirror reality."[20]

During his tenure on the Ninth Circuit, Kennedy's departure from originalism was evident in his analysis of the military's policy of discharging homosexuals. Although Kennedy—like Bork and Scalia—voted to uphold the policy, his difference in approach is apparent. In *Dronenburg v. Zech,* the D.C. Court of Appeals—in an opinion written by Bork and joined by Scalia—upheld the policy against constitutional challenge based on a methodology of text and specific tradition. Homosexuals had demonstrated no right "solidly based in constitutional text and history" to engage in sodomy, Bork writes. The activity "was never before protected, and indeed traditionally condemned." Thus, "we can find no constitutional right to engage in homosexual conduct," and, "as judges, we have no warrant to create one." Because no such fundamental right exists, the U.S. Navy's regulation was subject only to the rational basis test. "We have said that legislation may implement morality," Bork writes. "So viewed, this regulation bears a rational relationship to a permissible end." Further, Bork argues, courts have no authority to protect rights that are not explicitly stated in the Constitution or traditionally accepted by American society. "If the revolution in sexual mores that appellant proclaims is in fact ever to arrive," he writes, "we think it must arrive through the moral choices of the people and their elected representatives, not through the judicial ukase of this court."[21]

Four years earlier, as a Ninth Circuit judge, Kennedy had also upheld the military policy of discharging homosexuals.[22] But his opinion in *Beller v. Middledorf* found the constitutional issue more complex. This case, he writes, "does not require us to address the question whether consensual homosexual conduct is a fundamental right, as the term is used in equal protection and some due process cases" (807). He rejects the "all or nothing" approach Bork would employ in *Dronenburg* as well as the "misunderstanding" promoted by relying on the right to privacy. Rather, in language similar to that of his later confirmation testimony, Kennedy writes in *Beller* that claims of substantive due process require judicial consideration of "the nature of the individual interest allegedly infringed, the importance of the government interests furthered, the degree of infringement, and the sensitivity of the government entity responsible for the regulation to more carefully tailor alternate means of achieving its goals" (807).

Beller's specific claim may lack protection "by virtue of its inadequate foundation in the continuing traditions of our society." But Kennedy introduces a further, moral standard. When government "seriously intrudes into matters which lie at the core of interests which deserve due process protection," he writes, additional scrutiny is required. "The reasons which have led the Court to protect some private decisions intimately linked with one's personality, see e.g. *Roe,* and family living arrangements beyond the core nuclear family," he writes, "suggest that some kinds of government regulation of private consensual homosexual behavior may face substantial constitutional challenge" (810). Kennedy upheld the policy of discharging homosexuals because of "the unique accommodation between military demands and what might be constitutionally protected activity in some other contexts" (812). Yet he admits "private consensual homosexual behavior" in other contexts may merit some constitutional protection. Further, his decision transcends text and specific tradition to rely on larger moral conceptions of individual liberty and personality by engaging in a substantive evaluation of these interests against the particular needs of government in this specific circumstance.

Kennedy's opinion in *Beller*—combined with his public comments before coming to the Court—demonstrates his departure from originalism. Although, like Bork and Scalia, he upheld the policy, he rejected the idea that judges should protect only activities stated explicitly in the text of the Constitution or that have been accepted by a specific tradition. Judges have an obligation to determine independently whether a claim to constitutional protection should be enforced by the judiciary and not rely on a presumption of constitutionality. To Kennedy, text and tradition provide a starting point, but the moral concepts embodied by the text of the Constitution—and not prior understandings or interpretations of these concepts—provide the basis for determining the extent of the personal liberty that courts have a duty to enforce. Kennedy's statements before coming to the Court—in his speeches, his confirmation testimony, and his *Beller* opinion—broadly outline a substantive theory of personhood and liberty.

LEE V. WEISMAN: COERCION AND CONSCIENCE

Kennedy's majority opinion in *Lee v. Weisman* relies on these moral considerations of dignity, liberty, and coercion. In previous and later cases, Kennedy
reads the Establishment Clause to allow for flexible accommodation of religion, including religious displays on public property and even government
funding of religious institutions and schools on the same neutral basis as
other recipients.[23] Even in *Lee,* Kennedy initially voted to uphold clergy-led
prayer at public school graduations. Ultimately, however, he reaffirmed his
ideal of liberty of conscience against government coercion. Kennedy's opinion
in *Lee* employs morality and social science to discover violations of human
dignity and conscience caused by government pressure on dissenters to participate in a religious exercise.

Flexible yet Sensitive Accommodation
In his first major Supreme Court opinion involving religion,[24] Kennedy articulated his coercion principle in a way that appears consistent with originalism. In *Allegheny County v. Greater Pittsburgh ACLU,*[25] which upheld a
menorah displayed on public property but struck a crèche display, Kennedy
voted to uphold both. He accuses the majority of an "unjustified hostility toward religion" that is "inconsistent with our history and precedents" (655).
The Constitution, properly understood, he writes, "permits government some
latitude in recognizing and accommodating the central role religion plays in
our society." Kennedy explicitly rejects the metaphor of a wall of separation,
claiming that it sends "a clear message of disapproval" and "would border on
latent hostility toward religion" (657).

For Kennedy, "the border between accommodation and establishment"
rests on "two limiting principles." The first is that "government may not coerce
anyone to support or participate in any religion or its exercise." The second is
that government cannot, "in the guise of avoiding hostility or callous indifference, give direct benefits to religion in such a degree that it in fact 'establishes a
religious faith, or tends to do so'" (659). To Kennedy, the Free Exercise and Establishment clauses have "the great object" of preserving "the freedom to worship as one pleases without government interference or oppression." He ties
this interpretation to his larger conception of liberty. "It would be difficult indeed to establish a religion," he argues, "without some measure of more or less
subtle coercion." But coercion need not be direct compulsion under penalty of

law: the school prayer invalidated in *Engel v. Vitale,* he writes, "was unquestionably coercive in an indirect manner" (660 fn. 1).

Even so qualified, Kennedy's ideal of coercion does not require complete separation of government from religious expression. The fact that "speech may coerce in some circumstances," he writes, "does not justify a ban on all government recognition of religion" (661). He outlines a state role for "passive and symbolic" accommodation (662). The Establishment Clause is not breached unless government action "benefits religion in a way more direct and more substantial than practices that are accepted in our national heritage" (662–663). Yet his conception of coercion establishes a substantive—not merely historical—standard.

Under this standard, Kennedy finds both the menorah and crèche challenged in this case to be examples of "noncoercive government action" falling "within the realm of flexible accommodation" (662). Forcing governments to recognize only the secular dimension of the season "would signify . . . callous indifference toward religious faith" and "signal not neutrality but a pervasive intent to insulate government from all things religious." These displays, he writes, did not compel individuals to profess faith or advance one faith over the other. Further, "no one was compelled to observe or to participate in any religious ceremony or activity," and no government body "contributed significant amounts of money to serve the cause of one religious faith." The displays were "passive symbols." People could easily avoid or ignore them, "just as they are free to do when they disagree with any other form of government speech." As a result, Kennedy concludes, "no realistic risk" exists that these displays "represent an effort to proselytize or are otherwise the first step down the road to an establishment of religion" (663–664).

Kennedy's articulation of the coercion principle in *Allegheny County* appears at first to be consistent with originalist text- and history-based ideals of interpretation. Scalia did join his opinion. But Kennedy's analysis moves beyond history. Although Kennedy states that Establishment "is to be determined by reference to historical practices and understandings" (670), he uses selected aspects of history as benchmarks to define a substantive moral standard of coercion. Kennedy thus asserts an independent judicial role to measure the level of coercion of a government practice on individual liberty. Though arriving at the same result as justices committed to text and specific tradition, Kennedy moves beyond history to justify an independent standard of coercion.

In *Westside Community Board of Education v. Mergens,*[26] Kennedy again outlined a coercion test sensitive to considerations of conscience. He upheld federal legislation that required secondary schools receiving federal aid to allow equal access after school hours to student groups based on "religious, political, philosophical or other content." Religious groups may receive "incidental benefits," but those benefits do not "lead to an establishment of religion." They merely place religious groups on the same footing as other groups (260). Kennedy finds no evidence that "demonstrates that enforcement of the statute will result in the coercion of any student to participate in a religious activity" (261).

More significantly, Kennedy reiterates a broader definition of coercion that is substantive rather than formal or historical. It asks "whether the government imposes pressure upon a student to participate in a religious activity." Government pressure can take many forms, Kennedy states; thus the coercion test "must be undertaken with sensitivity to the special circumstances that exist in secondary schools where the line between voluntary and coerced participation may be difficult to draw" (261–262). Kennedy finds no such coercion in *Mergens*. But, as in *Allegheny County,* he indicates that coercion of individual conscience may result from more than just direct government action. Further, courts must show "special sensitivity" to coercion in the public school context.

Lee v. Weisman *and Coercion of Conscience*

In *Lee v. Weisman,* Kennedy voted at conference during November 1991 to uphold clergy-led graduation prayer at a public school graduation against challenge under the Establishment Clause. According to Justice Blackmun, Kennedy reiterated his coercion principle but did not find it applicable to this case. *Lee* was not a free exercise case: The graduation was a public event, and no one could interpret mere student attendance as participation in prayer. He also feared that striking the prayer would "undermine confidence with the people."[27] The Court divided 5–4 to uphold the graduation prayer, and after the conference vote Chief Justice Rehnquist assigned Kennedy to the job of writing for the five-justice majority.

Kennedy did not circulate an opinion for more than three months. On March 30, 1992, he sent a memo to Blackmun, the senior justice in dissent. "After writing to reverse in the high school graduation prayer case," he wrote, "my draft looked quite wrong. So I have written it to rule in favor of the objecting student, both at the middle school and high school exercises." Kennedy admitted that "after the barbs" in *Allegheny County*, "many between the two of us, I thought it most important to write something that you and I and the others who voted this way can join. That is why this took me longer than it should have."[28] Three days later, Blackmun—the senior member of the new majority—reassigned the majority opinion to Kennedy.[29]

In the final majority opinion in *Lee v. Weisman*,[30] Kennedy applied the coercion principle, latent in *Allegheny County* and *Mergens*, to strike official-led prayer in the context of public school graduations. He focused not on the potential establishment of religion by government but on the dissenting student's right of conscience. He was joined by none of the justices who had signed his Allegheny dissent. Rather than a shift from Allegheny, Kennedy's opinion in *Lee* is best read as a defense of personal liberty, dignity, and conscience.

To Kennedy, the prayer challenged in this case violates a "central principle" of the Establishment Clause: that "government may not coerce anyone to support or participate in religion or its exercise" (587). The involvement of school officials was "pervasive, to the point of creating a state-sponsored and state-directed religious exercise in a public school." In contrast to the displays in *Allegheny County*—where passersby could merely turn away—this prayer took place at an event of great importance where "attendance and participation . . . were in a fair and real sense obligatory" (586). The invocation and benediction constituted "an overt religious exercise in a secondary school environment," one where "subtle coercive pressures exist, and where the student had no real alternative which would have allowed her to avoid the fact or appearance of participation" (588).

Kennedy builds the coercion argument by describing the state's involvement in the ceremony. School officials decided to include an invocation and benediction, invited a specific religious official, and gave him guidelines for composing the prayer. Kennedy concedes the "good faith" of the school officials in "attempting to make the prayer acceptable to most persons." Nevertheless, "a cornerstone principle" of the Establishment Clause is "that it is no part of the business of government to compose official prayers for any group of the American people to recite as part of a religious program carried on by the government." By seeking "to produce a prayer to be used in a formal religious exercise" at an event "which students, for all practical purposes, are obliged to attend," the school violated the Establishment Clause (588–589).

Kennedy argues that religious belief and expression are essential aspects of individual personality "too precious to be either proscribed or prescribed by the State." The Constitution provides "that the preservation and transmission of religious beliefs and worship is a responsibility and a choice committed to the private sphere, which itself is promised freedom to pursue that mission" (589). Although the Free Exercise Clause "embraces a freedom of conscience and worship that has close parallels in the speech provisions of the First Amendment," the Establishment Clause adds "a specific prohibition on forms of state intervention in religious affairs" to protect "freedom of conscience in a religious matter" (591).

The Establishment Clause, to Kennedy, serves as a positive protection of individual conscience from direct or indirect government pressure. "In the hands of government," he writes, "what might begin as a tolerant expression of religious views may end in a policy to indoctrinate and coerce." Kennedy fears "a state-created orthodoxy" that "puts at great risk that freedom of belief and conscience which are the sole assurance that religious faith is real, not imposed" (591–592). When government—however well-meaning—engages in "state-sponsored religious exercises"—however composed not to offend— "the State disavows its own duty to guard and respect that sphere of inviolable conscience and belief which is the mark of a free people." Kennedy turns to his substantive approach to tradition, focusing not on specific past practices but on the coercion principle as embodied in the Constitution's guarantee of liberty. "To compromise that principle today," he writes, "would be to deny our own tradition and forfeit our standing to urge others to secure protections of that tradition for themselves" (592).

Kennedy uses this tradition to extend his reading of coercion and individual conscience. He defines coercion not from the perspective of the "reasonable observer" of O'Connor's endorsement test but from the view of the dissenting student. Further, he examines not just the formal action of the school but the effect of the entire event. The invocation and benediction in this ceremony "bore the imprint of the State" and "put school-age children who objected in an untenable position" (590). From the perspective of the dissenter, the government was using "social pressure to enforce orthodoxy" (593–594). "In a school context," Kennedy writes, religious activities carry "a particular risk of indirect coercion."

In language reminiscent of *West Virginia v. Barnette*, Kennedy writes that to the young dissenter, the graduation prayer "may appear an attempt to employ the machinery of the State to enforce a religious orthodoxy" (592). The controlled presentation of a high school graduation ceremony—combined with the "public pressure, as well as peer pressure on attending students to stand as a group or, at least, maintain respectful silence"—gives the dissenting student "the reasonable perception that she is being forced by the State to pray in a manner her conscience will not allow." To the dissenter who feels this "subtle and indirect" pressure, Kennedy writes, "the injury is no less real" than direct coercion (593).[31]

Kennedy thus concludes that "a reasonable dissenter in this milieu could believe that the group exercise signified her own participation or approval of it." The situation, created by government, puts "objectors in the dilemma of participating, with all that implies, or protesting." It produces an "intrusion" on conscience that is "real." The government prayer "gives insufficient recognition to the real conflict of conscience faced by the young student" (597). In this context, the Court must "guard and respect that sphere of inviolable conscience which is the mark of a free people" (592).

Scalia's dissent highlights Kennedy's departure from a jurisprudence of text and specific tradition.[32] After citing a passage from Kennedy's *Allegheny* opinion, Scalia observes that the majority opinion in *Lee* "is conspicuously bereft of any reference to history" (631). The Court "lays waste to a tradition that is as old as public school graduation ceremonies themselves, and that is a component of an even more longstanding American tradition of nonsectarian prayer to God at public celebrations generally" (632). To Scalia, prohibitions under the Establishment Clause "must have deep foundations in the historic practice of our people." The long-standing practice of prayers at public school graduations "displays with unmistakable clarity that the establishment clause does not forbid the government to accommodate it" (632, 645).

Scalia limits Establishment to "coercion of religious orthodoxy and financial support by force of law and threat of penalty" (640). To Scalia, Kennedy's substantive conception of harm to conscience is "ersatz" and a "psycho-coercion test" unsupported by the Constitution (644). "Interior decorating," he writes, "is rock-hard science compared to psychology practiced by amateurs" (636). Scalia mentions nothing about social pressure, freedom of conscience, or the perspective of the dissenting student. He focuses on the brevity of the prayer, argues that student silence implies neither participation nor approval, and fears the Pledge of Allegiance will "be the next project for the Court's bulldozer" (639).[33] For Scalia, coercion is defined by legal penalties;

for Kennedy, unconstitutional coercion includes not just legal penalties but "pressures upon a student to participate in a religious activity." Scalia advocates a standard of coercion that focuses formally on government action and inaction, whereas Kennedy focuses on the injury to the person and her right of conscience.

Most significantly, Scalia and Kennedy differ about the essential place of religion in public life. Scalia considers public prayer as unifying, not divisive. Throughout American history, he writes, "religious men and women of almost all denominations have felt it necessary to acknowledge and beseech the blessing of God as a people, and not just as individuals" (645). In this context, "to deprive our society of that important unifying mechanism in order to spare the nonbeliever what seems to me the minimal inconvenience of standing, or even sitting in respectful nonparticipation," Scalia writes, "is as senseless in policy as it is unsupported in law" (646). By taking the perspective of "religious men and women of almost all denominations," Scalia balances away the minimal inconvenience of the dissenter against the unifying social effect of public prayer, whereas for Kennedy, "the suggestion that government may establish an official or civic religion as a means of avoiding the establishment of a religion with more specific creeds strikes us as a contradiction that cannot be accepted" (590).

Scalia's dissent in *Lee* underscores Kennedy's departure from the originalist method of specific tradition and emphasizes his reliance on a substantive ideal of human liberty. These differences in methodology and substance were obscured when both used the word "coercion" to validate government involvement in religious speech. What Scalia mocks as "psychology practiced by amateurs" serves as a foundation of Kennedy's jurisprudence of human dignity. Kennedy looks beyond formal tests of coercion to the larger pressure that government action can place on individuals to take part in religious exercises. Where there is a simple religious display, Kennedy upholds it. Those who object can just look away. Where schools and government buildings offer after-hours extracurricular religious programs in public schools, Kennedy upholds those as well. If a student objects, he or she can leave.[34] It is only when the government activity requires participation and attendance that it truly constitutes coercion of the dissenter. The ideals of conscience and human dignity—obscured in earlier religion cases—become visible in *Lee* when they ultimately lead him to strike government action as a substantive injury.

LAWRENCE V. TEXAS: OVERTURNING THE
DEMEANING PRECEDENT OF BOWERS V.
HARDWICK

In *Lawrence v. Texas*, Kennedy wrote for a majority striking Texas's law criminalizing homosexual sodomy and overturning the Court's 1986 decision in *Bowers v. Hardwick*.[35] Kennedy's opinion in *Lawrence* reflects opposition to *Bowers* that he expressed publicly just a month after it was decided in a speech to the Canadian Institute for Advanced Legal Studies.[36] The speech outlined the problems he considered inherent in *Bowers*, criticized the terminology of a right to privacy, listed a broad spectrum of moral and practical factors that judges should consider, contrasted *Bowers* with a decision from the European Court of Human Rights, and rejected arguments from equality for others based on liberty. In rhetoric and substance, Kennedy's address foreshadowed the result and reasoning of his Supreme Court opinion in *Lawrence* seventeen years later.[37]

Kennedy's address focuses on the disadvantages of relying so heavily on privacy. He contrasts the U.S. decision in *Bowers* with the European Court of Human Rights' decision five years earlier in *Dudgeon v. United Kingdom*,[38] which struck a similar law. Personal privacy is a value explicitly protected by Article 8 of the European Convention on Human Rights (ECHR),[39] but Kennedy agrees with a dissenting ECHR justice that "mere invocation of the word 'private' does not resolve the question. . . . It simply restates the problem" (8). Further complications exist in the American context, Kennedy states, when a court is "faced with the question under a constitution which does not contain the word 'private' or 'privacy' at all" (9). Kennedy here finds serious problems with judicial reliance on privacy. "If a court begins by announcing such a right," he states, "it seems to go, on the one hand, beyond the case before it by adopting a phrase more extensive than required for its resolution of the case." Yet, "on the other hand, it goes not far enough because there remain so many further issues to be resolved" (9).

Kennedy expresses concern that "debate then shifts to the word 'privacy,' rather than to a constitutional term, such as 'liberty.'" After quoting Keats on heard and unheard melodies, Kennedy states that privacy "is good inspiration for poets, but promises considerable misunderstanding for judges charged with enforcing a written constitution." Introducing such a term serves to "create more uncertainties than we solve" (9–10). "I prefer to think of the value of privacy as being protected by the liberty clause," Kennedy later testified. "Maybe that is a semantic quibble, maybe it is not."[40]

Shifting the debate from privacy to liberty solves an interpretive problem, Kennedy admits, but not the substantive constitutional issue. Essential questions about the meaning and application of liberty remain unresolved, including

> whether the word embraces a substantive right of autonomous choice; if so, whether that choice insures the manifestation of one's personality and if so, whether it extends to conduct with others; whether it was legitimate for the legislature to regulate on the question of morals; what the morals and religious values of the particular community were; and whether those concerns were in fact advanced by the law in question. (9)

Some of these considerations are factual, but many of them involve essentially moral considerations similar to the ones Kennedy would enumerate in his confirmation testimony. Using the word "liberty" in place of "privacy" avoids a textual objection, and it brings moral and practical considerations to the forefront of constitutional adjudication.

While Kennedy initially appears sympathetic to the *Dudgeon* dissenters, he expresses forceful criticism of the U.S. Court's majority opinion in *Bowers*. He finds "a tension in methodology" (13) between Byron White's "reluctance" to support substantive due process and precedents involving constitutional protection for family, education, and child raising such as *Meyer v. Nebraska*[41] and *Pierce v. Society of Sisters*.[42] Kennedy clearly accepts these precedents. "The broad formulation of fundamental rights announced in *Meyer* is one of the richest in all our case law," Kennedy states, "yet the *Bowers* Court cautions that such language is not necessarily the authorization for a judicial creation of a whole new catalog of rights" (12). *Bowers* might be justified "by pointing to the lack of traditional approval for homosexual conduct," Kennedy concedes. Even so, "the tension in methodology remains." Given his broad ideal of personal liberty, his willingness to move beyond text and specific tradition, and his earlier opinion in *Beller*, it is unlikely Kennedy would accept traditional disapproval and continuing disapproval by a majority alone as a sufficient state interest to override a law that interferes with an individual's free choice and development of his or her own identity.[43]

Kennedy also rejects the alternative of striking Georgia's law on grounds of equal protection—the position Justice O'Connor later advocated in her separate concurrence in *Lawrence*. Using equality "seems problematic," he writes, "especially if the analytic framework simply repeats what has already been rejected under the Due Process Clause." He expresses concern that "equal protection litigation has tended to become based on the claims of classes of persons" rather than individual claims of personal liberty (14). More generally, Kennedy prefers broad, individualistic readings of liberty to class-based arguments for equality. Both the move away from privacy and the broad definition of liberty predominate in the final opinion in *Lawrence*.[44]

Kennedy concedes that "the constitutional text and its immediate implications, traceable by some historical link to the ideas of the Framers, must govern the judges." Yet he rejects originalist attempts to rely solely on text and long-standing tradition. "Saying the constitutional text must be our principal reference," he writes, "is in a sense simply to restate the question of what the text means" (20). As Kennedy stated in his confirmation hearings, "the concept of liberty is quite expansive, quite sufficient, to protect the values of privacy that Americans legitimately think are part of their constitutional heritage." Though he was unwilling to discuss the Court's reasoning in *Griswold v. Connecticut* finding a constitutional right to privacy based on a penumbra formed by emanations of several constitutional guarantees,[45] he admitted that "if you were going to propose a statute or a hypothetical that infringed upon the core values of privacy that the Constitution protects, you would be hard put to find a stronger case than *Griswold*." Yet he also admitted that "with reference to the right of privacy, we are very much in a stage of evolution and debate. I think that the public and the legislature have every right to contribute to that debate. The Constitution is made for that kind of debate."[46]

Before coming to the Court, Kennedy criticized both the terminology of the right to privacy and the wholesale rejection of substantive due process as insufficiently protective of the textual guarantee of liberty.[47] Invoking "liberty," he admits, cannot alone decide constitutional issues. Focusing on liberty, however, brings practical and moral considerations to the forefront of judicial decision-making. As Kennedy concludes, "uncertainty over precise standards of interpretation does not justify failing in the attempt to construct them, and still less does it justify flagrant departures."[48] These standards cannot be reduced to a simple formula that requires mere "lawyer's work" to discern the "facts" of text and tradition.[49] Before coming to the Court, then, Kennedy searched for an effective balance that would allow judges to enforce the full and necessary meaning of liberty while avoiding the interpretive and substantive difficulties raised by the right-to-privacy terminology. Kennedy's Canadian Institute speech provides contemporaneous evidence for his statement in *Lawrence* that *"Bowers* was not correct when it was decided."[50]

Kennedy's opinion for the Court in *Lawrence* has deep rhetorical and substantive roots in his prenomination statements. It begins with an expansive definition of personal liberty and ends by defending an expansive judicial duty to protect it. It incorporates his contemporaneous criticisms of *Bowers* and the terminology of the right to privacy, and it approves references to the law of other nations, including the European Court of Human Rights decision in *Dudgeon*. The opinion in *Lawrence* also includes a deeper analysis of the effect of sodomy laws on the dignity of homosexual persons.

Read in light of his commitments prior to coming to the Court, the foundations of Kennedy's interpretive project in *Lawrence* become evident. Kennedy's opinion begins with the word "liberty" and ends with the word "freedom."[51] *Lawrence*'s opening passage further justifies why courts should focus on liberty rather than privacy. To Kennedy, liberty "protects the person from unwarranted governmental intrusions into a dwelling or other private places." In addition, "there are other spheres of our lives and existence, outside the home, where the State should not be a dominant presence." Liberty "presumes an autonomy of self that includes freedom of thought, belief, expression, and certain intimate conduct." This statement parallels but expands the inclusion of marriage within the First Amendment right of association in *Griswold* as well as Blackmun's attempts in *Bowers* to fit both of these under the right to privacy.[52] To Kennedy, "the instant case involves liberty both in its spatial and more transcendent dimensions" (571–572).[53]

Kennedy rejects *Bowers* as contrary to personal liberty and human dignity. He reiterates the "broad statements of the substantive reach of liberty under the Due Process Clause," citing *Meyer* and *Pierce*. Yet he states that "the most pertinent beginning point is our decision in *Griswold v. Connecticut*" (564). Kennedy focuses on considerations of human dignity, personality, and potential. The sexual expression criminalized in this case "can be but one element in a personal bond that is more enduring" (567). White's opinion in *Bowers*, by focusing narrowly on a right to homosexual sodomy, "discloses the Court's own failure to appreciate the extent of the liberty at stake." Kennedy clearly attempts to make this opinion about more than homosexual rights and sodomy. Phrasing the issue as narrowly as White did in *Bowers* "demeans the claim the individual put forward," Kennedy writes, "just as it would demean a married couple were it to be said marriage is simply about the right to have sexual intercourse." In both cases larger considerations of liberty are at stake. "Adults may choose to enter upon this relationship in the confines of their homes and their own private lives," Kennedy writes, "and still retain their dignity as free persons" (567).

Kennedy recognizes the moral concerns of the majority that motivated Texas's law but finds them insufficient to justify its constitutionality.[54] *Bowers* rightly noted "that for centuries there have been powerful voices to condemn homosexual conduct as immoral." To many individuals, Kennedy concedes, "these are not trivial concerns but profound and deep convictions accepted as ethical and moral principles to which they aspire and thus determine the course of their lives." For Kennedy, however, there exists a crucial distinction between private belief and government policy. "The issue," he writes, "is whether the majority may use the power of the State to enforce these views on the whole society through operation of the criminal law." Kennedy then cites a statement from his opinion in *Casey* justifying constitutional protection for abortion rights: "Our obligation is to define the liberty of all, not to mandate our own moral code" (571, quoting *Casey* at 850).

To define this liberty, Kennedy moves beyond history and specific tradition. As in his 1986 address, he cites political and legal developments in the last half of the twentieth century in the United States and Europe. The developments, he writes, "show an emerging awareness that liberty gives substantial protection to adult persons in deciding how to conduct their private lives in matters pertaining to sex"—one which "should have been apparent when *Bowers* was decided" (571–572). In his confirmation hearings Kennedy emphasized the Western concept of individuality and human dignity: Given the decision in *Dudgeon* and the actions of several legislatures, he said, these developments taken together stand "at odds with the premise that the claim put forward was insubstantial in our Western tradition" (573).

As in 1986, Kennedy rejects O'Connor's proposal to uphold *Bowers* but strike Texas's law on equal protection grounds. (O'Connor had been a member of the majority in *Bowers* upholding a sodomy law that applied to heterosexuals as well as homosexuals.) Kennedy finds the questions connected: "Equality of treatment and the due process right to demand respect for conduct protected by the substantive guarantee of liberty are linked in important respects." He focuses, however, on larger considerations of liberty and human dignity. If *Bowers* remained good law, he says, "the stigma" of sodomy laws "might remain even if it were not enforceable as drawn for equal protection concerns." Aside from its substantive deprivation of liberty, to Kennedy the reasoning of the *Bowers* decision itself "demeans the lives of homosexual persons." This affront to dignity is practical as well as jurisprudential. Homosexuals found guilty suffer the "stigma" of a being found a criminal by the state "with all that imports for the dignity of the persons charged" (575).

Kennedy's other references to comparative law respond to Scalia's assertion that overruling *Bowers* would create legal and social uncertainty. To the contrary, Kennedy writes, "*Bowers* itself causes uncertainty, for the precedents before and after its issuance contradict its central holding" (577). To support this argument, Kennedy cites precedents in the American context before 1986—*Griswold* and *Roe*[55]—and two later majority opinions he authored—*Casey* and *Romer v. Evans*.[56] The ECHR had followed not *Bowers* but *Dudgeon* in three later cases.[57] Other nations and courts follow *Dudgeon*, not *Bowers*. To Kennedy, these developments have normative consequences that confirm his 1986 judgment. "The right the petitioners seek in this case has been accepted as an integral part of human freedom in other countries," Kennedy writes. "There has been no showing that in this country the governmental interest in circumscribing personal choice is somehow more legitimate or urgent" (576–577). He ultimately combines considerations of dignity and liberty. Under the Fourteenth Amendment, he writes, "the petitioners are entitled to respect for their private lives" (578).

The final paragraph of *Lawrence* reinforces Kennedy's rejection of originalism, his focus on "emerging awareness" rather than specific tradition, and his defense of an assertive judicial role in defining the essentially moral content of liberty:

> Had those who drew and ratified the Due Process Clauses of the Fifth Amendment or the Fourteenth Amendment known the components of liberty in its manifold possibilities, they might have been more specific. They did not presume to have that insight. They knew that time can blind us to certain truths and later generations can see that laws once thought necessary and proper in fact serve only to oppress. As the Constitution endures, persons in every generation can invoke its principles in their own search for greater freedom. (578–579)

By focusing on text and specific tradition, the *Bowers* majority misunderstood the claim before it and demeaned those who presented it. In *Lawrence*,

Kennedy makes an appeal to truth. "It sometimes takes humans generations to become aware of the moral consequences of their own conduct," Kennedy stated at his nomination hearings. "That does not mean that moral principles have not remained the same."[58] On the basis of this principled argument for liberty, his Ninth Circuit opinion in *Beller,* and the 1986 Canadian Institute address, Kennedy can creditably state in *Lawrence* that "*Bowers* was not correct when it was decided, and it is not correct today."[59]

Scalia's dissent warns of actual and potential changes wracked by Kennedy's majority opinion. Overruling *Bowers,* Scalia writes, does cause a social disruption; by rejecting majoritarian morality as a legitimate state interest, the Court eliminates justification for laws against same-sex marriage, bigamy, adult incest, bestiality, prostitution, and obscenity (590). More significantly, Scalia criticizes Kennedy's expansive definition of liberty as "the passage that ate the rule of law" (588).

Scalia then attempts to divorce Kennedy's reasoning from *Griswold* and connect it to *Lochner v. New York,* the infamous 1905 case where the Supreme Court struck a maximum hours law as a violation of liberty of contract protected under the Fourteenth Amendment.[60] Scalia admits Texas's law may limit liberty in some absolute sense. But, he writes, "so do laws prohibiting prostitution, recreational use of heroin, and, for that matter, working more than 60 hours a week in a bakery." For Scalia, "there is no right to 'liberty' under the Due Process Clause." Rather, the clause "*expressly allows* States to deprive their citizens of 'liberty,' *so long as 'due process of law' is provided.*" If a liberty is not fundamental—"deeply rooted in this Nation's history and tradition"—it "may be abridged or abrogated pursuant to a validly enacted state law if that law is rationally related to a legitimate state interest" (593, all emphases in original).

Perhaps surprisingly, Scalia turns to the majority opinion in *Griswold* for support.[61] And he even finds merit in William O. Douglas's method, if not in his result. Scalia states that *Griswold* "*expressly disclaimed* any reliance on the doctrine of 'substantive due process.'" Rather, it "grounded the so-called 'right to privacy' in penumbras of constitutional provisions other than the Due Process Clause." Further, to Scalia, *Griswold* recognized a right of privacy "penumbral to the *specific* guarantees in the Bill of Rights, and not a 'substantive due process' right" (595, all emphases in original).

At least in *Lawrence,* Scalia casually dismisses Kennedy's citation of the opinions of other courts and nations. Fundamental rights, he argues, arise not from an "emerging awareness" but must be "deeply rooted in this Nation's history and traditions." Rights do not exist because states have repealed laws; "much less do they spring into existence, as the Court seems to believe, because foreign nations decriminalize conduct." The Court's citation of other nations is "meaningless dicta." Yet it is "dangerous," Scalia writes, because it may provide cover for judges to "'impose foreign moods, fads, or fashions on Americans'" (598).[62] Scalia further notes that most of these repeals occurred not through the actions of the people or their elected representatives, but through judicial decisions.[63]

Under the guise of liberty, Scalia argues, the Court has betrayed democracy and taken the side of "a law-profession culture that has largely signed on to the so-called homosexual agenda." By striking Texas's law, "the Court has taken sides in the culture war, departing from its role of assuring, as neutral observer, that the democratic rules of engagement are observed" (602). The constitutional text may protect liberty, Scalia writes, but judgments about its content "are to be made by the people, and not by a governing caste that knows best" (604).

Kennedy's majority opinion in *Lawrence* fulfills the promise of his 1986 Canadian Institute speech. It incorporates his contemporary criticism of the Court's decision in *Bowers*. It shifts constitutional locations from privacy to liberty. It includes considerations of human dignity and respect. It appeals to international law and the decisions of other constitutional courts to illuminate those considerations. *Lawrence* exhibited the most prominent use of comparative materials in a majority opinion by the U.S. Supreme Court up to that time.[64] Kennedy would use similar sources two years later in *Roper* and meet even more forceful criticism from Scalia.

ROPER V. SIMMONS: CRUELTY AND PERSONALITY

In *Roper v. Simmons,* Kennedy wrote for a five-justice majority ruling that a death sentence for a person who commits a capital crime before turning eighteen constitutes cruel and unusual punishment. *Roper* overturned the Court's 1989 holding in *Stanford v. Kentucky,* a majority Kennedy had joined.[65] As in *Lawrence,* Kennedy cited comparative and international law as well as psychological studies and political developments in America to support his independent judgment. His opinion attracted another spirited dissent from Scalia, who criticized Kennedy's result and his use of political consensus, psychology, and "alien law."[66] At bottom, Kennedy's use of "objective" sources provided support for his independent judgment about the nature of human dignity and individual personality.

At the beginning of his *Roper* opinion, Kennedy says "we must determine, as an exercise of our own independent judgment, whether the death penalty is a disproportionate punishment for juveniles."[67] According to Supreme Court precedent, the Eighth Amendment "must draw its meaning from the evolving standards of human decency that mark the progress of a maturing society."[68] To support his independent judgment of the meaning of decency in a maturing society, Kennedy argues that "objective indicia of consensus"—repeal by five states, infrequency of imposition by juries—demonstrate an evolving consensus that juveniles "are less culpable than the average criminal" (1192, 1194). These "objective indicia" of political development serve as referents to support Kennedy's larger conception of human personality.[69]

Kennedy's discussion in *Roper* about the nature of human psychological development contains several parallels to his opinions in *Lee* and *Lawrence*. As in *Lee*, he argues that "juveniles are more vulnerable or susceptible to negative influences, including peer pressure." More significantly, Kennedy writes, "the character of a juvenile is not as well formed as that of an adult. The personality traits of juveniles are more transitory, less fixed." For evidence he cites Erik Ericson's 1968 classic *Youth and Crisis* as well as other psychological and sociological studies (1195). To Kennedy, the incomplete nature of human personality during adolescence makes the death penalty for crimes committed during that stage cruel and unusual. "When a juvenile offender commits a heinous crime," he writes, "the State can exact forfeiture of some of the most basic liberties, but the State cannot extinguish his life and his potential to attain a mature understanding of his own humanity" (1197).

Kennedy devotes the opinion's concluding Part IV to a discussion of international law, noting "the United States is the only country in the world that continues to give official sanction to the juvenile death penalty." He admits that "this reality does not become controlling, for the task of interpreting the Eighth Amendment remains our responsibility." Nevertheless, in the exercise of "independent judgment," judicial consultation of the laws of other nations can be "instructive" (1198). Kennedy cites Article 37 of the United Nations Convention on the Rights of the Child—which the United States did not sign—as expressly prohibiting execution for crimes committed before the age of eighteen. Only seven nations—Iran, Pakistan, Saudi Arabia, Yemen, Nigeria, Congo, and China—have executed juvenile offenders since 1990, and all now claim to repudiate the practice (1199). "In sum," Kennedy writes, "it is fair to say that the United States now stands alone in a world that has turned its face against the juvenile death penalty" (1199). Kennedy finds these international developments to be relevant to his ideal of human dignity and personality, "resting in large part on the understanding that the instability and emotional imbalance of young people may often be a factor in the crime." The decision remains one made by this Court, Kennedy writes; nevertheless, "the opinion of the world community, while not controlling our outcome, does provide respected and significant confirmation for our own conclusions" (1200).

Kennedy closes by defending his citation of international law within an expansive judicial duty to define and enforce the full and necessary meaning of liberty. Although the Constitution "sets forth, and rests upon, innovative principles original to the American experience," Kennedy writes, it also includes "broad provisions to secure individual freedom and preserve human dignity" (1200). He finds these commitments "central to the American experience" and "essential to our present-day self-definition and national identity." "Not the least of the reasons we honor the Constitution," Kennedy says, "is because we know it to be our own." But there are other, higher reasons to respect the Constitution: "It does not lessen our fidelity to the Constitution or pride in its origins," he concludes, "to acknowledge that the express affirmation of certain fundamental rights by other nations and peoples simply underscores the centrality of those same rights within our own heritage of freedom" (1200).

For Kennedy, the Constitution fundamentally deserves respect because of its larger commitment to liberty. In earlier speeches and opinions, he emphasized the uniqueness of the American experience, including its innovative vision of sovereignty in the areas of federalism and separation of powers.[70] Here Kennedy seeks to use judicial power to enforce one true understanding of liberty. As in *Casey* and *Lawrence*, Kennedy ends *Roper* with the word "freedom," a cognate to "liberty." *Roper* illustrates that Kennedy will consider claims of liberty based on his own independent judgment, even if that requires overturning past precedents and recanting an earlier vote.

As in *Lee* and *Lawrence*, Scalia objects to Kennedy's result and reasoning.[71] In exercising "independent judgment," he says, the Court "proclaims itself the sole arbiter of our Nation's moral standards": "I do not believe . . . that the meaning of our Eighth Amendment, any more than the meaning of our other provisions of our Constitution, should be determined by the subjective views of five Members of this Court and like-minded foreigners" (1217). Scalia further rejects the idea "that American law should conform to the rest of the world" (1226). Many aspects of U.S. law—such as the exclusionary rule, the reading of establishment of religion, and the constitutionality of abortion legislation—differ from those of other nations (1227–1228). "To invoke alien law when it agrees with one's own thinking, and ignore it otherwise," Scalia writes, "is not reasoned decisionmaking, but sophistry" (1228).

Scalia concludes by responding to Kennedy's closing oratory. Consistent with his commitment to text and specific tradition, Scalia finds most relevant "the centuries-old American practice—a practice still engaged in by a large majority of the relevant states—of letting a jury of 12 citizens decide whether, in the particular case, youth should be the basis for withholding the death penalty." For the majority, Scalia writes, "what these foreign sources 'affirm,' rather than repudiate, is the Justices' own notion of how the world ought to be, and their diktat that it shall be so henceforth in America" (1229). To Scalia, Kennedy's use of comparative law—no less than the use of political consensus and social science research—cloaks personal preference in legal citation.

DIGNITY, PERSONALITY, AND CATHOLICISM

Kennedy's reliance on liberty and human dignity—criticized by Scalia as merely Kennedy's personal preference—is likely inspired by his Catholicism.[72] His language in these cases finds parallels in several post–Vatican-II era pronouncements, particularly *Dignitatis Humanae*.[73] While the subject of that declaration is religious liberty, it provides a basis for the larger conception of human dignity expressed in *Lee, Roper,* and *Lawrence*. Theological fidelity aside, Kennedy's rhetoric of liberty and human dignity appears to be profoundly shaped by his Catholicism.

The clearest rhetorical connection to Catholic thought is found in Kennedy's coercion principle and its articulation in *Lee*. *Dignitatis Humanae* affirmed the right to religious freedom based on the "dignity" of all human beings "because they are persons, that is, beings endowed with reason and free will and therefore bearing personal responsibility" (1.2, 2.9, 3.11–12). From this dignity and nature, "human beings should respond to the word of God freely, and . . . therefore nobody is to be forced to embrace the faith against their will." All persons "are to be guided by their own judgments and to enjoy freedom" (2.9, 2.11), including those "who do not live up to their obligation of seeking the truth and adhering to it" (1.2).

To ensure this search for truth is free and genuine, all persons must "enjoy both psychological freedom and immunity from external coercion" (1.2, see also 2.12). That command, like Kennedy's statement in *Lee,* moves beyond formal penalties by government to embody a broader freedom from all social coercion and a broader freedom of conscience and judgment. As the declaration states, "people nowadays are subjected to a variety of pressures and run the risk of being prevented from acting with their own free judgment." Because "the act of faith of its very nature is a free act, in religious matters *every* form of human coercion should be excluded," no matter the source (2.11, my emphasis). To allow all persons to gain a "deeper knowledge of truth," "no one is to be coerced into believing" or "to be forced to embrace the faith against their will" (1.3, 1.8, 2.10). Acts of true faith "cannot be commanded or forbidden by any merely human authority" (1.3). As a result, "the individual must not be forced to act against conscience" or "be prevented from acting according to conscience, especially in religious matters" (1.3).

Freedom for the religious is limited by the fundamental considerations of the human dignity of dissenters that form the foundation of Kennedy's reasoning in *Lee.* All individuals and groups, including government, thus must avoid coercing persons who dissent from or do not accept majority views. "The search for truth," the declaration states, "must be carried out in a manner that is appropriate to the dignity and social nature of the human person; that is, by free enquiry with the help of teaching or instruction, communication and dialogue." This search must be personal and cannot be compelled by others or by government. "In spreading religious beliefs and in introducing religious practices," the declaration states, "everybody must, at all times, avoid any action which seems to suggest coercion or dishonest or unworthy persuasion." Groups or individuals have the right to persuade others of their moral views, but actions that force others to act contrary to conscience "must be considered an abuse of one's own right and an infringement of the rights of others" (1.4). The rhetoric—and perhaps the substance—of Kennedy's conceptions of human dignity and personality, his opposition to coercion, and his ideal of a social dialogue were influenced by ideas such as those stated in *Dignitatis Humanae.*[74]

Kennedy's opinion in *Roper* also includes considerations of human personality, dignity, and capacity for redemption that resonate in Catholic thought. For Kennedy, the idea that juveniles do not have a sufficiently developed personality is fundamental to the argument that executing them for an act committed at that age constitutes cruel and unusual punishment. This ideal is consistent with the Catholic catechism, which states that the "traditional teaching of the Church does not exclude recourse to the death penalty." In *Roper*, Kennedy does not question the constitutionality of the death penalty as a general matter.[75] Nevertheless, the Catholic catechism advises that if nonlethal means are available, "authority will limit itself to such means, as these are more in keeping with the concrete conditions of the common good and more in conformity to the dignity of the human person."

While the Catholic Church says such circumstances are "very rare, if not practically nonexistent," it also emphasizes that the state, "by rendering one who has committed an offense incapable of doing harm," can maintain public safety and order "without definitely taking away from [an offender] the possibility of redeeming himself."[76] In *Roper*, Kennedy applies this possibility of redemption to those who commit capital crimes as minors, finding that "it is difficult even for expert psychologists to differentiate between the juvenile offender whose crime reflects unfortunate yet transient immaturity, and the rare juvenile offender whose crime reflects irreparable corruption."[77] If one's personality may not yet be fully developed, a chance for redemption remains. This possibility for redemption appears again in his 2008 opinion for the Court in *Kennedy v. Louisiana.*

Even Kennedy's opinion in *Lawrence* employs characteristically Catholic language of human dignity. As *Persona Humanae* (1975) states, the church has traditionally drawn a distinction between homosexual inclination and homosexual acts.[78] This distinction may have led to Kennedy's opinion in *Romer v. Evans* striking a state constitutional amendment that created a legal classification of homosexual persons. (I discuss *Romer* in more depth in Chapter 4.) *Persona Humanae* admits that some homosexuals may have that orientation "because of some kind of innate instinct or a pathological constitution judged to be incurable." Such people "must certainly be treated with understanding," and "their culpability will be judged with prudence" (8.3–8.4).

Yet the same declaration states that homosexual acts are "intrinsically disordered and can in no case be approved of." This idea was emphasized in 1986, when, in a letter from John Paul II that included the name of then-cardinal Joseph Ratzinger as prefect, the Vatican reiterated that "as in every moral disorder, homosexual activity prevents one's own fulfillment and happiness by acting contrary to the creative wisdom of God. The Church, in rejecting erroneous opinions regarding homosexuality, does not limit but rather defends personal freedom and dignity realistically and authentically understood."[79] Even this letter states that "it is deplorable that homosexual persons have been and are the object of violent malice in speech or in action." The church writes that "such treatment deserves condemnation" and "reveals a kind of disregard for others which endangers the most fundamental principles of a healthy society. The intrinsic dignity of each person must always be respected in word, in action and in law" (10.1).

In *Lawrence,* Kennedy seems to create a Dworkinian distinction: he agrees with the church's larger concept of human dignity but disagrees with its application to laws regarding homosexual behavior. The church claims that homosexuality is "a disordered sexual inclination which is essentially self-indulgent." As a result, "homosexual activity prevents one's own fulfillment and happiness by acting contrary to the creative wisdom of God." With this teaching, the church claims that it "does not limit but rather defends personal freedom and dignity realistically and authentically understood." The church, however, "warns against generalizations in judging individual cases." More generally, "what is at all costs to be avoided is the unfounded and demeaning assumption that the sexual behavior of homosexual persons is always and totally compulsive and therefore inculpable." "What is essential," the letter states, "is that the fundamental liberty which characterizes the human person and gives him his dignity be recognized as belonging to the homosexual person as well" (11.2).

These essential ideals of human dignity are evident in Kennedy's opinion in *Lawrence.* To Kennedy, homosexuality is not necessarily a hindrance to one's personality; rather, it can be an essential component of it. By showing how laws such as Texas's lead to additional discrimination and diminished status in the community and how the *Bowers* precedent itself demeans, Kennedy focuses on how such criminal laws—and their constitutional defense—can harm homosexuals in both the public and private sphere. The church warns against giving same-sex relationships the same legal status as marriage, and Kennedy's opinion in *Lawrence* states in at least two places that the Constitution does not require governments to recognize same-sex relationships. Kennedy concludes, however, that forming such relationships "is within the liberty of persons to choose without being punished as criminals." Striking Texas's law allows all citizens—including homosexuals—to "retain their dignity as free persons."[80] For Kennedy, the harm to dignity involves both the practical harm of allowing such laws and the jurisprudential harm of the reasoning of *Bowers*.

These sources of Catholic thought suggest possible explanations for the rhetoric and perhaps even for the substantive roots of Kennedy's ideals of liberty and human dignity. They provide a substantive basis and—along with social science research, political development, and comparative constitutional law—serve as an objective referent to the subjective considerations of personality that Kennedy articulated in his confirmation hearings. The similarities between the language of Kennedy's opinions in *Lee, Roper,* and *Lawrence* and prominent writings in Catholic social thought with which he is likely familiar are significant.

CONCLUSION

Although these cases involve different constitutional provisions, Kennedy's opinions for the Court in *Lee, Lawrence,* and *Roper* demonstrate how he seeks to define constitutional liberty. In method, he moves beyond history and tradition to adopt an approach with parallels to Ronald Dworkin's moral reading of the Constitution, William Brennan's reliance on human dignity, and Randy Barnett's presumption of liberty. Kennedy believes that the Western concepts of liberty and human dignity serve as foundations for the U.S. Constitution, and that the duty of the judiciary is to discover and enforce the full and necessary meaning of liberty. Substantively, this conception of liberty requires judicial sensitivity to the many ways in which government actions, supported by the majority, can prevent individuals from fully developing their own personalities.

Kennedy's approach does raise the objection mentioned in confirmation hearings by Senator Gordon Humphrey, and later, on the Court, by Justice Scalia. While Kennedy claims to find objective referents for his conclusions, Humphrey and Scalia argue that he in fact seeks to impose his own preferences through subjective standards that are easily manipulated. Kennedy's citation of social science research, the direction of political consensus, and comparative constitutional law arises from his search for objective referents to support a vision of human dignity with apparent rhetorical and substantive foundations in Catholic teachings. Scalia—a Catholic born in the same year as Kennedy—criticizes Kennedy for engaging in "psychology practiced by amateurs," for importing the views of the "law profession culture," and for invoking the views of "like-minded foreigners." To Scalia, Kennedy does little more than "rattle off a collection of adjectives that simply decorate a value judgment and conceal a political choice" based only on "personal predilection." These questions of personal liberty and dignity, Scalia believes, are simply value judgments that judges cannot show to be true or false. And "value judgments," he notes, "should be voted on, not dictated by courts."[81]

Scalia's criticisms of the Court's use of social science research, political consensus, and comparative law cut to the heart of Kennedy's jurisprudential project.[82] Such efforts to define and enforce the full and necessary meaning of liberty, Scalia believes, are not based on statements of fact (which can be true or false), but on values. "I am not looking for the evolving standards of decency of American society; I'm not looking for what is the best answer in my mind as an intelligent judge," he states in a 2005 public debate with Breyer. "I try to understand what it meant, what was understood by the society to mean when it was adopted. And I don't think it changes since then." The use of foreign law in judicial decision-making, he warns, is "manipulation" and a way to impose a judge's own "moral perceptions" on society.[83] It is this personalization that he has long found to be the greatest danger in judicial interpretation of any law.[84]

Essentially, Scalia defines the debate over the use of comparative materials as one about the larger role of judges and courts. He believes that any argument for the use of comparative materials in American constitutional interpretation "assumes that it is up to the judge to find THE correct answer." He believes the cases where the Court has used foreign materials mostly "involve moral sentiments," and thus "you're not going to come up with a right or wrong answer." To Scalia, decisions on these questions made by other nations and other courts are thus irrelevant. "I'm sure that intelligent men and women abroad can make very intelligent arguments," he states. "But that's not the issue, because it should not be up to me to make those moral determinations." If you think the law violates morality, "persuade your fellow citizens and repeal the laws." Scalia's larger objection arises from his belief that the greatest danger in judicial interpretation is that judges will read their own preferences into the law and thus deny the power of the people under an essentially democratic Constitution.

In contrast to Scalia, Kennedy believes that the U.S. Constitution protects ideals of individual liberty and dignity. Those ideals have right answers and objective meaning discoverable by judges. The concept of liberty is amorphous, Kennedy admits, and lines can be difficult to draw. To interpret the document faithfully, however, judges have an obligation to define the scope of those concepts and apply them. Kennedy employs sources outside the American legal tradition—comparative law, social science, and political developments—because of what he sees as his official duty to provide "objective referents" for these conclusions. His opinions in *Lee, Lawrence,* and *Roper*—and his jurisprudence as a whole—should be viewed not as verbal rationalizations of preexisting ideological attitudes, or, as Scalia puts it, as manipulation of sources that "simply decorate a value judgment and conceal a political choice" at bottom based only on "personal predilection." Rightly understood, Kennedy's jurisprudence should be judged as a continuing duty to discover and enforce the full and necessary meaning of personal liberty.

2. Still Struggling:
Anthony Kennedy and Abortion

I am still struggling with the whole abortion issue and
thought it proper to convey this in what I wrote.
—HANDWRITTEN CORRESPONDENCE FROM
KENNEDY TO HARRY BLACKMUN, JUNE 21, 1990

Justice Anthony M. Kennedy's opinion for the Court in *Gonzales v. Carhart* (2007),[1] upholding a federal criminal ban on intact dilation and extraction ("partial-birth") abortions, generated as much controversy for its rhetoric as for its result. Dissenting Justice Ruth Bader Ginsburg criticized its reliance on "ancient notions about women's place in the family."[2] Commentators characterized it as confused, paternalistic, patronizing, and preachy.[3] Others wrote that the opinion "treats women as symbols rather than actual people,"[4] found it "inconsistent" with "the otherwise libertarian arguments" Kennedy "has employed in other abortion cases,"[5] or speculated that it was motivated by the majority justices' Catholicism.[6]

Ginsburg went further, stating "the Court's hostility to the right *Roe* and *Casey* secured is not concealed."[7] Her claim that *Gonzales* indicates hostility to *Roe v. Wade*[8] and *Planned Parenthood v. Casey*[9] raises a paradox. According to many scholars—and even Justice Ginsburg herself[10]—the plurality opinion in *Casey* (1992), which was coauthored by Kennedy, placed the abortion right announced in *Roe* on a sounder constitutional foundation.[11] Yet *Gonzales* is neither the first time Kennedy has used paternalistic and moralistic language in his abortion opinions[12] nor the first time it has provoked responses from fellow justices.

In this chapter I situate Kennedy's *Gonzales* opinion within his larger behavior in abortion cases. I begin by assessing his position before the decision in *Casey*, including his role in *Webster v. Reproductive Health Services*[13] as well as his opinions in two 1990 cases involving parental notification and consent requirements for minors, *Hodgson v. Minnesota*[14] and *Ohio v. Akron Center for Reproductive Health*.[15] Kennedy's actions reflected his stated desire to narrow *Roe* without overturning it, something he would achieve by changing its constitutional foundations from privacy to liberty in ways consistent with his prenomination statements. His rhetoric aroused opposition from within the Court—particularly from the chambers of Justice Blackmun—and an admission from Kennedy that he was "still struggling with the whole abortion issue."

I then focus on Kennedy's role in the *Casey* decision, his success in recasting the foundations of the abortion right from privacy to liberty, and his introduction of a new state interest in promoting respect for fetal life. I examine Kennedy's dissents in two abortion-related cases from 2000: *Stenberg v. Carhart*,[16] the first partial-birth abortion case arising from Nebraska, and *Hill v. Colorado*,[17] a First Amendment case decided on the same day involving protests on public grounds around health-care facilities. In *Hill*—a dissent read from the bench—Kennedy sketches what he considers a "reasoned, careful" constitutional balance[18] concerning abortion. In both cases he outlines an increasing government interest in promoting profound respect for fetal life. Finally, I revisit Kennedy's rhetoric in *Gonzales*, trace it to the larger conceptions of human dignity, liberty, and regret with foundations in Catholic social thought, and assess how Ginsburg's recent dissent echoes Blackmun's earlier criticisms of Kennedy's approach.

Rightly understood, Kennedy's rhetoric in *Gonzales* does not signal his intention to overturn *Roe* or *Casey.* It does, however, highlight a significant tension that exists throughout his abortion opinions. Kennedy attempts to justify a role for government as a moral instructor promoting profound respect for fetal life within a larger jurisprudence based on a judicial ideal that "our obligation is to define the liberty of all, not to mandate our own moral code."[19] The emotional and moralistic language in Kennedy's opinions reveals this tension within his jurisprudence and undermines his project to articulate a reasoned, careful balance to the abortion issue.

FROM *WEBSTER* TO *CASEY:* FROM PRIVACY TO LIBERTY

Material from the papers of Justice Harry A. Blackmun shows Kennedy wrestling with the abortion issue during his early years on the Court. Prior to coming to the Court, Kennedy embraced an expansive role for judges in defining and enforcing constitutional liberty. But he also expressed concern about using the terminology of a right to privacy to invalidate most government attempts to regulate abortion. In *Webster* and other cases, Kennedy acted not to overturn *Roe* but to refine and limit it in a way that would allow more government regulation of the procedure while retaining a judicial role in enforcing individual liberty.

In these cases from 1989 to 1992, even as Kennedy sided with Chief Justice William H. Rehnquist and Justice Byron White—the two dissenters in *Roe*—the opinions he wrote and joined included rhetorical and substantive changes that reflected his concerns. These opinions never sought directly to overrule *Roe*, but they did seek to narrow it substantially. Kennedy's own opinions in two cases from 1990—particularly *Ohio v. Akron Center for Reproductive Health*[20]—preview the language he would later use in *Casey, Hill,* and *Gonzales.* His position and rhetoric did not escape criticism within the Court, and that rhetoric created what appeared to be a jurisprudence of doubt.

Roe *and* Webster

Kennedy first faced the abortion issue during his first full term on the Court in *Webster,* which involved, among other provisions, Missouri's requirement that doctors test for fetal age before performing an abortion if they had reason to believe the fetus was twenty weeks or older. A fractured Court upheld the requirement as a reasonable regulation for promoting its interest in the potentiality of human life, even though the regulation—which reaches into the second trimester—would have been found unconstitutional under the trimester framework established in *Roe v. Wade.*[21]

Although Kennedy did not write separately in *Webster,* Blackmun's papers suggest that his involvement was critical to the outcome of the case and the conflicted nature of the Court's opinions. At conference, Kennedy admitted that this requirement would be "invalid under *Roe*" and *Colautti.*[22] Despite these precedents, Kennedy voted to save Missouri's law. Thus he "would cut back on this" line of precedent.[23]

Although the existence of a constitutional right to abortion was not directly implicated by this case, in conference Kennedy also expressed his larger position on *Roe.* "On pure *stare decisis,*" he stated, he "would leave" *Roe* "alone." Nevertheless, *Roe* "continues to do damage to the Court and judicial review and conception of judge's proper position and role." Kennedy would find the abortion right not as a fundamental right under the right of privacy or the Equal Protection Clause, but as a protected liberty.[24] Such a change would "return this debate to the democratic process," which, he said, would "protect the rights of young women." As a result, Kennedy would "reach merits and alter the methodology and structure of *Roe*." He would thus consider abortion not as part of a right to privacy, but more directly as a liberty protected under Fourteenth Amendment Due Process Clause. Further, he would overturn the "rigid" trimester system established in *Roe* to allow for more government regulation of the abortion procedure.

The position expressed by Kennedy in conference concerning *Roe* likely influenced several changes to Rehnquist's plurality opinion. *Webster* attempts to distinguish *Roe* from *Griswold*, a case Kennedy had approvingly cited in his confirmation hearings. "Unlike *Roe*," Rehnquist writes, *Griswold* "did not purport to adopt a whole framework, complete with detailed rules and distinctions, to govern the cases in which the asserted liberty interest would apply."[25] Rehnquist's earlier draft criticized *Roe* because it "sought to establish a constitutional framework for judging state regulation during the entire term of pregnancy" and "to balance once and for all by reference only to the calendar the claims of the State to protect the fetus as a form of human life against the claims of a woman to decide for herself whether or not to abort a fetus she was carrying."[26] "The rigid trimester analysis," Rehnquist writes, ended up "making constitutional law in this area a virtual Procrustean bed."[27] The Court, as a result, "would modify and narrow *Roe* and succeeding cases" (521).

An additional change to *Webster* reflects the liberty-based approach and faith in the democratic process that Kennedy expressed in conference. Rehnquist rejects Blackmun's raising of the "great debate" in constitutional interpretation. "There is wisdom," he writes, "in not unnecessarily attempting to elaborate the abstract differences between a 'fundamental right' to abortion . . . a 'limited fundamental constitutional right,' which Justice Blackmun treats *Roe* as having established, or a liberty interest protected by the Due Process Clause, which we believe it to be" (547). To Rehnquist, "the goal of constitutional interpretation is surely not to remove inexorably 'politically divisive' issues from the ambit of the democratic process, whereby the people, through their elected representatives, deal with matters of concern to them." Rather— echoing Kennedy's comments in conference—"the goal of constitutional interpretation is to hold true the balance between that which the Constitution puts beyond the reach of the democratic process and that which it does not. We think we have done that here today."[28]

Rehnquist criticizes Blackmun for insinuating "that legislative bodies, in a Nation where more than half of our population is women, will treat our decision today as an invitation to enact abortion regulation reminiscent of the Dark Ages." By doing so, Blackmun thus "not only misreads our views but does scant justice to those who serve in such bodies and the people who elect them" (522). These passages in Rehnquist's opinion reiterate support for *Griswold*, recast abortion as a liberty interest rather than a fundamental right under the right of privacy, and reiterate the protections of the democratic process without overturning *Roe*. Each of these decisions demonstrates Kennedy's influence.

Justices from each side criticized this approach in Rehnquist's opinion, claiming that the plurality "would effectively overrule *Roe v. Wade*." Scalia criticizes the majority for acting to "contrive" not to overrule *Roe*, and he characterizes the plurality's ruling as "the most stingy possible," "indecisive," and "the least responsible course" (532, 535, 537). As Scalia writes, "the mansion of constitutionalized abortion law, constructed overnight in *Roe v. Wade*, must be disassembled doorjamb by doorjamb, and never entirely brought down, no matter how wrong it might be" (536).

Blackmun states that *Roe* and the abortion right "survive but are not secure." The plurality, he says, "implicitly invites every state legislature to enact more and more restrictive abortion regulations in order to provoke more and more test cases, in the hope that somewhere down the line the Court will return the law of procreative freedom to the severe limitations that actually prevailed in this country before January 22, 1973." The plurality "foments disregard for the law and our standing decisions" and has "gone about its business in . . . a deceptive fashion" (537). He finds "tucked away at the end of its opinion . . . a radical reversal in the law of abortion" (541). To Blackmun, the criticism of the trimester framework by the plurality proves "merely an excuse for avoiding the real issues embedded in this case and a mask for its hostility to the constitutional rights that *Roe* recognized" (547, fn. 7). From a "contrived" conflict, the plurality develops a new standard under which, "for all practical purposes, *Roe* would be overruled" (555).

The *Webster* plurality ignored this great debate and produced a confusing opinion that continued a jurisprudence of doubt. While Scalia and Blackmun saw the opinion as silently overruling *Roe*,[29] some insightful scholars—like Daniel Farber—read the plurality's language as a reaffirmation of some abortion right.[30] While Farber attributed this change of view to Rehnquist, the more accurate explanation is that Kennedy fundamentally disagreed with

Rehnquist and White about the status of *Roe* and the answers to these larger questions.

Hodgson *and* Akron Center

One year after *Webster,* Kennedy wrote his first abortion opinions in two cases involving regulations involving minors seeking abortions. In *Hodgson v. Minnesota,*[31] Kennedy voted to uphold a statute requiring teenagers to notify two parents, and he would have upheld it even if the law did not include a provision for a minor to bypass the notification requirement by gaining permission from a judge. In *Ohio v. Akron Center,*[32] decided the same day, Kennedy upheld a law requiring a minor to obtain the consent of one parent. In both opinions, Kennedy uses language about the nature of the abortion decision that previews his rhetoric in *Casey* and *Gonzales,* and in *Akron Center* his language attracts charges of paternalism similar to the ones made after *Gonzales.*

In *Hodgson,* Kennedy justifies the two-parent notice requirement by emphasizing the importance of family ties for minors making abortion decisions. He begins the opinion by quoting the Court's earlier decision in *Bellotti v. Baird*[33] that abortion "is a grave decision, and a girl of tender years, under emotional stress, may be ill-equipped to make it without mature advice and emotional support."[34] Kennedy identifies two relevant state interests: promoting "the welfare of pregnant minors," and "acknowledging and promoting the role of parents in the care and upbringing of their children" (481). The family bond, for Kennedy, is paramount: "We have held that parents have a liberty interest, protected by the Constitution, in having a reasonable opportunity to develop close relations with their children" (484). Furthermore, notification provides more than medical benefit: "To deny parents this knowledge," he writes, "is to risk, or perpetuate, estrangement or alienation from the child when she is in the greatest need of parental guidance and support" (486). Minnesota's notification law "does not place an absolute obstacle before any minor seeking an abortion, and it represents a considered weighing of the competing interests of minors and their parents" (496). Its purpose "rests upon a tradition of a parental role in the care and upbringing of children that is as old as civilization itself" (501).

Kennedy admits that this tradition is based on an ideal. "For all too many young women," he writes, "the prospect of two parents, perhaps even one parent, sustaining her with support that is compassionate and committed is an illusion." Studies chronicling abuse and neglect, he writes, "are but fragments of the evidence showing the tragic reality that becomes day-to-day life for thousands of minors." Nevertheless, in striking the two-parent notification provision without bypass, "the Court errs in serious degree when it commands its own solution to the cruel consequences of individual misconduct, parental failure and social ills." Minnesota sought "to recognize and promote the primacy of the family tie," Kennedy writes, "a concept which this Court now seems intent on declaring a constitutional irrelevance" (501).

In *Akron Center*—announced on the same day as *Hodgson*—Kennedy wrote for a majority upholding Ohio's one-parent consent law that included a judicial bypass. As in *Hodgson*, most of Kennedy's opinion focuses on the importance of parental liberty in the upbringing of minor children.[35] But the concluding passage (Part V) is most revealing. The Ohio law, he writes, "does not impose an undue, or otherwise unconstitutional burden on a minor seeking an abortion."[36] He also states that "the legislature acted in a rational manner" (520). Perhaps in an attempt to attract O'Connor's vote, he obscures the test he employs. But whatever his alternative, with these words Kennedy rejects *Roe*'s trimester system and its strict scrutiny of all abortion legislation.

Kennedy then employs language that previews his rhetoric in *Casey*. A woman's decision about whether to have an abortion, he writes, is a grave one that "will embrace her own destiny and personal dignity, and the origins of the other human life that lie within the embryo." This language about destiny and human dignity resonates with the list of considerations Kennedy discussed in his confirmation hearing as components of personal liberty. But the second part of the sentence emphasizes the importance of the value of fetal life. Given the significance of the abortion decision to the woman and to the larger culture, Kennedy writes, "a free and enlightened society may decide that each of its members should attain a clearer, more tolerant understanding of the profound philosophic choices confronted by a woman who is considering whether to seek an abortion" (520). He characterizes the abortion decision as a philosophical choice that implicates the woman's personal destiny and dignity. By including the ideal of a free and enlightened society, Kennedy lays the foundation for state interests in both ensuring free and informed choices and promoting respect for fetal life. These state interests apply to all women—not just minors—and exist at all stages of pregnancy.

Returning to the case before him, Kennedy argues for the specific requirement of parental consent: "The State is entitled to presume that, for most of its people, the beginnings of that understanding will be within the family, society's most intimate association." Ohio can require parental notice because "in most instances, the family will strive to give a lonely or even terrified minor advice that is both compassionate and mature." To Kennedy, "it would deny all dignity to the family to say that the State cannot take this reasonable step in regulating its health professions to ensure that, in most cases, a young woman will receive guidance and understanding from a parent" (520). Although Kennedy rests his opinions on the constitutionally recognized family tie, his rhetoric acknowledges the moral gravity of the abortion decision as well as moral concerns that would justify state regulation. He also recognizes a greater state interest in regulating the health profession, one he would later emphasize in *Stenberg* and *Gonzales*.

Although Kennedy wrote for a majority in *Akron Center*, Part V spoke only for a plurality; O'Connor wrote, "I join all but Part V of your opinion."[37] O'Connor often wrote separately in abortion cases, acting as a "concurring voice" to "shape the development of legal doctrine."[38] She may have refused to join Part V because of its equivocation about whether the proper standard of review was the "rational basis" test indicated by the plurality in *Webster* or the "undue burden test" long advocated by O'Connor that would later emerge in *Casey*. Her refusal may have also reflected unease at the opinion's moral characterization of women who seek abortions. Justice John Paul Stevens also decided not to join Part V, leaving it the plurality view of only Kennedy, Scalia, White, and Rehnquist.

The more visible response to Part V came from Justice Blackmun, who replies in dissent that Kennedy "engages in paternalistic comments."[39] "Some" of Kennedy's observations "may be so 'in most cases,'" Blackmun writes, "and, it is to be hoped, in judges' own and other warm and protected, nurturing family environments." But "most cases need not rely on constitutional protections that are so vital for others." Blackmun—himself not immune to using emotional language—continued: "It is the unfortunate denizens of that world, often frightened and forlorn, lacking the comfort of loving parental guidance and mature advice, who most need the constitutional protection that the Ohio Legislature set out to make as difficult as possible to obtain" (541).

Blackmun objects to Ohio's "stridently and offensively restrictive" law. Yet he also implicitly attacks Kennedy's attempt both to retain and to narrow *Roe*. As Blackmun writes, "it is as if the Legislature said, 'If the courts of the United States insist on upholding a limited right to abortion, let us make that

Dear Harry,

After much hesitation, I decided it best for our collegial relation and, I hope, mutual respect to tell you that I harbor deep resentment at your paragraph on page 17 in Ohio v. Akron Center. You say my hypothesis is to incite an inflamed public. To write with that purpose would be a violation of my judicial duty.

I am still struggling with the whole abortion issue and thought it proper to convey this in what I wrote. Though I have not read it, I am told L. Tribe's just issued work "[A] Clash of Absolutes," makes the same point, though perhaps at more length.

I do not question the depth of your compassion and understanding, but neither do I yield to the charge that my own is somehow a mask for some improper purpose.

In any event, though it is late in the

Kennedy's handwritten note to Blackmun, June 21, 1990, where he states that he is "still struggling with the whole abortion issue." Copy reproduced from the Blackmun Papers, Box 544, Folder 2. Manuscript Division, Library of Congress, Washington, D.C.

abortion as difficult as possible to obtain' because, basically, whether on professed moral or religious grounds or whatever, 'we believe that is the way it must be'" (541–542). In response to Kennedy's faith in the democratic process, Blackmun writes that "few are the instances where the injustice is so evident and the impediments so gross as those inflicted by the Ohio Legislature on these vulnerable and powerless young women" (542).

Blackmun's initial criticism of Kennedy's rhetoric about the nature of the abortion decision, the state of women who face such decisions, and the ultimate state of *Roe* was even sharper. His first draft stated that the plurality opinion "concludes. . . . with hyperbole that can have but one purpose: to further incite an American press, public and pulpit already inflamed by the pronouncement made by a plurality of this Court last Term in *Webster*."[40] In response to this draft, Kennedy sent a handwritten note to Blackmun's chambers. "I harbor deep resentment at your paragraph on page 17 in *Ohio v. Akron Center*," Kennedy wrote. "You say my hyperbole is to incite an inflamed public. I am still struggling with the whole abortion issue and thought it proper to convey this in what I wrote."[41]

Kennedy then turns to the implications of Blackmun's criticism. "I do not question the depth of your compassion and understanding," he writes, "but neither do I yield to the charge that my own is somehow a mask for some improper motive." Kennedy hopes that "perhaps" his note would cause Blackmun "to reconsider what is a most unfair attribution of motives not consonant with the conscientious discharge of my office."[42] To "assuage your feelings," Blackmun responded, in the final opinion he would change "purpose" to "result."[43]

By 1990, Kennedy's struggle over abortion was not about whether to overturn *Roe.* It was about how to modify and narrow *Roe* to allow for more democratic regulation of abortion while retaining it as a judicially enforceable liberty. His opinions cast abortion as a grave philosophical moral issue, one that primarily affects the individual woman and that should thus be protected. Nevertheless, the decision also implicates the rights of others, including parents. To Kennedy, the profound moral and practical effects of the abortion decision produces an additional state interest in ensuring a choice that is free and informed—a state interest that exists throughout pregnancy. In *Hodgson* and *Akron Center* Kennedy articulated a new government interest consistent with free and enlightened societies: promoting respect for life. This interest appears consistent with his vote in *Webster.* The struggle is over how to construct and articulate a new standard that recognizes the liberty of the woman as well as these relevant state interests. Given the balance of the rest of the Court, Kennedy's individual struggle with the abortion issue produced a jurisprudence of doubt.

CASEY: CROSSING THE RUBICON?

Kennedy's pivotal role in *Planned Parenthood v. Casey* is well known, and the plurality opinion should be seen as evidence of the success of his larger jurisprudential project. While retaining the "core holding" of *Roe,* the plurality shifted the abortion right's constitutional foundations from privacy to liberty and articulated an undue burden standard to allow for more state regulation of abortion. More significantly, the Court recognized a new state interest in promoting respect for fetal life. In articulating this state interest in morality, however, Kennedy introduced a tension within a jurisprudence based on the ideal that "our obligation is to define the liberty of all, not mandate our own moral code." This tension—largely latent in *Casey*—would emerge to play a central role in later cases involving abortion.

Casey *in Chambers*

Planned Parenthood of Southeastern Pennsylvania v. Casey involved challenges to changes to the Pennsylvania abortion code made during the late 1980s, including some passed after the Court's decision in *Webster*. These changes included requirements that a woman seeking an abortion receive informed consent about the procedure, that a woman wait twenty-four hours after receiving this information before undergoing an abortion, that a minor seeking an abortion have the informed consent of one parent or a court order, and that a married woman sign a statement affirming that she had notified her husband about the abortion. The law included definitions of medical emergencies that would excuse these requirements, and it imposed certain reporting requirements on facilities providing abortions. The Court of Appeals—employing O'Connor's undue burden standard rather than *Roe*'s trimester framework—upheld all of the law except for the spousal notification requirement.[44]

According to Blackmun's conference notes, Kennedy initially voted to uphold all of Pennsylvania's requirements—including spousal notification—as "neutral provisions." As at the *Webster* conference, Kennedy said he would "overrule parts of *Akron* and *Thornburgh*."[45] Blackmun's notes include no indication that Kennedy would vote to overturn *Roe*. On May 27, 1992, Chief Justice Rehnquist circulated the first draft of an attempted majority opinion.[46] That draft—which sought to include Kennedy—stated that "we are now of the view that, in terming this right fundamental, the Court in *Roe* read the earlier opinions upon which it based its decision much too broadly." The Court "reached too far when it . . . thereby deemed the right to abortion fundamental."[47] As in *Webster*, Rehnquist's draft clearly attempts to attract Kennedy by seeking to narrow *Roe* but not overturn it.

Soon after the Rehnquist draft circulated, Kennedy sent a note to Blackmun stating, "I need to see you as soon as you have a few free moments. I want to tell you about some developments in *Planned Parenthood v. Casey*, and at least part of what I say should come as welcome news."[48] According to Blackmun's notes about this meeting—which apparently took place on May 30[49]—Kennedy was "delegated" by O'Connor and David Souter. Kennedy said the plurality had determined that *Roe* was sound, "though not the trimester system." The spousal notification requirement would be struck—a shift in Kennedy's position. Otherwise, he said, the Pennsylvania statute was constitutional. The Court would retain *Roe,* but overturn the 1983 decision in *Akron v. Akron Center for Reproductive Health* and the 1986 decision in *Thornburgh v. American College of Obstetricians.* Souter's section of the opinion would focus on the value of *stare decisis* that should be accorded to *Roe,* and "The 3"—as Blackmun called them—would adopt O'Connor's undue burden standard as the test for constitutionality of abortion regulations.

Blackmun's notes of his impressions about this meeting with Kennedy are particularly revealing in light of their exchanges two years earlier regarding *Akron Center.* Blackmun first writes, "Can I jam some RC agony and Harlan." Assuming RC stands for Roman Catholic, the note implies that Blackmun believed that Kennedy was still engaged in a moral and jurisprudential struggle with the abortion issue. (I'll return to explore this aspect later in the chapter.)

The influence of Justice John M. Harlan II in the final plurality opinion is evident. Part II includes an extended discussion of Harlan's liberty-based approach to substantive due process, with two long block quotations. The plurality cites Harlan's opinion in *Poe v. Ullman* to support the view that substantive due process requires judges to "exercise that same capacity which by tradition courts always have exercised: reasoned judgment. Its boundaries are not susceptible of expression as a simple rule."[50] Blackmun also notes that "election is urel." He was apparently convinced (or noted Kennedy's attempt to convince him) that the upcoming 1992 presidential election was "unrelated" to the decision to affirm *Roe.*[51] Nevertheless, in his published *Casey* opinion, Blackmun would describe the joint opinion as "an act of personal courage and constitutional principle."[52]

The first draft of the plurality opinion contained sharp criticisms of the initial decision in *Roe* consistent with the sentiments Kennedy had expressed three years earlier in the *Webster* conference. In Part II, the plurality states that the main problem with *Roe* was "not the strength of the woman's interest" but the undervaluing of "the interest of the State in the protection of potential life." This interest in protecting life is vital to Kennedy. "Had we been Members of the Court when the valuation of the State interest came before it as an original matter," he wrote, "we cannot say that we would have concluded, as the *Roe* Court did, that its weight is insignificant to justify a ban on abortions prior to viability even when it is subject to certain exemptions."[53]

Blackmun's notes from meeting with Kennedy, May 30, 1992. Copy reproduced from the Blackmun Papers, Box 601, Folder 6. Manuscript Division, Library of Congress, Washington, D.C.

Nevertheless, as he said in the *Webster* conference, "the matter is not before us in the first instance." Nearly twenty years later, he stated, "We are satisfied that the immediate question is not the soundness of *Roe*'s resolution of the issue, but the precedential force that its holding is entitled to be accorded."[54] This view is consistent with Blackmun's report of Souter's commitment to *stare decisis* and with Kennedy's conference statement in *Webster*. This passage would be dropped—at Stevens's request—to gain a majority for this section.[55]

This draft included a sharper critique of *Roe*'s trimester system. "A framework of this rigidity," it states, "was unnecessary and in its later interpretation contradicted the State's reasonable exercise of its powers."[56] To Kennedy, "the Constitution established a framework of democratic decisionmaking within the rule of law." Under that "system of ordered democracy," he writes, "decisions are reached through the efforts of the executive, legislative and judicial branches, each operating within its field of legitimate authority."[57] Although these passages were eventually deleted, their early inclusion reflects Kennedy's efforts in *Webster* and later cases to reconcile expansive judicial review with a confidence in the democratic process.

The draft also exhibits what some would deem paternalistic phrasing. Given the state interest in promoting potential life, Kennedy writes, "it follows as well that the State can enact reasonable measures to assure that the woman's decision is cautious, mature and informed." By using the adjectives "cautious" and "mature" to describe the abortion decision—and using them to describe decisions made not just by minors, but by all women—Kennedy accepts increasing state power to influence women. In the final opinion, this passage was moved to Part IV, with the wording changed from "cautious, mature and informed" to "informed" and "more informed and deliberate." The waiting-period and informed-consent requirements, the final draft said, would "facilitate wise exercise of the right."[58]

The Opinion in Casey: Ending the Jurisprudence of Doubt?

This background within the Court illuminates several aspects of Kennedy's contribution to the final plurality opinion in *Casey*. The opinion bases the constitutional right to abortion firmly on liberty rather than privacy. Kennedy's famous—or infamous—"heart of liberty" passage, which invited criticism first from Scalia, and later from Thomas and Ginsburg, is just one example of how the concept of liberty is emphasized in the opinion. The *Casey* opinion begins with the word "liberty," ends with the word "liberty," and emphasizes, "The controlling word in the case before us is 'liberty.'"[59] In his second draft, Kennedy added this passage: "It is a promise of the Constitution that there is a realm of personal liberty which the government may not enter."[60] Most significantly, the opinion states:

> These matters, involving the most intimate and personal choices a person may make in a lifetime, choices central to personal dignity and autonomy, are central

to the liberty protected by the Fourteenth Amendment. At the heart of liberty is the right to define one's own concept of existence, of meaning, of the universe, and of the mystery of human life.[61]

Although the "heart of liberty" passage has attracted the most rhetorical and substantive criticism, the sentence immediately following it presents an important clarification: "Beliefs about these matters could not define the attributes of personhood were they formed under compulsion of the State."[62] With this sentence, Kennedy connects the constitutional question of abortion to the broader moral conceptions of individual personality, liberty, free expression, and freedom from government coercion that form the core of his larger jurisprudence.[63] As he would put it in a later case, "at the heart of the First Amendment is the principle that each person should decide for him or herself the ideas and beliefs deserving of expression, consideration and allegiance."[64]

Elements of Kennedy's moral struggle with abortion do remain in the final opinion. This section of the opinion reflects Kennedy's portrayal of the abortion issue as essentially a moral one. People "of good conscience," he writes, can differ "about the profound moral and spiritual implications of terminating a pregnancy, even in its earliest stage."[65] Referring at least to himself, Kennedy admits that "some of us as individuals find abortion offensive to our most basic principles of morality, but that cannot control our decision." As judges, he says, "our obligation is to define the liberty of all, not to mandate our own moral code."[66]

Casey marks the limits of state power to enforce that belief against the liberty protected by the Constitution.[67] "The underlying constitutional issue," he states, "is whether the State can resolve these philosophical questions in such a definitive way that a woman lacks all choice in the matter."[68] Despite the philosophical nature of the abortion decision—one that ultimately requires constitutional protection—Kennedy steps back to define and limit the extent of this liberty. "Though the abortion decision may originate within the zone of conscience and belief," he writes, "it is more than a philosophic exercise" (852). Abortion is "a unique act," one that is "unique to the human condition and so unique to the law" (851).

That unique act is one "fraught with consequences," and the consequences he considers relevant warrant closer analysis. First are the consequences "for the woman who must live with the implications of her decision." Kennedy states that "the mother who carries a child to full term is subject to anxieties, to physical constraints, to pain that only she must bear." The sacrifices of a woman who bears a child, he writes, are "endured with a pride that ennobles her in the eyes of others and gives to the infant a bond of love." He would later use the "bond of love" language to different ends in *Gonzales*; in *Casey* he employs it to protect the core abortion right as one that belongs to the woman. The philosophical, psychological, and physical effects on the woman of denying the abortion decision prevent the conclusion "that the State is entitled to proscribe it in all instances." Given the anguish of the woman that would result from denying this choice, majority and historical beliefs about fetal life and the nobility of motherhood "cannot alone be grounds for the State to insist she make the sacrifice," he writes. "Her suffering is too intimate and personal for the State to insist, without more, upon its own vision of the woman's role" (852).

Kennedy then connects abortion to contraception and the precedent in *Griswold*. Both "involve personal decisions concerning not only the meaning of procreation but also human responsibility and respect for it" (852–853). Referring to both contraceptives and abortion, he says that "reasonable people will have differences of opinion about these matters." One position "is based on such reverence for the wonder of creation that any pregnancy ought to be welcomed and carried to full term no matter how difficult it will be to provide for the child and ensure its wellbeing." Another is that "the inability to provide for the nurture and care of the infant is a cruelty to the child and an anguish to the parent" (853).

In expressing these positions, Kennedy returns to the considerations of anguish and personality that he mentioned in his confirmation testimony. Individual beliefs about procreation "are intimate views with infinite variations," he writes, and "their deep and personal character" supported the decision in *Griswold* and decisions in later cases involving contraception. "The same concerns are present when the woman confronts the reality that, perhaps despite her attempts to avoid it, she has become pregnant," he observes. To Kennedy, "it was this dimension of personal liberty that *Roe* sought to protect." As Kennedy stated in the *Webster* conference, both substantive and precedential considerations led to this decision. Thus, "the reservations any of us may have in reaffirming the central holding of *Roe*"—reservations Kennedy had expressed more explicitly in the opinion's earlier drafts—"are outweighed by the explication of individual liberty we have given combined with the force of *stare decisis*" (853).

The opinion also outlines grounds for state regulation of the abortion procedure. It is personal, but not entirely private. The *Casey* plurality later states that "what is at stake is the woman's right to make the ultimate decision" is "not a right to be insulated from all others in doing so" (877). The opinion seeks to sketch principled and practical limits to the abortion liberty. In Part II, Kennedy states that the abortion decision has relevant consequences for others besides the mother: "for the spouse, family, and society, which must confront the knowledge that these procedures exist, procedures some deem nothing short of an act of violence against innocent human life; and, depending on one's beliefs, for the life or potential life that is aborted" (851). Abortion is a matter of belief with practical consequences; thus the final decision cannot be dictated by the state. Fetal life has a value, but that does not outweigh individual liberty; state power to enforce beliefs about the value of fetal life through an abortion ban must therefore be limited. "The destiny of the woman," Kennedy writes, "must be shaped to a large extent on her own conception of her spiritual imperatives and her place in society" (852).

In Part IV, the plurality adds a consideration not found in *Roe*. "Regulations which do no more than create a structural mechanism by which the State, or the parent or guardian of a minor, may express profound respect for the life of the unborn are permitted," the opinion states, "if they are not a substantial obstacle to the woman's exercise of the right to choose" (877). Government need not "remain truly agnostic"[69] or "abstain from indications of moral value."[70] Furthermore, "the woman's liberty is not so unlimited that from the outset the State cannot show its concern for the life of the unborn" (869). As this and later cases demonstrate, allowing states to act throughout pregnancy is essential to Kennedy's conception of the abortion right and his criticism of *Roe*. The Constitution allows government to recognize the moral value of fetal life; the woman's liberty limits the means by which states can promote that value.

In several other places, the *Casey* plurality asserts that because abortion is "fraught with consequences for others," the state can legislate to express this concern and to promote profound respect for fetal life. This interest in promoting profound respect for life is distinct from the protection of fetal life and justifies additional regulation of the woman's liberty (846). "A state measure designed to persuade [a woman] to choose childbirth over abortion," the plurality writes, "will be upheld if reasonably related to that goal" (878). This would include allowing a state to "require doctors to inform a woman seeking an abortion of the availability of materials relating to the consequences to the fetus, even when those consequences have no direct relation to her health," so long as that information is truthful (882). The intended effect may well discourage abortion: "Informed choice need not be defined in such narrow terms that all considerations of the effect on the fetus are made irrelevant" (883). As the plurality states, "requiring that the woman be informed of the availability of information relating to fetal development and the assistance available should she decide to carry the pregnancy to full term is a reasonable measure to ensure an informed choice, one which might cause the woman to choose childbirth over abortion" (883).[71]

In light of the earlier and later accusations of paternalism against Kennedy, the section of *Casey* striking the spousal notice requirement merits further attention. This is the one abortion provision that Kennedy has struck in his years on the Court, and one he voted at conference to uphold. The plurality differentiates spousal notice from parental consent, saying the latter is "based on the quite reasonable assumption that minors will benefit from consultation with their parents and that children will often not realize that their parents have their best interests at heart. We cannot adopt a parallel assumption about adult women" (895). The plurality admits that "there was a time, not so long ago, when a different understanding of the family and of the Constitution prevailed," citing *Bradwell v. Illinois*[72] and *Hoyt v. Florida*[73] as cases that exemplify views "no longer consistent with our understanding of the family, the individual or the Constitution" (896–897). The same section acknowledges that "it is an inescapable biological fact that state regulation with respect to the child a woman is carrying will have a far greater impact on the mother's liberty than on the father's" and that "women do not lose their constitutionally protected liberty when they marry" (896, 898). Although some— such as Justice Ginsburg—later find connections in this section with gender discrimination and equal protection,[74] the constitutional analysis in the *Casey* opinion focuses squarely on liberty.

By affirming the other provisions of Pennsylvania's statute, the *Casey* plurality focuses on the state interest of the abortion choice being—if not "mature"—at least free and informed. It supports the waiting period, saying that, assuming the delay "does not create any appreciable health risk . . . the idea that important decisions will be more informed and deliberate if they follow some period of reflection does not strike us as unreasonable" (885). An informed consent requirement "facilitates wise exercise of that, so long as the information is truthful, right" (887). The parental consent requirement for minors—with judicial bypass—in combination with the waiting period and informed consent requirements, "have particular force with respect to minors." They "may provide the parent or parents of a pregnant young woman the opportunity to consult with her in private, and to discuss the consequences of her decision in the context of the values and moral or religious principles of their family" (900).

From its first word to its last, the plurality opinion in *Casey* reflects Kennedy's success in influencing the Court. The decision modifies and narrows *Roe*, but does not overturn it. It recasts the foundation of the abortion right from privacy to liberty; it reaffirms a judicial duty to define and enforce the moral bases of that liberty; and it allows for greater democratic regulation of the procedure based on moral concerns. The *Casey* plurality emphasizes state interests in the abortion decision being free and informed, ratifies state preference for childbirth over abortion, and introduces an interest in promoting the profound respect and concern for fetal life that Kennedy expressed in *Akron Center.* The final paragraph also reaffirms Kennedy's rejection of originalism based on specific tradition and offers a final defense of judicial power based on a moral reading of the Constitution:

> Our Constitution is a covenant running from the first generation of Americans to us and then to future generations. It is a coherent succession. Each generation must learn anew that the Constitution's written terms embody ideas and aspirations that must survive more ages than one. We accept our responsibility not to retreat from interpreting the full meaning of the covenant in light of all our precedents. We invoke it once again to define the freedom guaranteed by the Constitution's own promise, the promise of liberty. (901)

In *Casey,* Kennedy affirmed his ideal of the full and necessary meaning of liberty while upholding regulations he believes will facilitate wise exercise of that right.

At the time, Kennedy considered *Casey* a personal crossing of the Rubicon.[75] The opinion in this case—along with his majority opinion earlier that term in *Lee v. Weisman*[76]—affirmed his commitment to a moral reading of liberty. Under the Constitution, the ultimate abortion decision is for the individual to make, but moral grounds also permit additional state regulation of the procedure. Kennedy's success in *Casey* suggests a practical challenge to his project: In what other ways can the government promote profound respect for fetal life consistent with its obligation to define the liberty of all? The *Casey* plurality admitted that justices operating from shared premises can come to different conclusions (878).[77] This would become apparent the next time the Court confronted the abortion issue.

STENBERG AND HILL: CASEY REPUDIATED?

Eight years after *Casey*, Kennedy would dissent from the Court's opinions in *Stenberg v. Carhart*, which struck Nebraska's criminal ban on partial-birth abortion, and *Hill v. Colorado*, which upheld a criminal prohibition of peaceful protest on public grounds near the entrance of health facilities, including abortion clinics. Aspects of Kennedy's dissent in *Stenberg* preview his 2007 majority opinion in *Gonzales*, and his *Hill* dissent delivered that same day provided a more systematic articulation of his view of the constitutional status of abortion. For Kennedy, the moral nature of the abortion issue requires a reasoned, careful balance of a woman's limited, defined liberty interest and government's moral authority. His sharp dissents in *Stenberg* and *Hill* reflected not regret about his decision to uphold the abortion right in *Casey* but revulsion at the abortion procedure and disgust at the lack of deference accorded by the Court to democratic decisions designed to promoting respect for life. Kennedy displayed this displeasure not only by reading his *Hill* dissent from the bench, but through the language he used in *Stenberg* to describe the late-term abortion procedure and the doctors who perform it. He emphasized the role of the state as not merely a facilitator of wise choice and a protector of the rights of others, but as a moral instructor—through the criminal law statutes—about the proper respect for fetal life.

In *Stenberg*, the Court by a 5–4 vote struck Nebraska's criminal ban on partial-birth abortion as an undue burden on the abortion right. Citing *Casey*, the Court found the law overly vague because it could apply to the procedure used in most pre-viability abortions, and it found the law an undue burden because it included no exception for circumstances that threatened the health of the woman. Kennedy believes the *Stenberg* majority—which included Justices O'Connor and Souter—"repudiates" the "central premise" of *Casey*. He believes "the States retain a critical and legitimate role in legislating on the subject of abortion, limited by the woman's right [that] the Court restated and again guaranteed." For Kennedy, government has a role and perhaps an obligation to assure some level of cultural or political agreement—even on a topic where men and women of good conscience disagree, and perhaps always will disagree. He considers this power essential, asserting that "the State's constitutional authority is a vital means for citizens to address these grave and serious issues, as they must if we are to progress in knowledge and understanding in the attainment of some degree of consensus."[78]

Kennedy's language reflects his moral revulsion at the dilation and extraction (D&X) procedure that Nebraska banned. In describing the practice, he uses the word "abortionist" thirteen times.[79] The first instance is revealing: "The majority" of the Court, he writes, "views the procedure from the perspective of the abortionist, rather than from the perspective of a society shocked when confronted with a new method for ending human life" (957). He then includes a three-page description of the procedure—including a statement that "the abortionist next completes the delivery of a dead fetus, intact except for the damage to the head and the missing contents of the skull."

Kennedy allows an expanded role for government in promoting respect for fetal life. "*Casey* is premised," he writes, "on the States having an important constitutional role in defining their interests in the abortion debate" (960). Those interests extend beyond promoting maternal health, protecting potential human life, and facilitating wise, free, and informed deliberation: states can legislate "to promote the life of the unborn and to ensure respect for all human life and its potential." They may not only speak out in favor of childbirth over abortion; they "also have an interest in forbidding medical procedures which, in the State's reasonable determination, might cause the medical profession or society as a whole to become insensitive, even disdainful, to life, including life in the human fetus." Abortion, he states, "has consequences beyond the woman and her fetus"; thus the state has an interest in regulating this "unique act" (957, 961–962).

Here he includes passages similar to the ones he tried to include in the first draft of *Casey* reaffirming the importance of the democratic process. Kennedy responds to the concurrences of Stevens and Ginsburg, who argued that the ban has no rational basis or purpose because the permitted, common dilation and evacuation (D&E) procedure appears to be just as gruesome.[80] To Kennedy, "the issue is not whether members of the judiciary can see a difference between the two procedures. It is whether Nebraska can" (962–963). Because the intact D&X procedure has a "stronger resemblance to infanticide," he says, Nebraska could find that it "presents a greater risk of disrespect for life and a consequent greater risk to the profession and society, which depend for their sustenance upon reciprocal recognition of dignity and respect" (963).

For Kennedy, as long as the more common D&E procedure exists, Nebraska's criminal ban on D&X presents no undue burden on a woman's right to have an abortion before the fetus reaches viability. The ban advances the interest stated in *Casey* of promoting "profound" respect for life. With this law, "Nebraska instructs all participants in the abortion process, including the mother, of its moral judgment that all life, including life of the unborn, is to be respected." The distinction between D&E and D&X, he writes, "is itself a moral statement, serving to promote respect for human life" (964).

Although Kennedy ties this moral distinction to the state's interest in promoting free and informed choice, he sees the promotion of respect for fetal life as a separate but related state interest. He clearly believes that this law could convince women not to have abortions even under the protected procedure. "If the woman and her physician in contemplating the moral consequences of the prohibited procedure conclude that grave moral consequences pertain to the permitted abortion process as well," he continues, "the choice to elect or not to elect abortion is more informed; and the policy of promoting respect for life is advanced" (964).

Kennedy is clearly horrified not just by the procedure but by the expressed policy of the doctor who challenged the law, Dr. Leroy Carhart, to perform a D&X in every abortion where the fetus was more than fifteen weeks old. To Kennedy, "requiring Nebraska to defer to Dr. Carhart's judgment is no different than forbidding Nebraska from enacting a ban at all; for now it is Dr. Leroy Carhart who sets abortion policy for the State of Nebraska, not the legislature or the people" (964). Striking the ban reflects a "physician-first view," Kennedy says, that the Court repudiated in *Casey*. He finds "substantial and objective medical evidence to demonstrate the State had considerable support for its conclusion that the ban created a substantial risk to no woman's health" (969). In evaluating the law, "courts must exercise caution (rather than require deference to the physician's treatment decision) when medical uncertainty is present" (970). Because the common D&E alternative remains legal, Nebraska's ban "deprived no woman of a safe abortion and therefore did not impose a substantial obstacle on the rights of any woman" (965).

At the conclusion of his dissent, Kennedy returns to a criticism he expressed prior to (and while writing) *Casey:* that the Court struck the law without allowing for the operation of the democratic process. When a federal district court struck the law on its face, it "denied each branch of Nebraska's government any role in the interpretation or enforcement of the statute," he said. "This cannot be what *Casey* meant when it said we would be more solicitous of state attempts to vindicate interests related to abortion." The majority "closes its eyes to these profound concerns" (979). The Court was striking a law that reflected the people's decision "that medical procedures must be governed by moral principles having their foundation in the intrinsic value of human life, including life of the unborn." With this ban, the state "chose to forbid a procedure many decent and civilized people find so abhorrent as to be among the most serious of crimes against human life, while the State still protected the woman's autonomous right of choice as reaffirmed in *Casey*" (979). To Kennedy, this law should have been upheld.

The moral foundations of Kennedy's abortion jurisprudence are even more evident in his *Hill* dissent, announced the same day as *Stenberg*. *Hill* involved a Colorado law making it a crime to

> knowingly approach another person within eight feet of such person, unless such other person consents, for the purpose of passing a leaflet or handbill to, displaying a sign to, or engaging in oral protest, education or counseling with such other person in the public way or sidewalk area within a radius of one hundred feet from any entrance door to a health facility.

Leila Jane Hill, who was engaged in peaceful protest and leafleting on a public sidewalk near an abortion facility, challenged the law as a violation of the First Amendment. The Court upheld it by a 6–3 vote, finding Colorado's law a permissible content- and viewpoint-neutral restriction on the time, place, and manner of speech. Although *Hill* primarily involves free speech,[81] Kennedy uses his dissent to articulate a careful, reasoned view of what he sees as the balance between the constitutionality of abortion legislation and his larger conception of the First Amendment.[82] To Kennedy, the majority's ruling "conflicts with the essence" of *Casey*.[83]

Writing in 2007, after the decision in *Gonzales v. Carhart*, professor Garrett Epps and journalist Dahlia Lithwick claimed to find no paternalistic language in Kennedy's earlier *Stenberg* dissent.[84] Nevertheless, Kennedy's statements later that same day in *Hill* about the importance of social and moral debate about abortion, the psychology of women considering abortion, and the possibility of postabortion regret clearly preview the later statements in *Gonzales*.

Kennedy begins his dissent in *Hill* by focusing on free-speech principles. Yet his discussion and application of them leaves little doubt of his substantive views about abortion. "For the first time," he writes, "the Court approves a law which bars a private citizen from passing a message, in a peaceful manner and on a profound moral issue, to a fellow citizen on a public sidewalk." He finds Colorado's law to be aimed "at a narrow range of topics—indeed one topic in particular."[85] "To say that one citizen can approach another to ask the time or the weather forecast or the direction to Main Street," he writes, "but not to initiate discussion on one of the most basic moral and political issues in all of contemporary discourse, a question touching profound issues in philosophy and theology, is an astonishing view of the First Amendment" (768). If the statute seeks "to protect distraught women who are embarrassed, vexed or harassed as they attempt to enter abortion clinics," he writes, such acts "should be prohibited in those terms" (777).

The First Amendment analysis employed by Kennedy is informed by his view of the constitutional and moral nature of abortion. *Casey* prevents "any plea to the government to outlaw some abortions." Thus those "who oppose abortion must seek to convince their fellow citizens of the moral imperative of their cause" (787–788). Protesters like Leila Jane Hill, he said, "want to engage in peaceful face-to-face communication with individuals the petitioners believe are about to commit a profound moral wrong" (780). As Kennedy writes, "nowhere is the speech more important than at the time and place where the act is about to occur"; in practice, "what this statute restricts is one person trying to communicate with another, which ought to be the heart of civilized discourse" (788).

By defending the right of protesters to use "the means of expression they deem best suited to their purpose" (781), Kennedy makes several assumptions about the psychology of women considering abortion. After stating that "merely viewing a picture or brief message on the outside of a leaflet might be critical in the choice to receive it," Kennedy returns to his belief—expressed in *Akron Center* and the first draft of *Casey*—that the abortion decision should be "cautious and mature." Peaceful protests can inform this decision. Suppose "the leaflet will contain a picture of an unborn child," Kennedy continues:

> One of the arguments by the proponents of abortion, I had thought, was that a young woman might have been so uninformed that she did not know how to avoid pregnancy. The speakers in this case seek to ask the same uninformed

woman, or indeed any woman who is considering an abortion, to understand and contemplate the nature of the life she carries within her. (789)

With this language, Kennedy assumes that the "young woman"—or "any woman who is considering an abortion"—can benefit from the information the protesters can provide. Citing the testimony of a "sidewalk counselor," Kennedy states: "It would be remiss, moreover, not to observe the profound difference a leaflet can have in a woman's decision making process" (790).

Kennedy also introduces more forthrightly than in prior decisions the idea that women who have abortions may regret their decision. "There are, no doubt, women who would testify that abortion was necessary and unregretted," he concedes. Nevertheless, "the point here is simply that speech makes a difference, as it must when acts of lasting significance and profound moral consequence are being contemplated" (790). In *Casey,* Kennedy stated that abortion is a decision of lasting consequence and profound moral significance; as a result, the ultimate decision must be protected as a personal liberty. But in *Hill,* because this is a decision that has consequences for the woman and for society, others can use their liberty peacefully to protest it.

By ruling against Hill, Kennedy writes, the Court "delivers a grave wound" both to free speech principles and "to the essential reasoning in the joint opinion in *Casey.*" He considers *Casey* to have "reaffirmed its prior holding that the Constitution protects a woman's right to terminate her pregnancy in the early stages." In doing so, however, the plurality "took care to recognize the gravity of the personal decision." With this decision—more even than with *Stenberg*—"the Court now strikes at the heart of the reasoned, careful balance I had believed was the basis for the joint opinion" (791).

In light of his focus in *Akron Center* and *Casey* on the moral dimension of the abortion decision, it becomes clear why in Kennedy's view *Hill* delivers a graver wound to the Constitution than even *Stenberg. Stenberg*—wrong as it was—merely misapplied the undue burden test and gave too little weight to the state's interest in promoting respect for life. *Hill,* "in a cruel way," fundamentally threatens the possibility of any social or political discourse about the morality of abortion.[86] The Court "in effect tells us the moral debate is not so important after all and can be conducted just as well through a bullhorn from an 8-foot distance as it can through peaceful, face-to-face exchange of a leaflet." It is thus understandable that Kennedy's deepest exploration of the moral dimensions of the abortion issue is found in *Hill.* In his view, "the vital principle" of *Casey* "was that in defined circumstances the woman's decision whether to abort her child was in essence a moral one, a choice the State could not dictate." Thus, "those who oppose it are remitted to debate the issue in its moral dimensions" (791).

Kennedy uses characteristically grand rhetoric to unite his constitutional views of abortion and free speech. "In a fleeting existence," he writes, "we have but little time to find truth through discourse." Kennedy's conception of the truth of this matter is clear. Further, "no better illustration of the immediacy of speech, of the urgency of persuasion, of the preciousness of time, is presented than in this case. Here the citizens who claim First Amendment protections seek it for speech which, if it is to be effective, must take place at the very time and place a grievous moral wrong, in their view, is about to occur."[87] With this decision, "the Court tears away from the protesters the guarantees of the First Amendment when they most need it." To Kennedy—as to Scalia—*Hill* and *Stenberg* signaled reactivation of the "ad hoc nullification machine"[88] they believed *Casey* had destroyed. "So committed is the Court to its course," Kennedy concludes, "that it denies these protesters, in the face of what they consider to be one of life's gravest moral crises, even the opportunity to try to offer a fellow citizen a little pamphlet, a handheld paper seeking to reach a higher law."[89]

Kennedy's emotional dissents in *Hill* and *Stenberg* reveal the moral and emotional foundations of his abortion jurisprudence. In *Stenberg*, his repeated references to "abortionists" and his extended description of the procedure indicate his moral revulsion. In *Hill*, he portrays the "young" women considering abortion as anguished, morally conflicted, and likely uninformed. They are liable to persuasion from a picture and—if they still decide to have an abortion—are likely later to suffer regret. Kennedy's rhetoric indicates his fear that the Court's decisions would foreclose political and (more importantly) cultural conversation about the morality of abortion. To Kennedy, these decisions strike at the heart of the liberty that forms the foundation of his jurisprudence.

GONZALES V. CARHART: MEDICAL UNCERTAINTY AND SELF-EVIDENT REGRET

Kennedy's more recent majority opinion in *Gonzales v. Carhart* upholding the federal ban on partial-birth abortion reiterates the themes of his *Stenberg* dissent and his other abortion writings. He recognizes the power of government—federal as well as state—to use the criminal law to promote respect for fetal life and reject what he considers a physician-first view of the abortion right. Kennedy also uses language reminiscent of his earlier abortion opinions. That language reflects his continuing approval of the constitutionality of democratic moral judgments intended to promote respect for life and his continuing hope to promote larger social dialogue about abortion. The considerations of anguish and harm that he used in *Casey* to support the abortion liberty are employed here to uphold the ban. In *Gonzales,* Kennedy emphasizes his assertion in *Hill* that women who have abortions will often suffer regret and psychological harm, while doctors who perform late-term procedures cannot be trusted to serve their patients' true interests.

Gonzales involved a challenge to a federal law signed in 2003 that criminalized the partial-birth abortion procedure. The law—like the Nebraska one struck seven years earlier in *Stenberg v. Carhart*—included an exception when the woman's life was in danger, but it did not include a health exception. Leroy Carhart, among other doctors, challenged the federal law as unconstitutional. By 2007, Justice O'Connor (a member of the *Stenberg* majority) had retired from the Court and been replaced by Samuel Alito. The 5–4 decision to strike the state law in *Stenberg* became a 5–4 decision to uphold the federal law in *Gonzales*. Kennedy moved from a dissenter in *Stenberg* to author of the majority opinion in *Gonzales.*

Kennedy tries to introduce distinctions between the federal law upheld in this case and the state ban struck in *Stenberg*. The federal ban is "more specific," he says, "concerning the instances to which it applies and in this respect more precise in its coverage" than the Nebraska ban struck in *Stenberg*.[90] Nevertheless, the holding in *Gonzales* does raise uncertainty about *Casey,* because the recent majority includes two justices who voted against the plurality in *Casey* and two justices who have expressed no position on it.[91] In any event, the interest in promoting respect for life that had been downplayed in *Casey* now becomes central. "Whatever one's view regarding the *Casey* joint opinion," Kennedy writes, "it is evident [that] a premise central to its conclusion—that the government has a legitimate and substantial interest in preserving and promoting fetal life—would be repudiated were the Court now to affirm the judgments of the Courts of Appeals."[92]

Kennedy again attempts to balance a woman's right to choose an abortion and society's power "to promote respect for life, including life of the unborn"

(1633). He goes further than in *Casey* and *Stenberg* in outlining the moral reasons for society to seek to promote respect for the life of the unborn. As in *Stenberg*, Kennedy recounts the partial-birth abortion procedure in great detail, even quoting testimony from doctors and nurses who have performed it (1620–1623). He then expands the discussion to consider how knowledge of the procedure might affect the decision of the woman contemplating abortion. The moral gravity of the abortion decision leads Kennedy to conclude that "the government may use its voice and its regulatory authority to show its profound respect for the life within the woman" (1633). Because abortion is fraught with consequences for those involved in the procedure and for society as a whole, he says, government has the power to regulate the practice on moral concerns.

Kennedy's opinion in *Gonzales* rests on assumptions about the psychology of women and childbirth. Echoing *Casey*, he states that "respect for human life finds an ultimate expression in the bond of love a mother has for her child" and that "whether to have an abortion requires a difficult and painful moral decision" (1634). In *Casey*, the moral and personal nature of this bond of love leads Kennedy to find ultimate protection for abortion as a constitutional liberty of the individual woman. In *Gonzales*, he focuses on the difficulty and pain of the moral decision. Although "we find no reliable data to measure the phenomenon," Kennedy writes, "it seems unexceptionable to conclude some women come to regret their choice to abort the infant life they once created and sustained" (1634). Kennedy admits his argument is based at most on anecdotal evidence. But that anecdotal evidence is itself revealing: he cites an amicus brief on behalf of Sandra Cano—the Mary Doe of *Doe v. Bolton*, the companion case to *Roe v. Wade*.[93]

This regret, Kennedy says, leads to both physical and psychological harm, as "severe depression and loss of self-esteem can follow." These statements echo the explanations he offered in his earlier opinions—in *Akron Center*, *Stenberg*, and *Hill*—regarding the regret women can feel following an abortion, and the ideal he advanced of promoting respect for life. Kennedy finds regret particularly relevant to the late-term D&X procedure: "It is self-evident," he writes, "that a mother who comes to regret her choice to abort must struggle with grief more anguished and sorrow more profound when she learns, only after the event, what she once did not know: that she allowed a doctor to pierce the skull and vacuum the fast-developing brain of her unborn child, a child assuming the human form" (1634).

Kennedy further expands this ideal of regret, anxiety, and anguish in *Gonzales* in order to dismantle the broad health exception afforded in *Roe* and *Doe* for late-term abortions based on the judgment of the physician. "It is likely the case with the abortion procedures here at issue," Kennedy writes, that women "prefer not to hear all details, lest the usual anxiety preceding invasive medical procedures become the more intense" (1634). Kennedy moves from normal anxiety about surgery to moral anguish about the late-term abortion procedure. For Kennedy, knowledge about the D&X procedure would likely influence women to reconsider their decision to have an abortion—even under the allowed and protected methods.

Unlike in *Stenberg*, in *Gonzales* Kennedy does not refer to Carhart or others who perform the banned procedure as "abortionists." Instead he calls them "abortion doctors." But his moral condemnation of their actions is no less piercing. Kennedy rejects an unbounded health exception based on the "preferences of the physician" or "mere convenience" (1620), stating that "the law need not give abortion doctors unfettered choice in the course of their medical practice, nor should it elevate their status above other physicians in the medical community" (1636). Kennedy asserts that abortion doctors (or at least Dr. Carhart) cannot be trusted to provide information in the best interest of their patients. "In a decision so fraught with emotional consequence," he writes, "some doctors may prefer not to disclose the precise details of the means that will be used, confining themselves to the required statement of risks that the procedure entails." Yet "it is . . . precisely this lack of information concerning the way the fetus will be killed that is of legitimate concern to the State" (1634).

As in *Hill* and *Stenberg*, Kennedy connects state interests in protecting life with promoting respect for life. The federal law—like the state regulations upheld in *Casey* and the ones he would have upheld in *Stenberg*—is justified because government "has an interest in ensuring [that] so grave a choice is well informed." To Kennedy, a wise and well-informed choice may require moral as well as medical information. The federal ban is intended to inform not just the patient but also the doctor and the larger society. Kennedy argues that the state interest in respect for life embodied in this law may serve to inspire innovation to "different and less shocking methods to abort the fetus in the second trimester." Upholding the law, he hopes, will ultimately produce "a dialogue that better informs the political and legal systems, the medical profession, expectant mothers and society as a whole of the consequences that follow from a decision to elect a late-term abortion." Kennedy also sees the law as helping to reduce the rate of partial-birth abortions as well as abortions in general. The law could lead some doctors to avoid performing late-term abortions, or persuade some women not to have abortions at all. "It is a reasonable inference," he writes, "that a necessary effect of the regulation and the knowledge it conveys will be to encourage some women to carry the infant to full term, thus reducing the absolute number of late-term abortions" (1634).[94]

In *Gonzales*, as in *Stenberg*, the existence of "medical uncertainty" about comparative and significant health risks for the banned and allowed procedures "provides a sufficient basis to conclude in this facial attack that the Act does not impose an undue burden" (1637). For Kennedy, this uncertainty does not justify striking the ban in all its applications. The federal ban allows for standard D&E, "a commonly used and generally accepted method," for late-term abortions. Thus, the doctor's "mere convenience" or preference for D&X "does not suffice to displace" the moral judgment of the community. From this uncertainty about the comparative risks of each procedure, he writes, "it does not follow that the State is altogether barred from imposing reasonable regulations" (1638). Regulations that do not strike at the heart of liberty would be evaluated only under the rational basis standard that he stated in *Webster* and *Akron Center* (1639).

Kennedy's opinion remains open to challenges to the ban in particular circumstances where the woman's health is threatened. But he seeks to limit those challenges as a way of narrowing the broad scope of physician discretion allowed under *Roe* and *Doe*. He would uphold such challenges only "if it can be shown that in discrete and well-defined instances a particular condition has or is likely to occur in which the procedure prohibited by the Act must be used." Under such well-defined and limited circumstances, "the nature of the medical risk can be better quantified and balanced than in a facial attack." Kennedy seeks to avoid striking the law in all instances[95] and concludes "These facial attacks should not have been entertained" (1638–1639). For Kennedy, striking this law on its face and in all applications would resurrect what Scalia calls "the 'ad hoc nullification machine' which is our abortion jurisprudence."

Ginsburg's dissent, read from the bench, criticized Kennedy's rhetoric, reasoning, and consequences. She considers the Court's opinion "alarming" because "it refuses to take *Casey* and *Stenberg* seriously" (1640). Ginsburg's second footnote praises the opinion in *Casey*—and, perhaps implicitly, Kennedy's efforts in it—because it "described more precisely than did *Roe* the impact of abortion restrictions on a woman's liberty" (1641, fn. 2). But Ginsburg fundamentally attacks Kennedy's consideration of abortion rights solely as exercises of individual liberty. For Ginsburg, "legal challenges to undue restrictions on abortion procedures do not seek to vindicate some generalized notion of privacy." In her view, "they center on a woman's autonomy to determine her life's course, and thus to enjoy equal citizenship stature" (1641). Ginsburg's equal protection–based argument for the abortion right—similar to one she had expressed before coming to the Court and one later adopted by Blackmun[96]—should be read as a criticism of the "heart of liberty" or "mystery of life" passages in *Casey* and the larger liberty-based approach to abortion rights. Properly understood, Ginsburg's challenge to Kennedy's abortion position is no less fundamental than the previous attacks made by Scalia and Thomas.[97]

Ginsburg's reading of *Casey* minimizes that opinion's limitations on the abortion right. As in her *Stenberg* concurrence, Ginsburg argues that a ban on the D&X procedure serves no state's interest in protecting life. "The law saves not a single fetus from destruction," she writes, "for it targets only a *method* of performing abortion" (1647).[98] She rejects any state interest in promoting respect for life, as "the concerns expressed are untethered to any ground genuinely serving the Government's interest in preserving life" (1648). Moral concerns of promoting respect for life cannot justify "overriding fundamental rights." This law, she says, "would not survive under the strict scrutiny that previously attended state-decreed limitations on a woman's reproductive decisions" (1647, 1641). In neither *Casey* nor *Lawrence,* however, did Kennedy identify the liberty interest that he recognized as a fundamental right. Nor did he subject all regulations to strict scrutiny. Further, *Casey* recognized a state's moral concern in promoting respect for life—but Ginsburg does not. *Casey* expressed ambiguity about whether this interest in promoting profound respect for fetal life was a subset of protecting life or facilitating free and informed choice; in later cases, Kennedy clarified that this moral interest, though complementary to facilitating free and informed choice, is itself distinct.

Ginsburg most sharply attacks Kennedy's word choice. He relies on an "anti-abortion shibboleth," she writes: that "women who have abortions come to regret their choices, and consequently suffer from 'severe depression and loss of esteem.'" This language, she writes, "reflects ancient notions about women's place in the family and under the Constitution—ideas that have long since been discredited." To Ginsburg, Kennedy's words reflect a belief in "women's fragile emotional state" (1645). She admits that "the Court is surely correct that, for most women, abortion is a painfully difficult decision" (1648, fn. 7); however, "the solution the Court approves, then, is *not* to require doctors to inform women, accurately and adequately, of the different procedures and their attendant risks." "Instead," she writes, "the Court deprives women of the right to make an autonomous choice, even at the expense of their safety" (1649).

Ginsburg compares Kennedy's conception of the psychology of women considering abortion to that of *Muller v. Oregon*[99] and *Bradwell v. Illinois*, cases now seen to have relied on outdated gender stereotypes. "Though today's majority may regard women's feelings on the matter as 'self-evident,'" she writes, in *Casey* "the Court has repeatedly confirmed that 'the destiny of the woman must be shaped . . . on her own conception of her spiritual imperatives and her place in society" (1649). As in her discussion of the state interest in promoting respect for life, Ginsburg replaces *Casey*'s key qualifying phrase—"to a large extent"—with ellipses.

When Ginsburg argues that "the Court's hostility to the right *Roe* and *Casey* secured is not concealed," she identifies the core tension within Kennedy's abortion jurisprudence. In doing so, she echoes Blackmun's language in *Webster*.[100] "One wonders," she writes, "how long a line that saves no fetus from destruction will hold in the face of the Court's 'moral concerns.'" Ginsburg criticizes Kennedy's use of terms such as "abortion doctor," "unborn child," and "baby" as well as his references to "second trimester pre-viability abortions as 'late term'" and physicians' judgments as "'preferences[,] motivated by 'mere convenience'" (1650). What Ginsburg does not note—but Helen Knowles does—is that Kennedy's opinion in *Gonzales* never uses the word "liberty."[101] As Ginsburg concludes, "the Act, and the Court's defense of it, cannot be understood as anything other than an effort to chip away at a right declared again and again by this Court—and with increasing comprehension of its centrality to women's lives" (1653).

A REASONED, CAREFUL BALANCE? THE CATHOLIC ROOTS OF KENNEDY'S ABORTION RHETORIC

Ginsburg's dissent in *Gonzales* about Kennedy's paternalistic language and assumptions echoes Blackmun's objections in the years before *Casey*. Nevertheless, it is a mistake to read the *Gonzales* opinion as a sign that Kennedy regrets his vote in *Casey* or to suppose that he may in the future recant his position that abortion is a constitutionally protected liberty.[102] Kennedy's liberty-based approach to constitutional interpretation is integral to his conception of the judicial role, and his behavior in abortion cases should be seen as part of a long-standing project to devise a "reasoned, careful balance" to the abortion issue. It seeks to avoid the perceived excesses of either (1) following *Roe*, recognizing abortion as a fundamental right under either privacy or equal protection, and striking most abortion legislation under strict scrutiny, or (2) overturning *Roe* and leaving no judicially enforceable limits on abortion legislation.

To articulate this proper balance, Kennedy attempts to recast the abortion right in terms consistent with his larger moral reading of the Constitution and a judicial duty to define and enforce the full and necessary meaning of liberty. Abortion is a profound and grave moral issue for Kennedy, one that involves philosophical, physical, and psychological components. The ultimate decision thus falls within the "heart of liberty," which must belong to the individual.

Nevertheless, a woman's exercise of this liberty affects society as a whole, and this justifies state regulation of the procedure. Abortion can be regulated not only to protect fetal life and maternal health, but on other grounds. The first matter, he believes, is to ensure that the choice is free and informed, that an act of such profound consequence is undertaken with full knowledge. The choice is personal, and it is a matter that naturally, for some, produces regret. An informed choice, Kennedy theorizes, is one that is informed by the majority's moral judgment—in his view, a true one—that fetal life is entitled to profound respect throughout pregnancy and especially late in the term. Women who are aware of the medical and moral arguments are in a better position to exercise the abortion right wisely and less likely to regret their decision in the future. Kennedy's project to narrow *Roe* but not overturn it required changing its foundations and allowing a state interest in promoting free and informed choice as well as profound respect for fetal life. Kennedy therefore advanced his project in *Webster*, achieved success in *Casey*, lost ground in *Hill* and *Stenberg*, and prevailed in *Gonzales*. Yet the success of Kennedy's project, and the rhetoric of his opinions in these cases, reveal a larger rhetorical (and perhaps substantive) tension within his jurisprudence.

The tension in Kennedy's jurisprudence likely reflects his attempt to articulate his moral opposition to abortion within the larger moral conception of

liberty that characterizes his jurisprudence. Much of his rhetoric about human dignity, liberty, and postabortion regret resonates with the language of
papal statements issued after Vatican II, including *Dignitatis Humanae* (*On
Religious Liberty*) and two other major writings from John Paul II—*Mulieris
Dignitatem* (*On the Dignity and Vocation of Women*) and *Evangelium Vitae*
(*On the Value and Inviolability of Human Life*). These sources may provide
"objective referents" to Kennedy's rhetoric about the nature of liberty and the
abortion decision.

The influence of the Catholic documents can be seen most clearly in
Kennedy's language in *Casey* about the mystery of life, the dignity of women,
and the nature of the abortion decision. The 1988 apostolic letter *Mulieris
Dignitatem*[103] devotes an entire section to motherhood. It states that "scientific analysis fully confirms" that motherhood "corresponds to the psycho-
physical structure of women" (18.4). Two paragraphs later, the letter uses
language strikingly similar to the most controversial passages in *Casey* written
four years later:

> Motherhood involves a special communion with the mystery of life, as it develops
> in the woman's womb. The mother is filled with wonder at this mystery of life,
> and "understands" with unique intuition what is happening inside her. In the
> light of the "beginning," the mother accepts and loves as a person the child she is
> carrying in her womb. This unique contact with the new human being developing
> within her gives rise to an attitude towards human beings—not only towards her
> own child, but every human being—which profoundly marks the woman's
> personality. (18.6)

This section also mentions the "anguish" and "suffering" women undergo
during pregnancy and childbirth (19.6, 19.7). Similarly, Pope Paul VI's "Address to Women" at the close of the Second Vatican Council states "you are
present in the mystery of a life beginning."

Other sections in *Mulieris Dignitatem* resonate with Kennedy's "bond of
love" passages in *Casey* and *Gonzales*. "In God's plan," the encyclical states,
"woman is the one in whom the order of love in the created world of persons
takes first root" (29.1). According to the letter, "a woman's dignity is closely
connected with the love which she receives by the very reason of her feminin-
ity; it is likewise connected with the love she gives in return" (30.1). At the
same time, "the man—even with all his sharing in parenthood—always remains 'outside' the process of pregnancy and the baby's birth." This statement
could justify Kennedy's eventual decision to strike the spousal notice provi-

sion, and it perhaps explains why Kennedy could not vote to overturn the abortion right despite his objections to *Roe*.

The language of *Evangelium Vitae*, written in 1995, seems similar to the language Kennedy increasingly employs in abortion opinions after *Casey*.[104] *Evangelium Vitae* reiterates that abortion "is an unspeakable crime" (56.1) and never justified. Yet commonality in language exists with Kennedy's opinions in *Hill* and *Gonzales*, particularly about the "bond of love" between mother and child. It describes the abortion decision as "tragic and painful for the mother" (56.4). The encyclical states that "the experience of motherhood makes you acutely aware of the other person and, at the same time, confers on you a particular task" (99.2), then quotes the "special communion" passage in *Mulieris Dignitatem*.

Evangelium Vitae contains a section on postabortion regret that resonates with Kennedy's rhetoric in *Stenberg, Hill,* and *Gonzales*. The encyclical devotes "a special word to women who have had an abortion" (99.3). It describes abortion as "in many cases . . . a painful and even shattering decision" and acknowledges that "the wound in your heart may not yet have healed" (99.3). The encyclical encourages women with these words: "Do not give in to discouragement and do not lose hope." "With the friendly and expert help and advice of other people, and as a result of your own painful experience," the encyclical writes, "you can be among the most eloquent defenders of everyone's right to life" (99.3). Kennedy's opinion in *Gonzales* includes such a statement. He cites an amicus brief submitted by Sandra Cano, the plaintiff in *Doe v. Bolton*, urging the Court to uphold the federal ban on partial-birth abortion. These sentiments about postabortion regret may explain why he finds these ideas unexceptionable and self-evident even though he can cite no empirical evidence to support them.

The conflict in Kennedy's abortion jurisprudence reveals itself in his adoption of this rhetoric. The papal documents provide one possible source for the "mystery of life" passage in *Casey* and "bond of love" passages in *Casey* and *Gonzales*. They may also help to explain his later concern with postabortion regret, latent in earlier cases but much more explicit in his opinions written after *Evangelium Vitae* was issued. But the religious influence did not just pervade Kennedy's role in *Gonzales* and other cases; it can be seen more broadly in the articulation of the concepts of liberty, human dignity, personality, coercion, and dialogue that is at the core of his jurisprudence.[105]

Kennedy's project to fashion a careful, reasoned balance to the abortion issue appears promising. He has succeeded in achieving a tenuous majority in *Casey* and, more recently, *Gonzales*. But the emotional and moralistic rhetoric he employs to articulate it—and the role he approves for government to serve not merely as a facilitator of information and social dialogue but as a participant and instructor in that debate—create a tension within his larger jurisprudential ideal of defining liberty without mandating one's own moral code. The conflicts in Kennedy's abortion jurisprudence reflect his view that "abortion is a unique act" involving liberty "in a sense unique to the human condition and so unique to the law."[106] At the time, he characterized his action in *Casey* as crossing the Rubicon. Kennedy's recent rhetoric in *Gonzales,* however, suggests that years later he is still struggling to articulate the proper scope of the abortion liberty protected under the Constitution.

3. Kennedy's Expansive Conception of Free Speech

At the heart of the First Amendment is the principle that each person should decide for him or herself the ideas and beliefs deserving of expression, consideration and allegiance.

—*TURNER BROADCASTING SYSTEM I V. FCC* (1994)

Anthony Kennedy has been no swing voter in cases involving free speech. He is the current justice most likely to strike government action for violating freedom of speech and association, and he has joined every majority that has found a federal statute unconstitutional on free-speech grounds.[1] From this record, Cass Sunstein considers Kennedy a nonminimalist concerning the First Amendment.[2] Others argue that his free-speech votes show "the limitations of labeling" individual justices as liberal or conservative or—noting Kennedy's "more liberal streak in free speech issues" across a wide variety of contexts—assert that he "veers away from an expected course of action."[3] No study, however, has explained why Kennedy exercises such a consistently broad conception of freedom of expression.

Kennedy's expansive ideal of free speech is not, however, a contradiction or aberration in his thought. Instead, it is a logical extension of the conception of human personality that drives his larger jurisprudence. During his confirmation testimony, Kennedy said he would employ judicial power to strike government policies resulting in "the inability of the person to manifest his or her personality, the inability of a person to obtain his or her self-fulfillment, the inability of a person to reach his or her own potential." Responding to Senator Orrin Hatch (R-Utah), Kennedy asserted that the First Amendment "endures the dialogue that is necessary for the continuance of the democratic process."[4] Its guarantee "applies not just to political speech," but, "really, to all ways in which we express ourselves as persons," including art and dance. For Kennedy, "these features of our freedom are to many people as important or more important than political discussion or searching for philosophical truth."[5] He states the principle more broadly in a later case: "At the heart of the First Amendment is the principle that each person should decide for him or herself the ideas and beliefs deserving of expression, consideration and allegiance."[6]

Kennedy moves beyond tradition and democracy to bring an expansive and substantive conception of free speech as a component of personal liberty to his judicial decision-making. His opinions show great sensitivity to the many ways government can shape, control, and compel expression directly and indirectly. Across a broad variety of contexts—political protest, compelled speech, campaign and commercial speech, the public forum, and sexually indecent expression—Kennedy consistently strikes government actions that prevent individuals from discovering, receiving, and debating political, social, artistic, and aesthetic truth. Just as characteristically, Kennedy recasts constitutional issues in other areas of law as questions that implicate First Amendment values to justify expanding the scope of judicial power.

PROTECTING POLITICAL PROTEST

Kennedy applies his broad conception of free speech most directly to political dissent. While his concurring opinion in *Texas v. Johnson*[7] may be best known, he has—at least until recently—consistently voted to uphold the right to disagree with government policy.[8] He seeks to ensure government neutrality, allowing individuals to decide for themselves what ideas they should express, consider, and ultimately support.

In *Johnson,* the Court by a 5–4 vote overturned Texas's law criminalizing flag desecration. Gregory Johnson had burned an American flag as part of a political protest during the 1984 Republican National Convention in Dallas, was arrested, and appealed his conviction. Kennedy wrote a short but powerful concurring opinion validating the right to dissent. He admits the flag "holds a lonely place of honor" and "is constant in expressing beliefs Americans share, beliefs in law and peace and that freedom which sustains the human spirit" (421). Nevertheless, to Kennedy the content of those beliefs "forces recognition of the costs to which those beliefs commit us," including the "poignant but fundamental" one "that the flag protects those who hold it in contempt." These beliefs cannot be instilled by government under force of law; they must be reconsidered, reevaluated, and reaccepted by individual citizens.

Kennedy clearly has contempt both for Johnson's views and the mode he chose to express them. "For all the record shows," he writes, "this respondent was not a philosopher and perhaps did not even possess the ability to comprehend how repellent his statements must be to the Republic itself." But the content and coherence of Johnson's views are irrelevant. "Whether or not he could appreciate the enormity of the offense he gave," Kennedy writes, "the fact remains that his acts were speech, in both the technical and the fundamental meaning of the Constitution" (421).[9]

Kennedy's most forceful defense of the right to dissent is found in *Hill v. Colorado,* involving protest on public grounds near facilities that perform abortions.[10] In this case, a majority of the Court upheld a statute making it a crime to be "engaging in oral protest, education or counseling . . . in the public way or sidewalk area within a radius of one hundred feet from any entrance door to a health care facility." Kennedy vehemently dissented, stating that the majority "acts to deny the neutrality that must be the first principle of the First Amendment" (789). He finds the law content-based: "We would close our eyes to reality," he writes, "were we to deny that 'oral protest, education, or counseling' . . . concern a narrow range of topics—indeed one topic in particular" (767).

Kennedy finds the Court's decision appalling. "To say that one citizen can approach another to ask the time or the weather forecast or the directions to Main Street but not to initiate discussion on one of the basic moral and political issues in all of contemporary discourse, a question touching profound ideas in philosophy and theology," he writes, "is an astonishing view of the First Amendment." The Colorado law is a "clever" viewpoint-based restriction that seeks not just to prevent individuals from persuading women considering abortion to rethink their options but to limit criticism of the Court's own decision in *Roe v. Wade.* "Laws punishing speech which protests the lawfulness or morality of the government's own policy," Kennedy writes, "are the essence of the tyrannical power the First Amendment guards against" (769).

Kennedy concludes that the Court majority shows a "disregard of the importance of free discourse and the exchange of ideas in a traditional public forum" (778). Colorado's law "seeks to eliminate public discourse on an entire subject and topic" (770). Such speech may be unpopular or unpleasant, but "our foundational First Amendment cases are based on the recognition that citizens, subject to rare exceptions, must be able to discuss issues, great or small, through the means of expression they deem best suited to their purpose." Reiterating his sentiments in *Johnson,* Kennedy writes that "it is for the speaker, not the government, to choose the best means of expressing a message" (781). In contrast, "what this statute restricts is one person trying to communicate with another, which ought to be the heart of civilized discourse" (789). By upholding this restriction on protest on public grounds near abortion facilities, Kennedy writes, the Court "delivers a grave wound to the First Amendment" (791).

Kennedy has upheld the right to criticize government in other cases. In *Gentile v. State Bar of Nevada,*[11] he voted to strike a bar association's censure of a lawyer for holding a press conference and publicly accusing local police of corruption. "Speech critical of the exercise of the State's power," he writes, "lies at the very center of the First Amendment." Criticisms of the judicial system—even by participants in a criminal trial—"have the full protection of the First Amendment" (1029, 1058). Kennedy has extended this right to dissent beyond speech to areas not directly related to freedom of expression. For example, in *Burdick v. Takushi*[12] his dissent would strike Hawaii's absolute ban on write-in voting. He admits that the First Amendment and freedom of expression are not directly involved in this case: The purpose of voting "is to elect public officials, not to serve as a general forum for political expression." But his analysis focuses on the opportunity of the voter "to cast a meaningful ballot" (447; see also 443). When candidates run unopposed, "some voters cannot vote for the candidate of their choice without a write-in option" (447). In *O'Hare Truck Service v. City of Northlake,*[13] Kennedy's majority opinion ruled that terminating a government contract for political reasons violates free speech because political affiliation is not a "reasonably appropriate requirement" for towing services.

Kennedy is especially sensitive to the ways in which government involvement and funding can affect the political content of speech critical of its actions. For example, he wrote for a majority invalidating a congressional prohibition that prevented lawyers funded through a federal program to provide legal services for the poor from challenging the constitutionality of federal welfare legislation.[14] The funding program established by Congress, he concludes, "was designed to facilitate private speech, not to promote a governmental message" (542). This specific restriction on lawsuits challenging federal welfare legislation serves to "prohibit speech and expression upon which courts must depend for the proper exercise of the judicial power" (545). The federal program seeks "to exclude from litigation those arguments and theories Congress finds unacceptable but which by their nature are within the province of the courts to consider" (546). As a result, this law "operates to insulate current welfare laws from constitutional scrutiny and certain other legal challenges, a condition implicating central First Amendment concerns" (547).

Kennedy reiterated his categorical approach to free speech in his concurring opinion in *Simon & Schuster v. Crime Victims Board*,[15] the "Son of Sam" case. He voted to strike a New York state law restricting authors and publishers who profit from reports of their own criminal activity, "using as its sole criterion the content of what is written" (124). To Kennedy, New York's law "amounts to raw censorship based on content, censorship forbidden by the text of the First Amendment and well-settled principles protecting speech and the press" (128). He admits that some categories of expression—such as obscenity, libel, or incitement to lawless action—allow for content-based regulation. Although such a categorical approach "would not, of course, eliminate the need for difficult judgments," Kennedy embraces it as a "surer test" that does not have "the capacity to weaken central protections of the First Amendment."

PROTECTING COMMERCIAL SPEECH

Kennedy has also been a leader on the Court in expanding protection for commercial and corporate speech.[16] In *Edenfield v. Fane*,[17] he struck a state law that prohibited public accountants from engaging in direct solicitation to obtain new clients. The First Amendment protects commercial speech because such expression, "like other spheres of our social and cultural life, provides a forum where ideas and information flourish." Scott Fane's solicitation included "truthful, nondeceptive information." For Kennedy, "the general rule is that the speaker and the audience, not the government, assess the value of the information presented" (765, 767).

Kennedy later dissented from a decision that upheld a Florida regulation banning personal injury lawyers from soliciting victims for thirty days after an accident or disaster. The majority found that the bar had "substantial interest both in protecting injured Floridians from invasive conduct by lawyers and in preventing the erosion of confidence in the profession."[18] Kennedy disagreed. He stated that the communication "may be vital to the recipient's right to petition the courts for a redress of grievances" (636). Free speech, he said, benefits the listener as well as the speaker. Although some recipients may be disgusted, "we do not allow restrictions on speech to be justified on the ground that the expression might offend the listener" (638). Those disgusted can throw this mail in the trash. Any effort to maintain the dignity of the legal profession "begins with more rational speech, not less." Florida's ban "is censorship pure and simple," one "manipulating public opinion by suppressing speech that informs us how the legal system works" (639–640). Under the First Amendment, "the public, not the State, has the right and power to decide what ideas and information are deserving of their adherence" (645).

Kennedy expressed his fervent opposition to compelled commercial speech in *United States Department of Agriculture v. United Foods.*[19] United Foods, a mushroom grower, objected to mandatory government assessments to pay for generic mushroom advertising. Although this issue may appear "minor," for Kennedy the case raises such fundamental free-speech concerns that he invokes *West Virginia v. Barnette,* the classic case involving required student recitation of the Pledge of Allegiance in public schools.[20] He admits United Foods' payment "does not compel the expression of political or ideological views." Nevertheless, "First Amendment values are at serious risk if government can compel a particular citizen, or discrete group of citizens, to pay special subsidies for speech on the side that it favors." Even though the speech here "may be of interest to but a small segment of the population," he writes, this program still requires that "producers subsidize speech with which they disagree" (410–411). All funds collected under this plan "are for one purpose: generic advertising" (412). Such advertising "does not require group action, save to generate the very speech to which some handlers object" (415). To Kennedy, such government-mandated financial support for a message infringes a producer's right not to speak.[21]

Kennedy has voted to strike other government programs of coerced financial support. In *Brown and Hayes v. Legal Foundation of Washington,* he writes in dissent that a state program using interest on lawyers' trust accounts to provide legal services for the indigent acts as a state "monopoly" resulting in "forced support of certain viewpoints." To Kennedy, this program acts not merely as a Fifth Amendment taking but is then used to "serve causes the justices of the Washington Supreme Court prefer." "One constitutional violation (the taking of property)," he writes, "likely will lead to another (compelled speech)."[22]

CAMPAIGN FINANCE REFORM

Kennedy extends constitutional protection of political protest to a larger protection for political expression and political parties. This leads him to strike most legislation involving limits on campaign finance and campaign speech. He considers campaign activities, even by corporations, to be avenues of political protest. Restrictions on campaign donations and campaign speech by individuals, organizations, and parties—including those ratified by the Court in *Buckley v. Valeo*[23]—constitute content-based restrictions of free speech and association. In Kennedy's view, government attempts to regulate campaign speech rarely promote democracy or prevent the perception of corruption.[24] More often, they distort the free flow of information in the political system, mask the true motivations behind regulations of speech, and serve in practice as censorship of speech essential to democracy. The system of campaign finance legislated by Congress and approved by the Court distorts and censors political speech by prohibiting and restricting certain speakers and messages. Such policies have the effect of insulating the actions of elected officials from meaningful scrutiny and challenge.

While Kennedy's most expansive elaboration occurs in *McConnell v. Federal Elections Commission* (2003), these lines of argument appear in his opinions throughout his tenure on the Court. Kennedy has consistently voted to strike both state and federal legislation limiting campaign finance and campaign speech.[25] In *Austin v. Michigan Chamber of Commerce*,[26] he dissented from a decision to uphold a state law preventing corporations from spending money out of their general treasury to support candidates for office. With its decision, he writes, the Court "adopts a rule that allows Michigan to stifle voices of some of the most respected groups in public life on subjects central to the integrity of our democratic system" (695–696). Kennedy justifies striking this law as necessary to vindicate "society's interests in free and informed discussion on political issues, a discourse vital to the capacity for self-government" (698). By prohibiting corporations from speaking in this way, the state enacts a restriction based on content, "the essence of censorial power." Corporations, he writes, "have unique views of vital importance to the electorate," but under this law they "must remain mute" (699). Though the First Amendment "exists to protect all points of view," Kennedy concludes, by striking this provision the Court "contravenes fundamental principles of neutrality for all political speech" (700).

Kennedy believes this regulation deprives citizens of information necessary in a democracy based solely on the identity of the speaker. Michigan's law "is aimed at reducing the quantity of political speech," he writes, but "the First Amendment rests on quite the opposite theory" (704). He rejects the possibility that wealthy corporations can skew public debate any more than do wealthy individuals and candidates protected under *Buckley*. Further, corporate speech "is of importance and value to the self-fulfillment and self-expression of their members, and to the rich public dialogue that must be the mark of any free society" (710). He finds the law's only justification "hostility to the corporate form used by the speaker." By upholding this regulation, he writes, the Court "imposes its own model of speech" and "itself becomes the censor" (713).

Even before *McConnell*, Kennedy had written several opinions affirming the First Amendment associational rights of political parties and organizations. In *California Democratic Party v. Jones*,[27] his concurring opinion struck California's "blanket" primary allowing citizens to vote in different party primaries for different offices. Kennedy admits "there is much to be said" for any effort to increase political participation. Nevertheless, here the state acts "to force a political party to accept a candidate it may not want, and, by doing so, to change the party's doctrinal position on major issues" (587). By shifting control of the nomination process from the party to the electorate, he writes, "the State seeks to direct change in a political party's philosophy by forcing upon it unwanted candidates and wresting the choice between moderation and partisanship away from the party itself" (587). "In a free society," he concludes, "the State is directed by political doctrine, not the other way around" (590).[28]

Kennedy expressed further support for the rights of political parties and further disapproval of *Buckley* in his concurring opinion in *Colorado Republican Federal Campaign Committee v. Federal Election Commission*.[29] In this case, the Colorado Republican Federal Campaign Committee challenged federal restrictions on how political party organizations could allocate funds to candidates. The requirement that party expenditures not be coordinated with its candidates, Kennedy writes, "is both burdensome and quite unrealistic" (627). If under *Buckley* an individual can spend his or her own money on political speech, parties should have the same right to support their candidates. There is "a practical identity of interests" between parties and candidates, Kennedy writes, for "in the context of particular elections, candidates are necessary to make the party's message known and effective, and vice versa" (630,

629). If candidate expenditures can be unlimited, then as a "joint First Amendment activity" party expenditures should be as well.

Kennedy reiterated his hostility to campaign finance regulations in *Nixon v. Shrink Missouri PAC*,[30] when he dissented from a decision to uphold state limits on contributions to candidates from political action committees. By according campaign donations and speech less protection than given to "a single protestor with a hand-scrawled sign" or "a few demonstrators on a public sidewalk," he writes, *Buckley* and later court decisions constituted a "serious distortion of the First Amendment" (406). Kennedy characterizes "soft money, usually funneled through political parties," as "covert speech" that "conceals" the "real purpose of the speech." Although soft money is protected under the Constitution, "straightforward speech, in the form of financial contributions paid to a candidate, speech subject to full disclosure and prompt evaluation by the public, is not." Current campaigns employ "covert speech" and are policed by an "indirect system of accountability that is confusing, if not dispiriting to the voter" (407). While "there are no easy answers" to quell the public perception of political corruption, Kennedy admits, "the Constitution relies on one: open, robust, honest, unfettered speech that voters can examine and assess in an ever-changing and more complex environment" (409).

Kennedy has reiterated his opposition to government restriction of political discourse during campaigns. His concurring opinion in *Republican Party of Minnesota v. White*[31] struck a state law preventing candidates for elected judgeships from announcing their positions on disputed political and legal issues. Kennedy considers this restriction content-based and says it "should be invalidated without inquiry into narrow tailoring or compelling government interests" (2544). "The political speech of candidates is at the heart of the First Amendment," he finds; thus, "direct restrictions on the content of candidate speech are simply beyond the power of government to impose." Although judicial integrity is an important value, Kennedy admits, the state cannot "censor what the people hear as they undertake to decide for themselves which candidate is most likely to be an exemplary judicial officer" (2545). Voters who object to statements of judicial candidates "can use their own First Amendment freedoms to protest statements inconsistent with standards of judicial neutrality and judicial excellence." To Kennedy, "free elections and free speech are a powerful combination" (2546).

Kennedy expresses his sharpest criticism of government regulation of political speech in *McConnell v. Federal Elections Commission*,[32] where he voted to invalidate most of the Bipartisan Campaign Reform Act (BCRA) of 2002, commonly known as the McCain-Feingold act. The Court upheld much of the statute against First Amendment challenge, and in his introduction Kennedy states his main concerns about both the legislation and the Court's decision to uphold it. "The First Amendment," he writes, "guarantees our citizens the right to judge for themselves the most effective means for the expression of political views and to decide for themselves which entities to trust as reliable speakers" (286). The BCRA "is an effort by Congress to ensure that civic discourse takes place only through the modes of its own choosing" (287). Yet "government cannot be trusted to moderate its own rules for suppression of speech" (288).

Kennedy first votes to strike the BCRA's limitations on the raising and spending of soft money by national parties. He concedes a compelling state interest in preventing corruption or its appearance. Yet Kennedy distinguishes between quid pro quo corruption and favoritism: "It is in the nature of an elected representative to favor certain policies, and, by necessary corollary, to favor the voters and contributors who support those policies," he writes. "Democracy is premised on responsiveness" (297). Soft money for party-building activity—as opposed to donations to specific candidates—"lacks a possibility for quid pro quo corruption of federal officeholders" (301). Further, Kennedy finds that the BCRA prevents political parties "from aiding other speakers whom the party deems more effective in addressing discrete issues" (305).

Kennedy then examines the consequences of BCRA. In practice, he finds, it "begins to look very much like an incumbent protection plan" (306). He observes that under the act "more lenient treatment [is] accorded to incumbency-driven politicians than to party officials who represent broad national constituencies." By protecting some politicians at the expense of others and weakening parties, the act, he says, puts a "practical burden on challengers." Incumbents already enjoy "name recognition and other advantages" (307), and enforcement of a formally even playing field only has the effect of providing advantages to those who already hold office.

Kennedy does uphold portions of BCRA—those that limit the solicitation by officeholders of soft money within the quid pro quo anticorruption rationale (308, 315). Nevertheless, he strikes most of the provisions of Title II of BCRA limiting and regulating electioneering and expenditures of corporations and labor unions because these provisions amount to government control of political discourse. To Kennedy, this section of the act "silences political speech central to the civic discourse that sustains and informs our democratic processes." Congress refers to some speech as "sham issue ads"; but for Kennedy, "what the Court and Government call sham . . . are the ads speakers find most effective" and the ones that prove "most potent" (323). He believes that the line "between independent expenditures for commenting on issues, on the one hand, and supporting or opposing a candidate, on the other, has no First Amendment significance" (326–327). In light of the law's exemption for media, Kennedy argues, "Congress is determining what future course the creation of ideas and the expression of views must follow" (305).

Under *Buckley,* corporations can only communicate through political action committees (PACs). With these and other regulations, Kennedy asserts, government is attempting to control the identity, form, and content of political discourse. The legal rules concerning the creation and regulation of PACs "create major disincentives for speech." These disincentives include not merely monetary costs but being "forced to assume a false identity while doing so" (332). This system produces a "scheme of compulsory ventriloquism" that serves "to diffuse the corporate message" (333). Kennedy would also strike the prohibition of corporate or union funding of a broadcast communication within sixty days of an election as "a severe and unprecedented ban on protected speech" (334). "A central purpose of issue ads is to urge the public to pay close attention to the candidate's platform on the featured issues," Kennedy writes. In preventing such advertising, government "shields information at the heart of the First Amendment from precisely those citizens who most value the right to make a responsible judgment at the voting booth" (335–336).

Kennedy concludes by summarizing how the BCRA—like other attempts at campaign finance reform—violates core justifications for free speech in a democracy. As he states in *Austin,* the BCRA and the majority of the Court focus on the identity of speakers rather than the speech itself. "The hostility toward corporations and unions that infuses the majority opinion," he writes, "is inconsistent with the viewpoint neutrality the First Amendment demands of all Government actors" (340). Kennedy emphasizes the BCRA's effect on "budget-strapped nonprofit entities" like the American Civil Liberties Union (ACLU) "upon which many of our citizens rely for political commentary and advocacy." To participate in elections, these groups must establish a separate entity "against their institutional identities" and comply with "a legal construct sanctioned by Congress" instead of using "the means of communication chosen and preferred by the citizenry" (340). To Kennedy, the BCRA is an attempt by politicians—now approved by the Court—to use federal criminal law to regulate the form, structure, and content of American political debate. Yet "the civic discourse belongs to the people and the Government may not prescribe the means used to conduct it." In upholding this law, he says, the Court "leaves us less free than before" and "breaks faith with our tradition of robust and unfettered debate" (341).

Most recently, in *Randall v. Sorrell*[33] Kennedy used his separate opinion to reiterate the arguments of his *McConnell* dissent. Kennedy agreed with the majority that Vermont's strict limitations on campaign expenditures and contributions violated the First Amendment, but he went further than the majority did to criticize prior legislation and court rulings. "The universe of campaign finance regulation," he writes, "is one this Court has in part created and in part permitted by its course of decisions." The system produced "may cause more problems than it solves." Citing *McConnell*, he writes that "political parties have been denied basic First Amendment rights." In practice, PACs and other groups have emerged. "As much the creatures of law as of traditional forces of speech and association," he writes, these novel groups "can manipulate the system and attract their own power brokers, who operate in ways obscure to the ordinary citizen."

Kennedy vigilantly applies the First Amendment to the political speech that he believes "ensures the dialogue that is necessary for the continuance of the democratic process." This dialogue requires protections for individuals who dissent from government policies or officials[34] as well as for those who want to influence the political process through campaign speech and campaign donations.[35] To Kennedy, government regulations cannot be based on content, the corporate identity of the speaker, or a generalized accusation of political corruption. These can easily become means for government to insulate its policies or officials from criticism. The only constitutional remedy for dissenting speech, he contends, is more transparent speech.

EXPANDING THE TRADITIONAL PUBLIC FORUM

Kennedy's expansive theory of free speech motivates him to enlarge the concept of the public forum to promote the expression of diverse views. Justices Scalia and Rehnquist focus on the traditional element of the traditional public forum. Kennedy, in contrast, interprets the concept of a public forum to recognize new social realities and new technologies that serve the same practical purpose that the public square did in the past.

Although Kennedy did uphold some state restrictions on expression in the public forum early in his career, these opinions attempted to ensure that they did not infringe upon the content or viewpoint of the expression. During his first full term on the Court, he wrote the majority opinion in *Ward v. Rock against Racism*[36] affirming New York City's regulation that all performers in Central Park had to use a city sound technician. The city's regulation does not "vary the sound quality or volume based on the message being delivered by performers," Kennedy writes, and the "city's policy is to defer to the sponsor's wishes concerning sound quality" (795). The regulation in practice is thus content- and viewpoint-neutral. While Thurgood Marshall, in dissent, states that the city failed "to adopt the least intrusive restriction necessary to achieve its goals" (803), Kennedy observes that "the city's guideline has no material impact on any performer's ability to exercise complete artistic control over sound quality" (802).

Kennedy has upheld other restrictions targeted at the solicitation of money in the public forum. In his opinions, however, he moves beyond historical examples, to redefine and expand the concept of the traditional public forum in order to recognize social and technological changes. In *United States v. Kokinda*,[37] although he agreed that the U.S. Postal Service could limit in-person solicitations on post office grounds, he disagreed with the majority's claim that the sidewalk in front of a post office is not a public forum. "As society becomes more insular in character," he writes, "it becomes essential to protect public places where traditional modes of speech and forms of expression can take place" (737). The ban on in-person solicitation of money, however, is neither content- nor viewpoint-based. It "goes no further than to prohibit personal solicitations on postal property for the immediate payment of money" (738). The restriction does not prohibit the political or social expression of any idea based on its content. It "expressly permits the respondent and all others to engage in political speech on topics of their choice and to distribute literature soliciting support, including money contributions, provided there is no in-person solicitation for payments on the premises" (738–739).

Kennedy reiterated his commitment to expanding the definition of the traditional public forum in *International Society for Krishna Consciousness v. Lee*.[38] A majority of the Court ruled that an airport terminal was not a public forum. It thus upheld the New York Port Authority's ban on the distribution or sale of literature and solicitation for immediate payment of money. Rehnquist's opinion, like one from Scalia earlier that term,[39] focuses on the word "traditional" in deciding whether a specific setting constitutes a public forum. "Given the lateness with which the modern air terminal has made its appearance," Rehnquist writes, "it hardly qualifies" (680).

Although Kennedy also voted to uphold the ban, he objects to Rehnquist's analysis. Kennedy claims that "our public forum doctrine ought not to be a jurisprudence of categories, rather than ideas" (693–694). One idea is that "at the heart of our jurisprudence lies the principle that in a free nation citizens have the right to gather and speak with other persons in public places" (696). The traditional public forum is defined not "by recourse to history." It includes "other forms of property, regardless of their ancient or contemporary origins," that in today's society have the same qualities. "If the objective, physical characteristics of the property at issue and the actual public access and uses that have been permitted by government indicate that expressive activity would be appropriate and compatible with those uses," he writes, "the property is a public forum" (698). The growth of air travel and the predominance of government-run air terminals, he writes, "makes it imperative to protect speech rights there" (700).

Although Kennedy found the air terminal to be a public forum, he upheld the ban on solicitation and receipt of funds—as he did in *Kokinda*—because it "reaches only personal solicitations for immediate payment of money" (704). Considering whether the ban is an attempt to restrict any message based on content or viewpoint, Kennedy observes that solicitation "creates a risk of fraud and duress" and that "the ban is directed at these abusive practices, and not at any particular message, idea, or form of speech." Thus, he writes, "the regulation is a content-neutral rule serving a significant government interest." Nevertheless, he would strike the ban on the sale of literature because that "would leave organizations seeking to spread their message without funds to operate" (708).

Kennedy's evolving conception of the traditional public forum also recognizes changes in technology, such as the growth of cable television franchises, where single owner-operators often benefit from monopolies granted by local government. Others, like Justice Thomas, argue that owners of cable licenses have essentially the same First Amendment rights as private individuals. For Kennedy, however, the role of government in the granting of cable licenses and social changes makes this medium a public forum. "Minds are not changed in streets and parks as they once were," he writes in a 1996 case. "The more significant interchanges of ideas and shaping of public consciousness occur in mass and electronic media." [40] Given the extensive government involvement in licensing and monopolies, regulations of cable content must be subject to the same scrutiny as other regulations to ensure that the government is not favoring or disfavoring a particular content or viewpoint. Within new places and new technologies, he writes, "it contravenes the First Amendment to give Government a general license to single out some categories of speech for lesser protection so long as it stops short of viewpoint discrimination."

Kennedy wrote the principal opinion in two cases upholding federal requirements that cable companies carry local broadcast stations. In both he articulates his larger ideals of free speech and individual liberty. "At the heart of the First Amendment," Kennedy writes in the first case, "lies the principle that each person should decide for him or herself the ideas and beliefs deserving of expression, consideration and adherence."[41] Furthermore, "government action that stifles speech on account of its message, or that requires the utterance of a particular message favored by the Government, contravenes this essential right." Such policies "suppress unpopular ideas or information or manipulate the public debate through coercion, rather than persuasion."

The must-carry rules for the cable companies are acceptable to Kennedy, however, because they "impose burdens and confer benefits without reference to the content of the speech." The local access requirement was "based only upon the manner in which speakers transmit their messages to viewers, and not upon the messages they carry." The regulation was passed "not to favor programming of a particular subject matter, viewpoint, or format, but rather to preserve access to free television programming for the 40 percent of Americans without cable" and to protect them "from what Congress determined to be unfair competition by cable systems." In the second *Turner Broadcasting System* case, Kennedy reiterates the content-neutrality of the must-carry requirement. Further, he writes, "Congress has an independent interest in preserving a multiplicity of broadcasters to ensure that all households have access to information and entertainment on an equal footing with those who subscribe to cable."[42] Allowing cable operators who benefit from local monopolies to limit the number of local broadcast stations, he says, would decrease the viewpoints available both to cable subscribers and (eventually) to those without cable.

Kennedy expressed his commitment to individual expression in his decisions to extend free-speech protections to religious speakers in the public forum and public schools. He has joined several opinions allowing religious speakers and groups access to government facilities on the same basis as other groups.[43] In *Rosenberger v. Virginia*,[44] his majority opinion interpreted the free-speech guarantee—against an Establishment Clause challenge—to require a university to fund the publication of a religious group in the same way it would fund the publication of any other recognized student organization.

The University of Virginia withheld funding from a student publication (*Wide Awake*) because, it claimed, the publication "primarily promotes or manifests a particular belief in or about a deity or an ultimate reality." Kennedy finds this a prime example of content and viewpoint discrimination. "Religion may be a vast area of inquiry," he writes, "but it also provides, as it did here, a specific premise, a perspective, a standpoint from which a variety of subjects may be discussed and considered" (831). Once the university establishes a public forum for student expression, it cannot discriminate against religious expression. Allowing the state "to examine publications to determine whether or not they are based on some ultimate idea," Kennedy writes, would threaten "vital First Amendment speech principles."

The university had acted "against a background and tradition of thought and experiment that is at the center of our intellectual and philosophic tradition," Kennedy writes. Allowing the state to classify speech in this way would result in "the chilling of individual thought and expression" (835–836) and constitute "official censorship" (844–845). Kennedy finds that "the viewpoint discrimination inherent in the University's regulation required public officials to scan and interpret student publications to discern their underlying philosophic assumptions regarding religious theory and belief." Such action "would risk fostering a pervasive bias or hostility to religion, which could undermine the very neutrality the Establishment Clause requires" (845–846).

Kennedy reiterated his commitment to government neutrality in the university public forum by upholding a mandatory university activity fee for extracurricular speech. In *Board of Regents of University of Wisconsin v. Southworth*,[45] students claimed they were being forced to fund groups "that engage in political and ideological expression offensive to their personal beliefs" (227). Kennedy finds the activities and groups funded by the university to be "diverse in range and content," unlike the compelled commercial speech in the case of the mushroom grower in *USDA v. United Foods* (223).

The university requires this fee "for the sole purpose of facilitating the free and open exchange of ideas by, and among its students" and not merely to promote views government favors, Kennedy asserts (229). He finds the fee here permissible "to sustain an open dialogue" (233). "It is all but inevitable that the fees will result in subsidies to speech which some students find objectionable and offensive to their personal beliefs," he states, but "when a university requires its students to pay fees to support the extracurricular speech of other students, all in the interest of open discussion, it may not prefer some viewpoints to others." Kennedy finds "symmetry" with *Rosenberger:* "Viewpoint neutrality is the justification for requiring the student to pay the fee in the first instance and for ensuring the integrity of the program's operation once the funds have been collected" (232–233).

Even when upholding some state regulations, Kennedy's behavior in these cases remains consistent with his larger First Amendment values and his fear of government suppression of disfavored ideas. He expands the concept of the traditional public forum beyond historically accepted limits to account for social and technological advances and to promote access to a diversity of voices and viewpoints.

SEXUALLY EXPLICIT SPEECH

Kennedy stated in his confirmation testimony that the First Amendment "applies, really, to all ways in which we express ourselves as persons." From this, he has repeatedly struck federal efforts to regulate and criminalize expression that is sexually oriented but not obscene. In fact, it is in cases involving sexual speech where he has expressed some of his strongest justifications for freedom of individual expression. Government may not approve of such speech, and it has a compelling interest in keeping such material from minors. Indecent but nonobscene speech, however, retains First Amendment protection, and government cannot seek to favor or disfavor this speech in a way that materially limits its expression or receipt by consenting adults.

His first significant opinion in this area was a dissent in *Alexander v. United States*,[46] where the majority upheld forfeiture of an entire bookstore after the owner was convicted of obscenity. Although only some materials were obscene, an entire inventory was taken. Kennedy finds the wholesale forfeiture "a grave repudiation of First Amendment principles." The forfeiture, he says, aims "to destroy an entire speech business and all its protected titles, thus depriving the public of access to lawful expression." Kennedy finds this a classic form of prior restraint. "As governments try new ways to subvert essential freedoms," he writes, "legal and constitutional systems respond by making more explicit the nature and the extent of the liberty in question." The wholesale forfeiture even of nonobscene materials "is not the power to punish an individual for his past transgressions, but the authority to suppress a particular class of disfavored [though still protected] speech." To Kennedy, "the destruction of books and films that were not obscene and not adjudged to be so is a remedy with no parallel in our cases."

Kennedy has extended First Amendment protection to sexually themed indecent speech in several cases involving emerging technologies. In *Denver Area Educational Telecommunications Consortium v. FCC,*[47] he voted to strike rules (1) permitting local cable operators to prohibit programming on leased and public access channels that depicted sexual activity "in a patently offensive manner," and (2) allowing them to segregate and block "patently offensive" programming to a single channel. Consistent with his public forum opinions, Kennedy considers the cable monopoly a common carrier and thus a public forum. With both regulations, "Congress singles out one sort of speech for vulnerability to private censorship in a context where content-based discrimination is not otherwise permitted."

Even though government has a compelling interest in preventing minors from exposure to indecent material, Kennedy finds the means here to have a chilling effect on protected speech. Echoing *Cohen v. California,* he writes that "indecency often is inseparable from the ideas and viewpoints conveyed, or separable only with the loss of truth or expressive power." The FCC regulations granted operators not general editorial license to remove all kinds of offensive speech, but merely "a veto over the one kind of lawful speech Congress disdains." The restrictions "present a classic case of discrimination against speech based on its content."

Kennedy's later majority opinion in *U.S. v. Playboy Entertainment Group*[48] struck federal requirements that cable operators must fully scramble or block channels devoted to sexually oriented programs or limit their transmission to overnight hours when children are unlikely to view them. He again finds the identification of "'sexually-oriented' programming" to be a content-based regulation of otherwise protected speech. Congressional hearings about this legislation specifically mentioned Playboy; to Kennedy, "laws designed or intended to suppress or restrict the expression of specific speakers contradict basic First Amendment principles" (812). Kennedy recognizes the interest in preventing unsupervised children from accessing this material, but technology can block these channels on a house-by-house basis. This method, Kennedy notes, is a less restrictive (and more effective) means of accomplishing the government's objective. "Even where speech is indecent and enters the home," he writes, "the objective of shielding children does not suffice to support a blanket ban if the protection can be accomplished by a less restrictive alternative" (814).

More significantly, Kennedy uses this opinion to expound upon the connection between free speech and the larger conception of personal liberty that forms the foundation of his jurisprudence. "It is through speech that our convictions and beliefs are influenced, expressed and tested," Kennedy writes. "It is through speech that we bring those beliefs to bear on Government and on society. It is through speech that our personalities are formed and expressed. The citizen is entitled to seek out or reject certain ideas or influences without Government influence or control" (817).

Kennedy's defense of free speech derives from his larger ideal of liberty, morality, and human personality. Kennedy rejects the idea that expansive protection of free speech "is influenced by the philosophy that one idea is as valuable as any other, and that in art and literature objective standards of style, taste, decorum, beauty and esthetics are deemed by the Constitution to be inappropriate, indeed unattainable." Such judgments—in art and in morality, as well as in politics—can and must be made. "The Constitution," he writes, "no more enforces a relativistic philosophy or moral nihilism than it does any other point of view" (818). The First Amendment does, however, prevent government from making and enforcing ultimate determinations about the truth of such propositions. "The Constitution exists precisely so that opinions and judgments, including esthetic and moral judgments about art and literature," as well as politics, "can be formed, tested, and expressed," he writes. "What the Constitution says is that these judgments are for the individual to make, not for the Government to decree, even with the mandate or the approval of a majority."

To Kennedy, the nature of a public forum or of the governmental interest in morality must reflect a changing society and the changing nature of public life. "Technology expands the capacity to choose," he writes, "and it denies the potential of this revolution if we assume the Government is best positioned to make these choices for us." Content-based restrictions such as this one prevent individual adults from being able to make their own choices. If government prevailed, Kennedy observes, "we would risk leaving regulations in place that sought to shape our unique personalities or to silence dissenting ideas."

Following from this larger theory of personality, Kennedy has struck other federal laws specifically targeting sexually oriented, though nonobscene, speech. His majority opinion in *Ashcroft v. Free Speech Coalition*[49] invalidated provisions of the Child Pornography Protection Act (CPPA), which criminalized any depiction "that is, or appears to be, of a minor engaging in sexually explicit conduct." CPPA also criminalized "virtual child pornography" or any material "that conveys the impression" that it includes a minor engaging in sexually explicit conduct.

CPPA "seeks to reach beyond obscenity," Kennedy writes, and "a law imposing criminal penalties on protected speech is a stark example of speech suppression" (1398). In general, he says, "the First Amendment bars the government from dictating what we see or read or speak or hear." Government cannot criminalize speech "because it concerns subjects offending our sensibilities" (1399). Kennedy fears application of this act to performances of *Romeo and Juliet* or recent films such as *American Beauty* and *Traffic.* Although even child pornography with literary or artistic value can be punished because such value "did not excuse the harm it caused to its child participants," CPPA reaches material that does not involve any child participants (1401). "The Government cannot ban speech fit for adults simply because it may fall into the hands of children," he writes. "The evil in question depends upon the actor's unlawful conduct, conduct defined as criminal quite apart from any link to the speech in question" (1402). Kennedy concedes that virtual child pornography may tend to lead to the actual abuse of children; even so, the depictions enjoy constitutional protection. "The mere tendency of speech to encourage unlawful acts," he writes, "is not a sufficient reason for banning it" (1404).

Kennedy has also been vigilant in prohibiting regulation of indecent but nonobscene material on the Internet. In *Ashcroft v. ACLU,*[50] his concurring opinion reiterates that content-based regulations "are presumptively invalid abridgments of the freedom of speech" (1717). Following the earlier decision in *ACLU v. Reno,* he finds that "the national variation in community standards constitutes a particular burden on Internet speech" (1720). Moreover, "the more venues the Government has to choose from, the more speech will be chilled by variation across communities" (1722).

As of 2008, Kennedy has voted in one case to affirm federal regulation of nonobscene sexual material. Even in this opinion, however, he remained conscious of the law's potential effect on adults to receive protected expression. In *U.S. v. American Library Association*,[51] he voted to uphold against facial challenge a federal requirement that public libraries receiving federal funds for Internet access install filtering software to block material harmful to minors. Kennedy's concurrence recognizes that government has a "compelling" interest "in protecting young library users from material inappropriate to minors" (215). Yet he remains vigilant in policing government policies that restrict adult access to protected speech. If "an adult user" can gain access to an unblocked terminal "without significant delay," he writes, "there is little to this case" (214). Should some substantial obstacle to adult access exist, courts should entertain a challenge in the particular case (215). If there is no such burden on adult access, the condition is constitutional.

Kennedy also retreated a bit from his categorical hostility to content-based regulation in *City of Los Angeles v. Alameda Books*.[52] In that case, he joined a majority to uphold a city zoning ordinance that limited the concentration of adult businesses based on secondary effects such as public intoxication, prostitution, and other criminal activity. Even in this opinion, however, he reiterates his vigilant examination of whether a facially neutral state regulation acts to minimize the expression of protected speech based on content. Kennedy had in the past upheld such neutral regulations,[53] but here he tries, with more success, to reconcile such zoning with his general hostility to content-based regulation. Ordinances regulating the places of business of sexually oriented speech, he admits, "are content based and we should call them so."

For Kennedy, however, zoning regulations are a constitutionally permissible content-based regulation "because they have a prima facie legitimate purpose: to limit the negative externalities of land use" (1741). The efforts do not always intend to limit the expression of protected materials; they may seek only to regulate the place and manner where such expression occurs. "A zoning law need not be blind to the secondary effects of speech," he writes, "so long as the purpose of the law is not to suppress it" (1740). Kennedy admits that "the ordinance may be a covert attack on speech," but given the legitimate state purpose, "we should not presume it to be so." But even zoning regulations with facially legitimate purposes must withstand searching judicial scrutiny: "A city must advance some basis to show that its regulation has the purpose and effect of suppressing secondary effects," he writes, "while leaving the quantity and accessibility of speech substantially intact" (1742). Courts should not defer to government zoning decisions; judges must assess for themselves the motivations and consequences of the challenged regulation.

The following year, in *Ashcroft v. ACLU*,[54] Kennedy upheld a lower court's injunction preventing enforcement of the federal Child Online Protection Act (COPA). COPA criminalized the knowing posting on the Internet, for "commercial purposes," of material "harmful to minors." Penalties under COPA included fines of up to $50,000 and prison sentences of up to six months for each occurrence. The law allowed an affirmative defense for those who employed certain means—credit-card or age verification screens, for example—to prevent minors from gaining access. Kennedy's majority opinion overturning the law emphasizes that "content-based prohibitions, enforced by severe criminal penalties, have the constant potential to be a repressive force in the lives and thoughts of a free people" (660).

Kennedy rejected the specified affirmative defenses allowed under COPA as the least-restrictive means of achieving the government's objective. The district court had considered whether blocking and filtering software proved less restrictive of First Amendment rights and more effective in preventing access to minors. For Kennedy, the key determination is that filters "impose restrictions on speech at the receiving end, not universal restrictions at the source" (667). Adults still have access to lawful material and can turn off their own filters. "Above all," Kennedy writes, "promoting the use of filters does not condemn as criminal any category of speech, and so the potential chilling effect is eliminated, or at least much diminished" (667). Further, filters can be more effective than COPA in blocking such material from minors because they can monitor all sites and "can be applied to all forms of Internet communication, including e-mail, not just communications available via the World Wide Web" (668).

Requiring filters "is not a perfect solution," Kennedy admits. But under the First Amendment, the burden remains on the government to demonstrate that its criminal sanction is less restrictive and more effective (668). He enumerates several steps government can take to promote its compelling interest in protecting minors. "Congress can encourage the use of filters," as the Court (and he) approved in *American Library Association* (669). It can use its voice to "promote" filtering software in the industry and encourage greater parental involvement in and supervision of the activities of their children. "By enacting programs that promote the use of filtering software," he writes, "Congress could give parents that ability without subjecting protected speech to severe penalties" (670).

There are other "important practical reasons," Kennedy writes, for maintaining the injunction against the law's enforcement. Given that protected speech is threatened, "the potential harms from reversing the injunction outweigh those of leaving it in place by mistake" (670). Remanding the case for trial allows the parties to provide further evidence on factual questions such as the relative effectiveness of filtering software, the pace of advancing technology, and the effect of new laws passed by Congress in the intervening years. For Kennedy, even when laws seek the compelling interests of protecting minors and captive audiences, courts should examine the practical burden on adults who seek to receive constitutionally protected expression.

Aside from obscene speech—which can be constitutionally prohibited—Kennedy would consider all remaining sexually oriented speech to be protected against content-based restrictions. Government cannot seek to privilege or disadvantage one class of protected expression over another based on content, no matter the justification. Government can regulate secondary effects or non-speech components to promote its compelling interests. But it should not seek to influence the expression or interchange of ideas in any way. When it does so through criminal law, government infringes on the liberty of individual citizens to make political, aesthetic, and moral judgments for themselves.

USING FREE SPEECH TO EXPAND JUDICIAL POWER

Kennedy's behavior in more recent free-speech cases appears paradoxical.[55] He has cast deciding votes against free-speech claims in some high-profile cases, although he wrote and joined opinions seeking to limit the scope of the holding and to address fears that government is limiting debate. At the same time, Kennedy has employed innovative arguments based on free speech and association to expand the scope of judicial power into other areas of constitutional law generally considered political questions.

Two recent cases find Kennedy ruling against free-speech claims in surprising ways. In *Garcetti v. Ceballos,* Kennedy wrote for a five-justice majority finding that an assistant district attorney can be disciplined for a memo criticizing his office written as part of his official job responsibilities. Kennedy distinguishes between the words of a government employee uttered as a citizen—which are protected—and those made as an employee—which can subject him to sanction by his employer.[56]

In *Morse v. Frederick*,[57] Kennedy joined a majority finding no violation when a high school principal suspended a student for unfurling a banner reading "Bong Hits 4 Jesus" at an event attended by his classmates. Kennedy joined a concurring opinion written by Justice Samuel A. Alito, Jr., that expressed Kennedy's characteristic concerns. Alito's opinion rejected the sweeping arguments presented in favor of the school and accepted in the concurrence of Justice Thomas. Accepting a broad government power to punish speech in the public school context, Alito writes, "strikes at the very heart of the First Amendment" and threatens censorship and viewpoint discrimination. Despite his general protection of political dissent, however, Kennedy joined Alito to uphold the school's discipline of Frederick." Speech advocating illegal drug use poses a threat to student safety that is just as serious, if not always as immediately obvious," as the speech leading to actual disruption, Alito writes.[58] The opinion's language and concerns resonate with Kennedy's prior writings.

More significantly, Kennedy has used free speech and association claims to expand the scope of judicial power. For example, despite his general invalidation of government policies that classify citizens by race (see Chapter 4), in *Grutter v. Bollinger*—involving Michigan's law-school admissions program—Kennedy affirms the constitutional permissibility of some programs of affirmative action in university admissions. He grounds this on the basis "of a tradition, founded in the First Amendment, of acknowledging a university's conception of its educational mission." Part of that conception allows discretion in valuing educational diversity, including the racial background of its students. Consistent with his neutral individualism, Kennedy states that the use of race must be "nonpredominant," "modest," and "limited"; the university's conception must be "supported by empirical evidence"; and its policy must be subject to "rigorous judicial review" and "strict scrutiny." Kennedy finds the University of Michigan's law school admissions program challenged in this case to fall short of all of these standards. Nevertheless, the high value Kennedy places on First Amendment freedoms explains why he allows "giving appropriate consideration to race in this one context."[59]

Kennedy's most creative use of the First Amendment to increase the scope of judicial power is to justify judicial intervention in electoral redistricting. One example is his separate concurring opinion in *Vieth v. Jublirer*.[60] In *Vieth*, Kennedy upheld a congressional redistricting plan against a challenge, based on the Equal Protection Clause, which said that district lines were drawn for partisan reasons. Yet he refuses to join the plurality's rule finding that all such partisan gerrymandering claims are political questions not justiciable by the Court. "A determination by the Court to deny all hopes of intervention," he writes, "could erode confidence in the courts as much as would a premature decision to intervene" (310).

Given Kennedy's penchant for recasting constitutional arguments from equality to liberty, it is no surprise that in *Vieth* he justifies the judicial role not under the Fourteenth Amendment but under the First Amendment. To Kennedy, free speech "may be the more relevant constitutional provision" because the right claimed is one of free association arising from government "not burdening or penalizing citizens because of their participation in the electoral process, their voting history, their association with a political party, or their expression of political views." Under redistricting, "First Amendment concerns arise where an apportionment has the purpose and effect of burdening a group of voters' representational rights" (314).

Kennedy prefers using the First Amendment because it provides a more "manageable" or "limited and precise rationale" and a "sounder and more prudential basis of intervention than the Equal Protection Clause" (306, 315). Equal protection, he writes, is appropriate when the constitutional claim of districting is based on race, "since classification by race is almost never permissible." A partisan gerrymander "presents a more complicated question . . . whether a generally permissible classification has been used for an impermissible purpose." In contrast to the sharp categorical use of equal protection, First Amendment analysis of burdens and interests "allows a pragmatic or functional assessment that accords some latitude to the States" (315). Although Kennedy does not find this particular district unconstitutional, he states in his conclusion that "legislative restraint was abandoned" (316). "If workable standards do emerge to measure these burdens," he concludes, "courts should be prepared to offer relief" (317).[61]

Kennedy also employs the First Amendment to expand the scope of judicial review into the electoral process. In *New York State Board of Elections v. Lopez Torres*,[62] a candidate for state supreme court justice challenged New York's process of nomination by party convention. The majority considered the claim a political question. "We are not inclined to open up this new and excitingly unpredictable theater of election jurisprudence," Scalia writes. "We decline to enter the morass" (800, 801).

Kennedy authored a separate concurrence that took the candidate's First Amendment challenge more seriously. Although "the present suit does not permit us to invoke the Constitution in order to intervene," Kennedy writes, it does raise constitutional issues the Court must resolve (803). New York allowed independent candidates access to the ballot if they gained a sufficient number of voter signatures. "Were the state-mandated-and-designed nominating convention the sole means to attain access to the general election ballot," Kennedy writes, "there would be considerable force" to the candidate's challenge (801). Here, he notes, "this requirement has not been shown to be an unreasonable one" (802). Although Kennedy votes to uphold the electoral system in *Lopez Torres*—just as he rules against the claims brought under the First Amendment in *Grutter* and *Vieth*—he uses free-speech arguments to expand judicial scrutiny into other areas of constitutional law.

CONCLUSION

Kennedy's expansive protection of free speech across several doctrinal areas follows from the broad theory of personal liberty he has expressed in other areas of his constitutional jurisprudence. Just as he finds that "the heart of liberty is the right to define one's own concept of existence, of meaning, of the universe, and of the mystery of human life,"[63] he finds that "the heart of the First Amendment is the principle that each person should decide for him or herself the ideas and beliefs deserving of expression, consideration and allegiance."[64] He applies this vision most forcefully to political speech and political dissenters, striking down instances of compelled and commercial speech, campaign finance reform, and restrictions on corporations and political parties. Though Kennedy concedes that government may regulate the secondary effects of speech, he has voted to expand the public forum beyond traditional conceptions to account for new social and technological realities and to provide more protections to commercial speech and sexually oriented speech. More significantly, he attempts to expand the accepted role of the courts in enforcing the First Amendment as a means for expanding judicial power into other areas. Kennedy's larger ideal of individual liberty and personality—combined with his broad conception of the judicial role—thus leads him to be the justice on the current Court who most often strikes government actions for violating constitutional guarantees of free speech, expression, and association.

4. Kennedy's Equality of Neutral Individualism

Central both to the idea of the rule of law and to our own Constitution's guarantee of equal protection is the principle that government and each of its parts remain open on impartial terms to all who seek its assistance.

—*ROMER V. EVANS* (1996)

As his pivotal opinion in the 2007 *Seattle* schools case illustrates,[1] Justice Kennedy has played a crucial role in cases involving equal protection. He has joined conservative majorities to strike policies of affirmative action, school desegregation, and majority-minority legislative districts, and he has joined liberal majorities to restrict other state efforts to classify citizens on the basis of race, religion, or sexual orientation. He has acknowledged educational diversity as a compelling state interest, yet voted to invalidate every race-conscious admissions plan presented to the Court. Kennedy's controlling opinions in this area merit greater scholarly attention.

Although his votes may appear to be ideologically inconsistent, Kennedy's equal protection opinions in fact serve to illuminate the moral conceptions of individual liberty and human dignity at the heart of his larger jurisprudence.[2] Kennedy's ideal of what I call neutral individualism does not derive solely from the constitutional text, from history, or from specific tradition. His moral conception claims foundations in two Supreme Court opinions: Justice John Harlan's statement in his *Plessy v. Ferguson* dissent that the Constitution "neither knows nor tolerates classes among citizens";[3] and Chief Justice Earl Warren's statement in *Brown v. Board of Education* that racial classifications produce "intangible considerations." To segregate children "from others of similar age and qualifications solely because of their race," Warren writes, "generates a feeling of inferiority as to their status in the community that may affect their hearts and minds in a way unlikely ever to be undone."[4] Although Warren's quote in *Brown* referred to the harm suffered by African American children forced by law to attend segregated schools, to Kennedy it embodies a universal harm to liberty suffered by all citizens when government classifies them on the basis of any characteristic—race, but also sex, religion, or sexual orientation—they are powerless to control.

Whenever government classifies individuals by group traits and makes policies based on these stereotypes, Kennedy argues, it violates essential ideals of individual identity and human dignity. It frustrates personal development of citizens by presuming that these unchangeable traits produce individuals with predictable political interests and intellectual viewpoints. Even racial classifications intended to assist disadvantaged groups produce resentment in those excluded and self-doubt among the individuals who benefit. Government classifications cause citizens to think of themselves and others primarily as members of groups. These policies threaten social balkanization and serve ultimately to endanger personal liberty and individual identity. Prior to coming to the Court, Kennedy expressed concern that "equal protection litigation has tended to become based on the claims of classes of persons" rather than claims of individual rights.[5] Consistent with his larger jurisprudence, Kennedy recasts questions about equality as matters of personal liberty.[6]

Kennedy's conception of neutral individualism is also consistent with other aspects of his approach to constitutional interpretation. It requires not only a moral argument but also an empirical assessment of the effects of these classifications on individuals and the larger society. Many of these moral assumptions find more explicit expression in opinions by Justices Scalia and Thomas in the rhetoric of "the color-blind Constitution." Kennedy, however, applies the moral principles of neutral individualism more consistently to government racial classifications, and he extends their premises to other government classifications by race, religion, and sexual orientation. More recently, in *Grutter v. Bollinger* and *Parents Involved in Community Schools v. Seattle School District No. 1*,[7] Kennedy explicitly distances himself from pure colorblindness to recognize a compelling state interest in promoting educational diversity. Even in these cases, he employs searching judicial scrutiny, striking programs in order to ensure that government treats each citizen not primarily as the member of a racial or ethnic group but as a unique individual.

THE FOUNDATIONS OF NEUTRAL INDIVIDUALISM

Kennedy expressed his individualistic view of constitutional equality before coming to the Court. He stated in his confirmation hearings that the Fourteenth Amendment, "by its very terms, of course, includes all persons, and I think it was deliberately drafted in that respect."[8] This truism masks the deeper substance he believes the text of the amendment to embody, "the concept of individuality and liberty and dignity that those who drafted the Constitution understood" (170–171). Kennedy's conceptions of individual liberty and dignity, evident in his opinions on other areas of law, find further development in his equal protection jurisprudence.

Kennedy's conception of equal protection derives from moral norms independent of the historical circumstances of the Fourteenth Amendment's enactment. He stated that the Equal Protection Clause—and the amendment as a whole—"has far more validity and far more breadth than simply what someone thought they were doing at the time" (151). The amendment states an enduring moral principle: it "was intended to eliminate discrimination in public facilities on the day that it was passed because that is the necessary meaning of the actions that were taken and of the announcements that were made" (149). Kennedy concludes this not through historical study but from an ideal of equality. "I just do not think that the 14th Amendment was designed to freeze into society all of the inequities that then existed," he testified. "I simply cannot believe it" (151).

Kennedy's application of these values is evident in two of his Ninth Circuit opinions. In *Flores v. Pierce*,[9] he upheld the damages award to two Mexican American restaurant owners, Barbaro and Alma Flores, who argued that the police chief and city council of Calistoga, California, had delayed granting them a liquor license because of their ethnicity. To Kennedy, "the essence of an equal protection violation on racial grounds lies in the intent or motive to discriminate." Despite claims that government policy is neutral on its face, Kennedy writes, "the effect of a law may be so harsh or adverse in its weight against a particular race that an intent to discriminate is not only a permissible inference but a necessary one" (1389).

Kennedy moves beyond the neutral phrasing of the city's liquor licensing ordinance to search for "other evidence" that "suggests a motive or intent to discriminate." The grounds asserted by Calistoga for delaying the license—"to prevent aggravation of an existing police problem" or "to prevent an undue concentration of licenses"—could not be demonstrated. Moreover, no protests had been filed against applications for licenses, except in areas that primarily served Mexican Americans, for at least thirty-four years, and no protests had been lodged when a license was previously issued to an establishment on the same property. The police chief stated that problems would be caused "by the large number of Mexican field workers in the area to harvest the grapes." From these facts, Kennedy concludes, "the defendants acted with reference to racial classifications and offered explanations which invoked stereotypes from which one could infer an attempt to adopt a racial classification." Kennedy concludes that the Floreses were victims of "selective protests" because of "a clientele that was almost exclusively Mexican-American." As a result of this record, Kennedy concludes, "the jury may well have concluded . . . that the explanations given by the defendants for their actions were simply pretexts to conceal an intent to act upon stereotypic classifications which resulted from a racial animus" (1390).

Kennedy's opinion in *Flores* foreshadows his approach to equal protection generally. He finds discriminatory intent from an examination of the law's operation in practice. He carefully scrutinizes government actions to determine whether they embody stereotypes about how members of a certain group act, or if they serve as a cover for hostility against individuals identified by an immutable trait. He wants to determine whether the action in question denies a citizen's right to neutral treatment from government.

A desegregation opinion from his time on the Ninth Circuit—*Spangler v. Pasadena*[10]—offers further insight into Kennedy's neutral individualism and his fear that racial classifications will play a predominant role in political decision making. In 1976, the U.S. Supreme Court returned *Spangler* to the Ninth Circuit[11] to determine whether the district court should retain jurisdiction over Pasadena's desegregation process under *Brown v. Board of Education* and *Brown v. Board of Education II*.[12] On remand, Kennedy voted to limit federal judicial oversight. To Kennedy, under *Brown* a district court's remedy "may not be more extensive than is necessary to eliminate the effects of the constitutional violation that was the predicate for the court's intervention." The termination of federal court jurisdiction reinforces the importance of local control and "serves to restore to the state and local agencies the legal responsibility for supervising a school system that is properly theirs" (1242).

Kennedy's support for local control reflected his concern that continued judicial oversight could cause governmental decisions to focus predominately on racial factors. Once the Supreme Court determined that Pasadena's plan was racially neutral, he notes, federal jurisdiction should have ended. The argument that "the school board is constitutionally obligated to provide for a certain racial mix in its schools" is "erroneous" (1244). He describes the dangers that continued district court jurisdiction poses to "important governmental and personal interests" (1247). Continued oversight makes it difficult to enact "legitimate changes in educational policy" because "a board may feel obligated to take racial factors into account in each of its decisions so that it can justify its actions to the supervising court." Judicial oversight "may make it more, rather than less, difficult to determine whether race impermissibly influences board decisions, for the subject is injected artificially into the decision process, and the weight that racial considerations might otherwise have had is more difficult to determine" (1247). In *Flores* and *Spangler*, Kennedy expresses fear that any injection of race into the political process—explicitly or covertly—will violate government's fundamental commitment to neutrality.

NEUTRAL INDIVIDUALISM AND RACE

On the Supreme Court, Kennedy has enforced his conception of equality as neutral individualism most prominently by joining majorities to invalidate race-based affirmative action policies, to limit federal court jurisdiction over school desegregation, and to overturn majority-minority legislative districts. Although government in each case defends its actions as benign and remedial, Kennedy strikes these policies under strict scrutiny. His neutral individualism shares many of the premises of the color-blind interpretation offered by Justices Scalia and Thomas. Like Scalia and Thomas, Kennedy derives these premises not solely from constitutional text, history, and tradition but from a moral conception of equality and personal liberty.[13]

To Kennedy, when government engages in racial classifications of individuals, it violates the Constitution's commitment to treating all citizens equally as individuals. Such policies are predicated on stereotypical ideas about members of racial groups. They foster resentment among those classes of individuals who are denied benefits or preferences and doubt among those who receive them, and they create a society of citizens more conscious of, and more preoccupied with, racial characteristics. Thus government should never take this first dangerous step—even for the best of intentions.

Affirmative Action
During his first full term on the Court, Kennedy expressed the moral foundations of his conception of equality in *Richmond v. J. A. Croson.*[14] The city

council of Richmond, Virginia, required contractors to set aside at least 30 percent of all contracts to Minority Business Enterprises, defined as groups at least 51 percent controlled by African Americans, Spanish speakers, Indians, Asians, Eskimos, or Aleuts. The city council claimed the policy was intended to remedy past discrimination. Croson—a plumbing and heating contractor—sued, claiming the race-based subcontracting requirement was a violation of equal protection.

At conference, Kennedy expressed his view that Richmond's definition of minority groups was too broad. He feared that allowing such a preference system would impose unfair burdens on innocent persons.[15] In his concurring opinion, he asserts that "the moral imperative of racial neutrality is the driving force of the Equal Protection Clause" (518). Kennedy agrees with the ideals behind Scalia's concurring opinion, "which would strike down all preferences which are not necessary remedies to victims of unlawful discrimination." The categorical approach "would make it crystal clear to the political branches, at least those of the States, that legislation must be based on criteria other than race" (518–519). Nevertheless—foreshadowing *Grutter* and the *Seattle* case—Kennedy accepts the more limited rule that "any racial preferences must face the most rigorous scrutiny by courts." Equal protection, he writes, "forbids the use even of narrowly drawn racial classifications except as a last resort" (519).

Kennedy finds no such last resort here. Although the set-aside was enacted by a majority-black, democratically elected body in the former capital of the Confederacy, no judicial or legislative record of discrimination was presented to support the policy. General claims of historical discrimination are not enough: the specific nature of racism in Richmond and the responsibility of the city government toward each identified class, Kennedy writes, "were all matters unmeasured, unexplored and unexplained by the city council" (519). As a result, the statute is "open to the fair charge that it is not a remedy but is itself a preference." If allowed, Kennedy says, this policy "will cause the same corrosive animosities that the Constitution forbids in the whole sphere of government and that our national policy condemns in the rest of society as well" (520).

Kennedy expressed further opposition to racial classifications the following year in *Metro Broadcasting v. Federal Communications Commission*.[16] In this case, the FCC defended a federal broadcast-licensing program that gave exclusive preference to minority applications as needed to promote viewpoint diversity. A majority of the Court upheld the program, but Kennedy—joined by Scalia—argued that the policy perpetuated racial stereotypes. At conference, Blackmun reports, Kennedy became "emotional" and called *Metro Broadcasting* "a watershed case." If affirmed, Kennedy contended, racial preferences would be "limitless" and "last for all time."[17]

Kennedy's emotion comes through in his written dissent. The "fundamental errors" of *Plessy v. Ferguson*—the 1896 U.S. Supreme Court decision that ratified "separate but equal" laws—he writes, "have disturbing parallels in today's majority opinion." The majorities in both *Plessy* and *Metro Broadcasting,* Kennedy writes, "upheld a state-sponsored race-conscious measure" as "reasonable" because the legislature was "at liberty to act with reference to the established usages, customs and traditions of the people with a view to their comfort" (631–632). Just as the *Plessy* majority affirmed the reasonableness of segregated railcars, the majority in *Metro Broadcasting* affirmed the FCC policy to satisfy "the listening pleasure of media audiences."

Allowing the FCC policy, Kennedy argues, threatens both personal identity and social unity. The broadcast diversity policy equates viewpoint with race, then rewards and denies applicants with licenses on that basis. "Once the Government takes the step, which itself should be forbidden, of enacting into law the stereotypical assumption that the race of owners is linked to broadcast content," he writes, "it follows a path that becomes even more tortuous. It must decide which races to favor" (632). With this reasoning, the current Court "exhumes *Plessy*'s deferential approach" and "turns back the clock" (632–633).

This racial classification is not saved by the government's claim that it seeks to be inclusive. "Although the majority is 'confident' that it can determine when racial discrimination is benign," Kennedy observes, "it offers no explanation as to how it will do so" (633). Kennedy then quotes again from *Plessy* and from a document from the South African government justifying apartheid. These examples demonstrate that "policies of racial separation and preference are almost justified as benign, even when it is clear to any sensible observer that they are not" (635).

Although judges cannot divine benign motivation, Kennedy argues, they can measure the divisive effects of these policies. This weighing of effects must be done "with attention to the cardinal rule that the Constitution protects each citizen as an individual, not as a member of a group" (636). Government may claim that racial classifications are benign, but they "are often not seen that way by individuals affected by them." He first examines the effect of the policy on those who benefit. The asserted interest in broadcast diversity, Kennedy writes, "seems based on the demeaning notion that members of defined racial groups ascribe to certain 'minority views' that must be different than those of other citizens." Classifications based on race "also can foster the view that members of favored groups are inherently less able to compete on their own" (636). This "stereotypical thinking," Kennedy writes, produces injuries that are psychological and intangible, but no less real.

Kennedy argues that the Court should also consider the "perceptions" and "stigma imposed upon the excluded class . . . with the unproven charge of past racial discrimination" (636). When members of one group benefit, members of other groups suffer. "Whether or not such programs can be described as 'remedial,'" Kennedy writes, "the message conveyed is that it is acceptable to harm a member of the group excluded from the benefit or privilege" and that "individual harms are simply irrelevant in the face of efforts to compensate for racial inequalities" (636–637).

To Kennedy, the "warning" of Justice Harlan's *Plessy* dissent against sowing "the seeds of race hate . . . is now all the more apposite." Any government classifying by race, no matter the motive, risks unintended consequences that divide society. "History suggests much peril in this enterprise," he writes, "and so the Constitution forbids us to undertake it." Kennedy concludes that the majority's correlation of intellectual viewpoint with racial identity, and its decision to allow government to classify on that basis, serve only to "move us from 'separate but equal' to 'unequal but benign'" (637).[18]

In these early affirmative action opinions, Kennedy moves beyond the moral interpretations of equality and of our constitutional tradition to examine the tangible and intangible effects of governmental racial classification on individual beneficiaries and those excluded. Because these programs categorize individuals by race and impute racial stereotypes about viewpoint and ability based on that categorization, they deny the fundamental dignity of every citizen. These policies encourage government, and thus the public, to see citizens first by their racial identity—a practice inconsistent with the constitutional commitments to individual rights and a successful multiethnic American democracy.

Kennedy's neutral individualism parallels the "liberal, individualistic conception of equality" advanced by former solicitor general Charles Fried,[19] and it follows from his own larger theory of human liberty and personality. This ideal does not rely on interpretations of the original intent of the Reconstruction Amendments, or on a specific reading of American history. It rests on a larger moral ideal of individual identity and personal dignity. This ideal is violated whenever government classifies citizens under law as members of racial groups.

School Desegregation

Expanding on his Ninth Circuit opinion in *Spangler,* Kennedy has limited the jurisdiction of federal courts in cases involving school desegregation. He fears that continued court supervision after the elimination of the de jure segregation pressures school boards to make policy decisions based on a preoccupation with race. Continued judicial supervision may encourage them to classify students by race, which Kennedy considers to be the very injury the decision in *Brown* intended to eliminate. When a school board has in good faith moved to comply with desegregation orders, Kennedy believes, federal judicial oversight should end and education policy should be returned to local control.

On the Supreme Court, Kennedy has joined majorities limiting the remedial power of district courts to redress de facto segregation in public schools. A prime example is *Missouri v. Jenkins,*[20] where a district court charged with desegregating Kansas City's schools issued an order raising taxes within the district to double the existing rate, even beyond the limits of state law. The Court unanimously overturned the order, and Kennedy wrote separately. As in *Spangler,* Kennedy notes that courts possess limited means to achieve what he considers the limited constitutional mandate of *Brown.* "District courts can and must take needed steps to eliminate racial discrimination and ensure the operation of unitary school systems," he writes. "But it is discrimination, not the ineptitude of educators or the indifference of the public, that is the evil to be remedied." Shifting this larger responsibility to courts will have dramatic and harmful political consequences. "An initial finding of discrimination," he adds, "cannot be used as the basis for a wholesale shift of authority over day-to-day school operations from parents, teachers and elected officials to an unaccountable district judge whose province is law, not education." The expansive remedy of taxation and spending to quell white flight ordered by the district court in this case is "part of a legitimate political debate over educational policy and spending priorities, not the Constitution's command of racial equality" (77).

To Kennedy, the district court's taxation order is "a stark illustration of the ever-present question whether ends justify means." "Few ends are more important than enforcing the guarantee of equal educational opportunity for our Nation's children," he admits, and "the historical record of voluntary compliance with the decree of *Brown v. Board of Education* is not a proud chapter in our constitutional history." Moreover, he praises the "courage and skill" of federal judges in enforcing *Brown* against public and governmental resistance. Nevertheless, judicial power "must be exercised with due regard for the proper and historic role of the courts" (80)—one that, in this context, Kennedy considers sharply limited.

Kennedy further limits continued federal jurisdiction in desegregation cases with his majority opinion in *Freeman v. Pitts*.[21] A district court may relinquish control over the aspects of a school system in compliance with a desegregation decree, he writes, even if—due to demographic changes—other aspects of the system remain segregated in fact. In his view, "the rationale and objective of *Brown I* and *Brown II*" aim solely "to eliminate the vestiges of the unconstitutional de jure school system." To justify this limitation on judicial power, Kennedy appeals again to the psychological and sociological considerations expressed in *Brown*. Under *Brown,* courts are charged to ensure that "the principal wrong of the de jure system, the injuries and stigma inflicted upon the race disfavored by the violation, is no longer present" (485). Local school districts cannot always be held responsible for the continuation of residential segregation. "Where resegregation is a product not of state action, but of private choices," Kennedy writes, "it does not have constitutional implications." Requiring a broader solution for these larger social problems "would require ongoing and never-ending supervision" that is "difficult to address through judicial remedies" (495). Although "vestiges of past segregation by state decree do remain in our society and in our schools," he writes, judicial power to rectify them is limited. "Though we cannot escape our history," in his view, "neither must we overstate its consequences in fixing legal responsibilities" (495–496).

Kennedy emphasizes that the Court's "ultimate objective," after "alleviating the initial constitutional violation," is "to return school districts to the control of local authorities" (489). Relinquishing partial jurisdiction serves as "a transition phase" that "is an appropriate means to this end" (490). This relinquishing of judicial control also vindicates the principle of racial neutrality at the heart of equal protection. Kennedy writes that "the potential for discrimination and racial hostility is still present in our country, and its manifestations may emerge in new and subtle forms after the effects of *de jure* segregation have been eliminated." The best way to ensure the flexibility needed to address new forms of discrimination is to allow elected local school boards to take the lead, not to empower unelected federal district court judges. "Where control lies," he concludes, "so too does responsibility."

For Kennedy and for a majority of the current Court, the constitutional commitment to equality and the imperative to move beyond race has important consequences in the context of school desegregation. The task of district courts under *Brown* is to monitor remnants of de jure segregation. When this task is completed, jurisdiction must cease and full control returned to local authorities even if de facto desegregation persists.[22] Continued judicial jurisdiction and monitoring of school board decisions for racial balance compels officials to make policy decisions with racial considerations propelled to the forefront. In the 2007 *Seattle* case, Kennedy would face conflicts between his commitments to local control and racial neutrality.

Majority-Minority Legislative Districts

Kennedy applies his opposition to government acting on racial motives to cases involving the creation of majority-minority legislative districts. Following the decision in *Shaw v. Reno*,[23] he has joined a majority of the Court in concluding that such state action violates the Equal Protection Clause because it assumes that people of certain ethnic or racial groups vote alike because they think alike. Although redistricting inherently involves political questions,[24] for Kennedy these decisions must still comply with the constitutional commands of racial neutrality and individual identity.

Kennedy has applied the ideal of racial neutrality in several opinions striking majority-minority districts. His concurring opinion in *Bush v. Vera*[25] applies neutral individualism to justify striking Texas's effort to create new majority–African American and majority-Hispanic congressional districts as violations of equal protection and unauthorized by the Voting Rights Act. "We would no doubt apply strict scrutiny if a State decreed that certain districts had to be at least 50 percent white," he writes. "Our analysis should be no different if the State so favors minority races" (996). Kennedy admits that redistricting is a political process: "States are not prevented from taking into account race neutral factors in drawing permissible majority minority districts" that may produce districts of a "bizarre" shape, he notes. But race cannot be considered just another political factor. When a district can only be explained by "gratuitous race based districting or use of race as a proxy for other interests," he writes, they "cause constitutional harm insofar as they convey the message that political identity is, or should be, predominately racial" (999).

In *Miller v. Johnson*, Kennedy applies this conception of racial neutrality to invalidate Georgia's attempt to maximize the number of majority-minority congressional districts.[26] He finds the resulting boundaries explicable only as "egregious, unjustified race based districting." As Kennedy interprets *Shaw*, white plaintiffs have an equal protection if redistricting, "on its face, has no rational explanation save as an effort to separate voters on the basis of race." Although "application of those principles to electoral districting is a most delicate task," he says, it is one the Court must undertake (905).

To apply these principles, Kennedy returns to the considerations of individual identity he expressed in *Metro Broadcasting*. He considers government separation of citizens by race into voting districts to be no different from the segregation of public parks, golf courses, and schools. "When the State assigns voters on the basis of race," Kennedy writes, "it engages in the offensive and demeaning assumption that voters of a particular race, because of their race, think alike, share the same political interests, and will prefer the same candidates at the polls." (911–912). Such policies embody crude stereotypes about individual behavior; they "also cause society great harm" by threatening to split it into "competing racial factions" (912). Government classifications violate the Equal Protection Clause, Kennedy writes, "not just when they contain express racial classifications, but also when, though race neutral on their face, they are motivated by a racial purpose or object." Kennedy rejects the argument that "redistricting by definition involves racial classification." This argument relies on "the very stereotypical assumptions the Equal Protection Clause forbids." It is "based on the demeaning notion that members of the defined racial groups ascribe to certain 'minority views' that must be different than those of other citizens." To protect the dignity and personality of individuals, the Constitution forbids "the precise use of race as a proxy."

This test requires Kennedy to draw fine lines. "The distinction between being aware of racial considerations and being motivated by them," he writes, "may be difficult to make" (916). He further concedes that "a State is free to

recognize communities that have a particular racial makeup, provided its action is directed toward some common thread of relevant interests" (920). But
these shared interests must include more than a shared race. "Where the State
assumes from a group of voters' race that they 'think alike, share the same political interests, and will prefer the same candidates at the polls,'" he writes, "it
engages in racial stereotyping at odds with equal protection mandates."

In *Miller*—as in his later affirmative action opinions—Kennedy emphasizes that his constitutional objection to the policy is not the ends sought but
the means employed. The Voting Rights Act, he concedes, "has been of vital
importance in eradicating invidious discrimination from the electoral process
and enhancing the legitimacy of our political institutions." The nation and its
people "share both the obligation and the aspiration of working toward this
end" of producing a state in which "all members of the polity share an equal
opportunity to gain public office regardless of race." But to Kennedy, "that
end is neither assured nor well-served . . . by carving electorates into racial
blocs." Interpreting the Voting Rights Act to require maximization of majority-minority districts is "to demand the very racial stereotyping the Fourteenth Amendment forbids" (927–928).

Kennedy reiterates that race "must not be a predominant factor in drawing
the district lines."[27] State governments must not be pressured—even by the
federal Justice Department—"to act based on an overriding concern with
race." Not only is government acting predominately on the basis of race in
creating these districts, but a state is being forced by the federal government
to inject race into the political process of redistricting. The federal act "is not
an all-purpose anti-discrimination statute," he notes. Like federal jurisdiction
in school desegregation cases, it only redresses "specific evils" traceable to past
discrimination.[28]

In cases involving majority-minority legislative districts and the Voting
Rights Act, Kennedy argues that government should not use race or ethnic
background as a proxy for the political views of constituents. As he wrote in
Rice v. Cateyano to justify striking a special trustee election where only those
classified as native Hawaiians could vote, "one of the principal reasons race is
treated as a forbidden classification is that it demeans the dignity and worth of
a person to be judged by ancestry instead of by his or her own merit and essential qualities."[29] When government makes policy predominately on the basis of
race, it inevitably resorts to stereotypes about what group members believe,
what they will say, and how they will act. These actions would produce a poli-

tics and a society where racial demographics, rather than individual thought and ability, become the currency of society, and where citizens see themselves and others first in terms of race. As Kennedy sees it, these policies do not produce equal representation and opportunity. Instead, they encourage a social balkanization that threatens the very possibility of individuals developing a unique personality and identity.

EXTENDING NEUTRAL INDIVIDUALISM
TO PEREMPTORY CHALLENGES

In cases involving affirmative action, school desegregation, and majority-minority legislative districts, Kennedy votes with Scalia and Thomas, who have more explicitly articulated the moral argument for the color-blind Constitution. Kennedy, however, breaks from them in applying neutral individualism more consistently to limit the use of peremptory challenges for racial reasons. In most court cases, parties are allowed to strike a certain number of potential jurors they believe to be biased without having to provide a reason. (This practice differs from the removal of jurors for cause, which parties must defend in open court.) Following its decision in *Batson v. Kentucky* in 1986,[30] the Supreme Court heard several cases where it was alleged that one party employed these strikes in a racial pattern or was motivated by racial considerations. By allowing parties in its courts to exclude citizens from civic duty as jurors for no stated reason—and perhaps based on racial or group stereotypes—Kennedy believes government violates its obligation to consider citizens under the law as individuals and not primarily as members of groups. To justify this extension, Kennedy again appeals to the lessons of *Plessy,* to the harm such classifications produce in those who are excluded from service, and to the potential social and political evils that result when the law allows classification of citizens based on characteristics beyond their control.

Kennedy first suggested this application of neutral individualism in *Holland v. Illinois,*[31] where a white defendant argued that the prosecution's removal of two African American members of the jury pool violated his right to be tried by a representative cross-section of the community. Kennedy joined Scalia's majority opinion rejecting the defendant's Sixth Amendment argument. Nevertheless, in a concurring opinion he states that this result "does not alter what I think to be the established rule, which is that exclusion of a juror on the basis of race, whether or not by the use of a peremptory challenge, is a violation of the juror's constitutional rights." Echoing Justice Marshall's dissent, Kennedy finds it "essential to make clear that if the claim here were based on the Fourteenth Amendment Equal Protection Clause, it would have merit" (488). It is irrelevant that the defendant is white, or that all jurors are subject to peremptory challenge. Race-based exclusion "is inconsistent with the equal participation in civic life that the Fourteenth Amendment guarantees" and the defendant's right to a jury "selected by non-discriminatory criteria" (489).

Kennedy again employs psychological considerations to justify allowing the defendant standing to raise this constitutional issue. Although individual jurors can sue for themselves, he writes, "the reality is that a juror dismissed because of his race will leave the courtroom with a lasting sense of exclusion from the experience of jury participation, but possessing little incentive or resources to set in motion the arduous process needed to vindicate his own rights" (489). Eliminating all perception of racial exclusion from government is necessary to protect individual rights and to preserve larger public confidence in an impartial jury system and in government generally.

Kennedy would fulfill this commitment in later cases. The following year, in *Powers v. Ohio,*[32] he wrote for a majority that allowed a white defendant, Larry Joe Powers, to sue when African American jurors were the subject of the prosecution's peremptory challenges. Although Kennedy acknowledges the right of the defendant "to be tried by a jury whose members are selected by nondiscriminatory criteria" (404), the harm to the excluded jurors and the damage done to public confidence in government are the most important considerations. The jury provides an "opportunity for ordinary citizens to participate in the administration of justice." Furthermore, it "preserves the democratic element of the law, as it guards the rights of the parties and insures continued acceptance of the laws by all of the people" (407). When a prosecutor—an agent of the government—excludes citizens from jury service solely because of their race, Kennedy writes, that action "forecloses a significant opportunity to participate in civic life" (409).

In *Powers,* as in other cases, Kennedy equates the permissibility of race-based peremptory challenges with state-enforced segregation. Scalia claims in dissent that since all jurors of all races are subject to race-based peremptory challenges, no equal protection violation exists. To Kennedy, this argument is "no more authoritative than the case which advanced the theorem," *Plessy v. Ferguson* (410). A peremptory challenge made solely on the basis of race "is a constitutional violation committed in open court at the outset of the proceedings." Such race-based action "casts doubt over the obligation of the parties, the jury, and indeed the court to adhere to the law throughout the trial of the proceedings" (412).

The harm suffered by the dismissed juror extends beyond not enjoying the right to participate in government. The juror, "excluded from service because of race," Kennedy writes, "suffers a profound personal humiliation heightened by its public character." From this experience, that citizen "may lose confidence in the court and its verdicts, as may the defendant if his or her objections cannot be heard" (413–414). For Kennedy, equal protection is a "mandate that race discrimination be eliminated from all official acts and proceedings of the State" (415).

Scalia's dissent appears to disavow the individualistic, color-blind position he expresses in his affirmative action opinions. African Americans as individuals suffer no injury when excused because of race-based peremptory challenges. "When a group, like all others, has been made subject to peremptory challenge on the basis of its group characteristic," he writes, "its members have not been treated differently, but the same" (424). Being stricken from jury service on basis of race "implies nothing more than the undeniable reality (upon which the peremptory strike is largely based) that all groups tend to have particular sympathies and hostilities—most notably, sympathies toward their own group members," Scalia writes. "There is no implied criticism or dishonor." To Kennedy, Scalia's assertion violates the very core of neutral individualism and is no more supportable than the majority's statement in *Plessy* that any inferiority implied by racial segregation arises "solely because" that group "chooses to put that construction upon it." Scalia concludes that the majority's "supposed blow against racism, while enormously self-satisfying, is unmeasured and misdirected." Its only practical consequence is that "crime goes unpunished and criminals go free" (431).

Kennedy later reiterated his commitment to "the impropriety of racial bias in the courtroom." In *Edmonson v. Leesville Concrete*[33] he extended the ban on race-based peremptory challenges in criminal trials to those used by private parties in civil trials. O'Connor's dissent argues that "a trial, particularly a civil trial, is, by design, largely a stage on which private parties may act." On this stage, "the government erects the platform; it does not thereby become responsible for all that occurs on it." The use of race-based peremptory challenges "is fundamentally a matter of private choice, not state action" (632).

To Kennedy the civic humiliation of race-based challenges "harms the excluded juror no less than discrimination in a civil trial" (619). The actions "are permitted only when the government, by statute or decisional law, deems it appropriate" (620). These actions could not occur "without the overt, significant assistance of the court," and they are "used in selecting an entity that is a quintessential governmental body" exercising "traditional functions of government" (624–625). Kennedy again argues that a race-based peremptory challenge "raises serious questions as to the fairness of the proceedings[,] . . . mars the integrity of the judicial system, and prevents the idea of democratic government from becoming a reality." These actions are just as illegitimate as other government policies that classify by race. "To permit racial discrimination in this official forum," he writes, "compounds the racial insult inherent in judging a citizen by the color of his or her skin" (628).

As in his opinions striking affirmative action and majority-minority legislative districts, in *Edmonson* Kennedy portrays the elimination of government policy based on race as a precondition for any society that protects the rights and dignity of all individuals. "If our society is to continue as a multiracial democracy," he writes, "it must recognize that the automatic invocation of race stereotypes retards that progress, and causes continued hurt and injury" (630–631). The legal process can play an important role in this progress when it "dispels fears and preconceptions respecting racial attitudes."

Kennedy's prohibition of race-based peremptory challenges would not eliminate challenges of individual jurors who may be impartial. It would only require parties to explain and justify them in open court on a case-by-case basis. "If a litigant believes that the prospective juror harbors the same biases or instinct," Kennedy writes, "the issue can be explored in a rational way that consists with the dignity of persons, without the use of classifications based on ancestry or skin color" (631). He asserts that "the quiet rationality of the courtroom makes it an appropriate place to confront race-based fears or hostility by means other than the use of offensive stereotypes." Scalia in dissent claims that the "great symbolic value" of the majority decision obscures the fact that it will deny "minority litigants who use our courts" the same ability to strike jurors based on race (645). Kennedy, however, seeks to preserve the practical and symbolic importance of a government that protects individual identity. "If race stereotypes are the price for acceptance of a jury panel as fair," he writes, "the price is too high to meet the standard of the Constitution" (630).

Kennedy extended this view in *Campbell v. Louisiana*,[34] writing for a majority that a white criminal defendant can object to a parish's systematic exclusion of blacks from the position of grand jury foreman. "Regardless of his or her skin color," Kennedy writes, "the accused suffers a significant injury in fact when the composition of the grand jury is tainted by racial discrimination" (398). Grand juries decide whether to charge suspects of crimes and what charges to apply. "The integrity of these decisions depends on the integrity of the process used to select the grand jurors," Kennedy notes. "If that process is infected with racial discrimination, doubt is cast over the fairness of all subsequent decisions" (399).

By allowing race-based exclusions during the grand jury process—even by private parties—government betrays its commitment to treat each person as an individual and threatens public confidence in government. Thomas opens his dissent by stating, "I fail to understand how the rights of blacks excluded from jury service can be vindicated by letting a white murderer go free" (403). But for Kennedy, these cases involving race-based peremptory challenges require an extension of the ideal of personal identity behind the color-blind Constitution, an extension that justices more vocal in the expression of the color-blind ideal in other cases refuse to accept.

In *J.E.B. v. Alabama*,[35] Kennedy applies his broader conception of neutral individualism to the use of peremptory challenges made on the basis of sex. As he writes, "The Equal Protection Clause and our Constitutional tradition are based on the theory that an individual possesses rights that are protected against lawless action by government." He then expands upon the substantive meaning of equality: "The neutral phrasing of the Equal Protection Clause, extending its guarantee to 'any person,' reveals its concern with the rights of individuals, not groups (though group disabilities are sometimes the mechanism by which the state violates the right in question)" (152).

The violation caused by classification by sex is the same as that of classification by race. "The injury," Kennedy writes, "is to personal dignity and to the individual's right to participate in the political process" (152–153). And those considerations apply to all citizens, no matter their race or sex. For Kennedy, the injury to personal dignity is independent of the right to participate in government. It derives from "the neutrality of the Fourteenth Amendment's guarantee" that applies to all persons. "It is important," he writes, "to recognize that a juror sits not as a representative of a racial or sexual group, but as an individual citizen." He rejects the idea "that persons of different backgrounds go to the jury room to voice prejudice." The jury system "must be representative of the community," but—as in the area of majority-minority districting—the purpose of representation "is a structural mechanism for preventing bias, not enfranchising it" (154).

Kennedy again aroused Scalia's dissent. For Scalia, neutrality is assured when each side can eliminate a certain number of jurors for any reason. "Since all groups are subject to the peremptory challenge (and will be made the object of it, depending on the nature of the particular case)," he writes, "it is hard to see how any group is denied equal protection" (159). The pattern of challenges "displays not a systematic sex-based animus, but each side's desire to get a jury favorably disposed to its case" (160). To Scalia, the majority decision acts "not to eliminate any real denial of equal protection, but simply to pay conspicuous obeisance to the equality of the sexes." Its only practical effect is "the vandalizing of our people's traditions" (163).

Kennedy's opinions involving peremptory challenges demonstrate his departure from justices who employ the rhetoric of the color-blind Constitution. Kennedy—unlike Scalia, Thomas, and O'Connor—believes that any classification based on stereotypical ideas of race or sex must be exterminated from the law. Government neutrality is necessary to protect the rights of individual citizens to civic participation and to equal treatment, to prevent the validation of stereotypes based on immutable characteristics, and to preserve public confidence in the courts and government as a neutral system of justice.

EXTENDING NEUTRAL INDIVIDUALISM
TO RELIGION

Kennedy extends his broader conception of neutral individualism beyond race to religion. In his view, the First Amendment's Free Exercise Clause parallels the Equal Protection Clause. Whenever government classifies individuals or individual behavior on basis of religion—either explicitly or implicitly—it engages in a religious gerrymander contrary to equality and individualism. Devising laws or political boundaries on the basis of religion thus is forbidden by the Constitution's commitments to neutrality and individualism, regardless of whether government intends to target religion or to accommodate it.

In *Church of Lukumi Babalu Aye v. City of Hialeah*,[36] Kennedy's judgment for the Court invalidated a Florida city's animal-cruelty ordinance because it infringed the free exercise rights of a Santeria religious group that engaged in ritual animal sacrifice. For Kennedy, principles of equality support the free exercise argument. As in his Ninth Circuit *Flores* opinion, he establishes the impermissible object of the law by looking past the apparent "facial neutrality" of the law. The Constitution "protects against government hostility which is masked as well as overt" (534).

To Kennedy, the Free Exercise Clause acts, at least in part, as an "anti-discrimination principle" that complements a substantive equality of neutral individualism (see Blackmun's opinion at 578). Kennedy considers the laws challenged in this case to be essentially "religious gerrymanders"[37] that violate fundamental constitutional commitments to equality. "Legislators may not devise mechanisms, overt or disguised, designed to persecute or oppress a religion or its practices," he writes (522). Because this hostility is more likely to be disguised than overt, courts must actively analyze state actions for any evidence of such discrimination. Although each action of the city of Hialeah might be justified as needed to prevent cruelty to animals and preserve public health, "when considered together," the laws "disclose an object remote from these legitimate concerns." The law in practice, with its many exceptions, "excludes almost all killings of animals except for religious sacrifice." Kennedy concludes that "Santeria alone was the exclusive legislative concern" and that "religious practice is being singled out for discriminatory treatment" (537–538).

In *Kiryas Joel v. Grumet*,[38] Kennedy extended this reasoning from a metaphorical religious gerrymander to a literal one. The state of New York decided to create a special school district to accommodate the needs of handicapped children in Kiryas Joel, a village owned and inhabited solely by members of Satmar Hasidim, a Jewish group. Based on his past decisions allowing greater government recognition and accommodation of religious belief, Kennedy might have been expected to approve New York's attempt to accommodate handicapped children of the Satmars against a taxpayer's Establishment Clause challenge.

Nevertheless, Kennedy voted to strike the law based on neutral individualism. "The real vice of the school district," Kennedy writes, "is that New York created it by drawing political boundaries on the basis of religion" (722). He traces the fundamental problem to earlier Supreme Court opinions in *Grand*

Rapids v. Ball and *Aguilar v. Felton*[39] preventing public funding of after-school tutoring in religious schools on Establishment Clause grounds—cases Kennedy would later join a majority of the Court in overruling.[40] To Kennedy, however, this accommodation is fundamentally different because it "requires the government to draw political or electoral boundaries" (728). In this way, he writes, "the Establishment Clause mirrors the Equal Protection Clause." Kennedy finds government line-drawing based on religion—no matter the motive—to be just as constitutionally dangerous as government line-drawing based on race. "Just as the government may not segregate people on account of their race," he writes, "so too it may not segregate on the basis of religion."

As with majority-minority legislative districts, the legislature in this case "knew that everyone within the village was Satmar when it drew the school district along the village lines, and it determined who was to be included in the district by imposing, in effect, a religious test" (729). To Kennedy, "the danger of stigma and stirred animosities is no less acute for religious line-drawing as for racial." By creating political boundaries on the basis of these characteristics, government reinforces existing group identity at the expense of individual development. These policies "will divide the multiracial, multi-religious communities that our Constitution seeks to create," he predicts, and "generated antagonisms based on race." Kennedy quotes Justice William O. Douglas in stating that such line drawing may create a society "in which communities seek not the best person but the best racial or religious partisan." Kennedy finds such a result "at war with the democratic ideal" (728–729).

Kennedy recognizes that there are essential differences between religious and racial classifications. Nevertheless, he writes, "there is more than a fine line between the voluntary association that leads to a political community comprised of people who share a common religious faith, and the forced separation that occurs when government draws explicit political boundaries on the basis of people's faith" (730). The Court played a role in creating this problem with its past misinterpretations of the Establishment Clause, Kennedy admits. "One misjudgment is no excuse, however, for compounding it with another" (731). For government to draw boundaries that separate citizens on the basis of religion—whether designed to harm or to assist members of those groups—is just as impermissible as similar actions based on race are. Such acts constitute, not permissible accommodation, but impermissible gerrymanders that increase social balkanization and erode the ability of each individual to find his or her unique identity.

ROMER V. EVANS: EXTENDING NEUTRAL INDIVIDUALISM TO HOMOSEXUALITY

In *Romer v. Evans,*[41] Kennedy wrote the majority opinion striking an amendment to the Colorado Constitution that would have repealed existing anti-discrimination protections for homosexuals. His opinion departs from standard equal protection doctrine. It does not declare homosexuals a protected or suspect class and finds no violation of a fundamental right. Rather, Kennedy struck the amendment under rational basis review, the most lenient test in American constitutional law, finding the law had no reasonable relation to a legitimate state purpose. In the aftermath of the decision, scholars argued that *Romer* implicitly declared homosexuals to be a protected class or found political participation a fundamental right.[42] Others claimed it implicitly overruled *Bowers v. Hardwick,*[43] or that it exhibits a principled or prudential silence about gay rights.[44] Still others found *Romer*'s reasoning "largely incomprehensible,"[45] or the product of a minimalist or even subminimalist approach to constitutional interpretation.[46]

Read in the context of Kennedy's other equal protection opinions, however, the theoretical foundations of *Romer* become apparent. Colorado's amendment is invalid on its face because it identifies and classifies one group of citizens based on an immutable trait. To Kennedy, there is no need to determine whether homosexuals should be classified as a suspect class. The amendment makes one class of people constitutionally separate from and unequal to all other citizens. That, for Kennedy, suffices to make it unconstitutional.

Kennedy signals the comparisons with segregation in the opening paragraph of his opinion. He begins by quoting from Harlan's statement in the *Plessy* dissent that the "Constitution 'neither knows nor tolerates classes among citizens'" and noting that *Romer* was decided exactly 100 years after *Plessy.* "Unheeded then," Kennedy writes, "those words now are understood to state a commitment to the law's neutrality where the rights of persons are at stake" (623).

Colorado claimed that the amendment—titled "No Protected Status Based on Homosexual, Lesbian or Bisexual Orientation"[47]—merely "puts gays and lesbians in the same position as all other persons" (626). In Kennedy's estimation, the amendment "does more." It "prohibits all legislative, executive, or judicial action at any level of state or local government designed to protect the named class" (624). He focuses on the "sweeping and comprehensive" constitutional change in the status of one identifiable group of citizens. "Homosexuals, by state decree, are put in a solitary class with respect to transactions and relations in both the private and governmental sphere," Kennedy writes. They alone are denied "specific legal protection from the injuries caused by discrimination" (627). In all dealings, "an official must determine whether homosexuality is an arbitrary and thus forbidden basis for decision" (630). Sexual orientation is thus artificially injected into governmental decisions. Although it goes too far to say that Kennedy equates Colorado's classification of homosexuals to a bill for attainder,[48] he clearly finds it a violation of government's essential commitment to neutral individualism.

Kennedy believes the amendment singles out homosexuals and "imposes a special disability upon those persons alone" (630). It denies them rights that other citizens enjoy: protection "against exclusion from an almost limitless number of transactions and endeavors that constitute ordinary civic life in a free society." The amendment "fails, even defies," traditional equal protection analysis. It "has the peculiar property of imposing a broad and undifferentiated disability on a single named group," he writes, and "identifies persons by a single trait and then denies them equal protection across the board" (632–633). This law is "unprecedented in our jurisprudence" and "not within our constitutional tradition" (633). To Kennedy, the relevant tradition is a moral one of neutral individualism: "Central both to the idea of the rule of law and to our own Constitution's guarantee of equal protection," he says, "is the principle that government and each of its parts remain open on impartial terms to all who seek its assistance." No appeal to precedent is necessary: one need only look to the text of the Fourteenth Amendment. "A law declaring that in general it shall be more difficult for one group of citizens than for all others to seek aid from the government," Kennedy writes, "is itself a denial of equal protection of the laws in the most literal sense" (633).

In *Romer*, Kennedy again looks beyond the facial neutrality of the law to examine its practical effect on the rights and status of individual citizens. The "sheer breadth" of the amendment, he writes, "is so discontinuous with the reasons offered for it that the amendment seems inexplicable by anything but animus toward the class it affects" (632). The animus results not from any personal intent of the voters of Colorado to insult the class of homosexuals, however, but from the wide-ranging symbolic and practical effects of the law. "In making a general pronouncement that gays and lesbians shall not have any particular protections from the law," Kennedy writes, the amendment "inflicts on them immediate, continuing and real injuries that outrun and belie any legitimate justifications that can be claimed for it." The passage of the amendment is itself a special act, "a status-based enactment" (635). As with other government actions that identify viewpoint and behavior with ascriptive characteristics, the harm is as much psychological as legal. But the injury is still real and clearly inconsistent with a fundamental legal commitment to treat citizens equally as individuals. Kennedy draws "the inevitable inference that the disadvantage imposed is born of animosity toward the class of persons affected" (634).

In dissent, Scalia asserts that Kennedy's opinion "has no foundation in American constitutional law, and barely pretends to." He claims the Colorado amendment is "rather a modest attempt by seemingly tolerant Coloradans to preserve traditional sexual mores against the efforts of a politically powerful minority to reverse those mores through use of the laws" (636). Scalia considers Amendment 2 part of a "cultural debate" about homosexuality. "Since the Constitution of the United States says nothing about the subject," he writes, "it is left to be resolved by normal democratic means" (636). Furthermore, the Amendment itself models neutral individualism, as it "prohibits *special treatment* of homosexuals, and nothing more." The only injury homosexuals suffer is that "they may not obtain *preferential* treatment without amending the state constitution" (638, emphases in original). In Scalia's view, Amendment 2 is "an entirely reasonable provision" that is "designed to prevent piecemeal deterioration of the sexual morality favored by a majority of Coloradans." By striking the law, the Court enters the culture war. Its decision, Scalia concludes, "is an act, not of judicial judgment, but of political will" (653).

But Kennedy sees nothing modest or reasonable about the amendment. Colorado justified it as a means of respecting freedom of religion and association as well as to conserve resources to combat other forms of discrimination. The scope of the amendment, Kennedy says, "is so far removed from these particular justifications that we find it impossible to credit them." It can only be seen as "a classification of persons undertaken for its own sake," one done "not to further a proper legislative end but to make them unequal to everyone else."

Such action is impermissible, as "a state cannot so deem a class of persons a stranger to its laws" (635). By this, Kennedy means not that homosexuals are unknown to the laws. Rather, under Amendment 2 they are considered literally strange, members of the only group of citizens constitutionally required to receive distinctive treatment by government. Government marks all dealings with them by seeing the individuals first as members of a class. For Kennedy, it is irrelevant whether homosexuals are considered a protected class under equal protection doctrine, or whether rational basis, intermediate scrutiny, or strict scrutiny is necessary. Whenever government classifies some of its citizens based solely on membership in an identifiable group outside of their control, it contradicts core constitutional principles of liberty and personal dignity.[49]

GRUTTER AND SEATTLE: A NEUTRAL INDIVIDUALISM BEYOND COLORBLINDNESS?

In two more recent cases involving racial classifications in education, *Grutter v. Bollinger*[50] and *Parents Involved in Community Schools v. Seattle School District No. 1*,[51] Kennedy appears to retreat slightly from the rhetoric of earlier opinions such as *Croson* and *Metro Broadcasting*. He reiterates that the Constitution neither knows nor tolerates classes among citizens. But—implicitly in *Grutter*, and explicitly in the *Seattle* case—he rejects the ideal of the colorblind Constitution and recognizes a compelling state interest in promoting educational diversity. Kennedy still, however, subjects these programs to "rigorous" judicial scrutiny, finding both to violate equal protection. The problem was not that government acted in a race-conscious manner, but that it classified and labeled applicants by race and failed to provide adequate safeguards to ensure consideration of each student as an individual.

In *Grutter* the Court affirmed the constitutionality of the University of Michigan's law school admissions program, which took race into account to admit a "critical mass" of students from three specific racial and ethnic groups. Kennedy dissented.[52] He claims that the *Grutter* majority departed from the requirement of Justice Lewis F. Powell, Jr.'s, separate opinion in *Regents of University of California v. Bakke*[53] "that a university admissions program may take account of race as one, nonpredominant factor in a system designed to consider each applicant as an individual."[54] Although he voted with Scalia and Thomas to strike the program, Kennedy explicitly breaks from color blindness. Thomas claims that educational diversity is nothing more than a "faddish slogan of the cognoscenti"[55]; Kennedy says the use of race in admissions "reflected a tradition, grounded in the First Amendment, of acknowledging a university's conception of its educational mission" (387). Kennedy's defense of educational diversity on First Amendment grounds is consistent with his expansive conception of free speech, expression, and association.

To Kennedy, however, Powell's principle in *Bakke* is a "unitary formulation." The First Amendment compels deference to the university's conception of diversity, but the Equal Protection Clause requires strict judicial scrutiny of the means chosen to achieve that end. The use of race in the admissions process must be "modest" and "limited." It is only permissible when "supported by empirical evidence" and when "the program can meet the test of strict scrutiny by the judiciary" (388, 387). Nevertheless, Kennedy retains his core belief that "preferment by race, when resorted to by the State, can be the most divisive of all policies, containing within it the potential to destroy confidence in the Constitution and the idea of equality" (388). The only way to restore such confidence is through the safeguard of "rigorous judicial review" to protect the rights of the individual.

Kennedy finds the majority's analysis "nothing short of perfunctory" (388). He describes Michigan's application of the need for a "critical mass" of students designated as minorities to be "a delusion used by the Law School to mask its attempt to make race an automatic factor in most instances and to achieve numerical goals indistinguishable from quotas" (389). For the final 15 to 20 percent of the class admitted, he writes, "any given applicant's chance of admission is far smaller if he or she lacks minority status." He notes a close connection between the number of students admitted from minority groups and the percentage of applicants from each group. This "raises an inference that the Law School subverted individual determination" (390). Moreover, he finds that "the law school made no effort to guard against this danger" and took no steps to ensure that "individualized assessment is safeguarded through the entire process" (392). While "there is no constitutional objection to the goal of considering race as one modest factor among many," at all stages the process must ensure that "race does not become a predominant factor" (393).

The Court's decision to uphold Michigan's policy under the guise of strict scrutiny, Kennedy fears, "will lead to serious consequences." He seeks to avoid excessive use of the "corrosive category" of race. He worries that by upholding the law school policy "courts will lose the talents and resources of the faculties and administrators in devising new and fairer ways to ensure individual consideration." Strict, continued judicial oversight "forces the law school faculties to undertake their responsibilities as state employees in this most sensitive of areas with utmost fidelity to the mandate of the Constitution." This "would force educational institutions to seriously explore race-neutral alternatives" (392, 394). Like Powell in *Bakke,* Kennedy cites policies of other universities to show that "programs do exist which will be more effective in bringing about the harmony and mutual respect among all citizens that our constitutional tradition has always sought" (394–395).

Instead, Kennedy writes, the court relies on "the Law School's profession of good faith." In matters of race, Kennedy will not rely on government's good faith. Accepting Michigan's purpose as benign and its means as rigorous, he writes, gives all schools "the latitude to administer programs that are tantamount to quotas." They "will have few incentives to make the existing minority admissions schemes transparent and protective of individual review" (394). Kennedy returns to his belief that racial classifications will create and exacerbate social divisiveness that will not end at the twenty-five-year deadline suggested in O'Connor's majority opinion (341–342). It will only serve "to perpetuate the hostilities that proper consideration of race is designed to avoid." To Kennedy, that, "of course, would be the worst of all possible outcomes." The majority's disavowal of "searching judicial review," he writes, "negates my authority to approve the use of race in pursuit of student diversity" (395).

In 2007, Kennedy again recognized a compelling government interest in racial diversity but struck the means used to achieve it as a violation of neutral individualism. In *Parents Involved in Community Schools,*[56] the Court by a 5–4 vote struck voluntary programs designed by elected school boards that classified students by race in the course of assigning them to a public school in order to ensure that the schools had a racial balance reflecting the population of the larger community. Kennedy agrees with the portions of Chief Justice Roberts's opinion that find the programs to be "patently unconstitutional" (2753). They embody a "limited notion of diversity" based on "working backward to achieve a particular type of racial balance, rather than working forward" (2754, 2757).

But Kennedy wrote a separate opinion concurring in the judgment. As in *Grutter,* he concedes that the schools' end of promoting diversity allows them to take race into account, but he finds the means employed inconsistent with the individualized consideration required by the Fourteenth Amendment. Kennedy criticizes "the state-mandated racial classifications at issue, official labels proclaiming the race of all persons in a broad class of citizens" (2788). Jefferson County classified students as black or nonblack, Seattle as white or nonwhite. To Kennedy, such a "blunt distinction" and "crude" categorization cannot advance true diversity (2790).

Kennedy's opinion also includes an explicit break with the rhetoric of the color-blind Constitution. Even though he had often cited Harlan's "our Constitution neither knows nor tolerates classes among citizens"—among other passages from the *Plessy* dissent—here he explicitly rejects the ideal of the first part of Harlan's sentence: that "our Constitution is color-blind."[57] "As an aspiration," Kennedy admits, "Justice Harlan's axiom must command our assent." Yet he retreats: "In the real world, it is regrettable to say, it cannot be a universal constitutional principle" (2791–2792). His rejection of colorblindness as a rule—cautious and qualified eighteen years earlier in *Croson*—and acceptance of educational diversity as a compelling constitutional interest—implicit in *Grutter*—becomes explicit here. "Diversity," Kennedy writes, "depending on its meaning and definition, is a compelling educational goal [that] a school district may pursue" (2789).

For Kennedy the definition of diversity must be consistent with a neutral individualism that sharply limits the ways that government can take race into account. It is permissible, he writes, "to consider the racial makeup of schools and to adopt general policies to encourage a diverse student body" (2792). Yet race-conscious means must be employed "in a general way and without treating each student in different fashion solely on the basis of a systematic, individual typing by race" (2792). Kennedy criticizes the school districts "assigning to each student a personal designation according to a crude system of racial classifications" (2792). Seattle, for example, used a "mechanical formula that has denied hundreds of students their preferred schools on the basis of three rigid criteria: placement of siblings, distance from schools, and race." This use of race—as a binary white/nonwhite category, and without sufficient consideration of other relevant factors—violates Kennedy's ideal of individual dignity. Kennedy also fears the consequences of a "classification that tells each student he or she is to be defined by race" (2792). He criticizes the "explicit, sweeping, classwide racial classification" as one that "tends to undermine well-accepted principles needed to guard our freedom." Should the dissenters prevail, the use of race could have "no principled limit" and would "invite widespread government deployment of racial classifications" (2793).

Kennedy reiterates his observation that nonracial means could have been used—or at least explored—to achieve the school districts' compelling interests. Districts may apply "neutral means" or "a more nuanced, individual evaluation of school needs and student characteristics that might include race as a component" (2793). Such a complex system would accommodate both the interest in diversity and individualized consideration. "If those students were considered for a whole range of their talents and school needs with race as just one consideration," he writes, "*Grutter* would have some application" (2794). But because Seattle "relies on a mechanical formula" that operates "on the basis of three rigid criteria"—none which take any individual factors of students into account—*Grutter*'s "important holding" does not apply (2793).

Near the end of his opinion, Kennedy addresses an argument presented by the Court of Appeals in favor of upholding the Seattle plan. That concurrence was written by Alex Kozinski, one of Kennedy's former clerks from his time on the Ninth Circuit.[58] Kennedy characterizes Kozinski's reasoning as follows: "If race is the problem, then perhaps race is the solution" (2796). Kennedy's description of this argument echoes the statement of Justice Blackmun in *Bakke:* "In order to get beyond racism, we must first take account of race. There is no other way. And in order to treat some persons equally, we must treat them differently."[59]

To Kennedy this line of argument "ignores the dangers presented by individual classifications" (2796). These dangers are both practical and moral. Government "must first define what it means to be of a race" (2796). He worries about the effect of such policies on students, for "to be forced to live under a state-mandated racial label is inconsistent with the dignity of individuals in our society." Most significantly, "it is a label that an individual is powerless to change" (2797). Kennedy reiterates his long-standing belief that government racial classifications "can cause a new divisiveness," leading "to a corrosive discourse, where race serves not as an element of our diverse heritage but instead as a bargaining chip in the political process" (2797).

The problem of racial isolation is compelling, Kennedy concedes, yet his reading of the Equal Protection Clause prevents government from addressing the problem in the most direct way. His response—consistent with his larger approach to constitutional interpretation—is to privilege individual liberty over equality. He believes that neutral individualism "reflects the duality of our history and our attempts to promote freedom in a world that sometimes seems set against it." Echoing *Planned Parenthood v. Casey* and his First Amendment jurisprudence, Kennedy states that "under our Constitution the individual, child or adult, can find his own identity, can define her own persona, without state intervention that classifies on the basis of his race or the color of her skin" (2797).

At the same time, Kennedy wants to allow room for government to address racial isolation. The "dangers" of government assessing racial considerations, he writes, "are not as pressing when the same ends are achieved by more indirect means." He acknowledges a "moral and ethical obligation" for government "to fulfill its historic commitment to creating an integrated society that ensures equal opportunity for all of its children" (2797). He admits schools have a compelling interest in cultivating a diverse student body where "race may be one component of that diversity." To protect individual identity, however, school officials must also consider other factors, including "special talents and needs" of individual students. In any case, "what the government is not permitted to do, absent a showing of necessity not made here, is to classify every student on the basis of race and to assign each of them to schools based on that classification" (2797). As in *Croson* and *Metro Broadcasting*, Kennedy fears that "crude measures of this sort threaten to reduce children to racial chits valued and traded according to one school's supply and another's demand" (2797).

Kennedy appears at least somewhat more open to race-conscious policies than he did in his Ninth Circuit decision in *Spangler* almost thirty years earlier and in *Croson* twenty years earlier. The plans challenged here "are unconstitutional as the cases now come to us" (2788). Classifications by race must be "a last resort," and "measures other than differential treatment based on racial typing of individuals first must be exhausted." These programs require "a showing of necessity," one "not made here" (2797).

Kennedy concludes by reasserting the "important work of bringing together students of different racial, ethnic and economic backgrounds." As in *Grutter*, he expresses hope that this goal can be achieved without explicit racial classification. Further, he sees the Court striking these policies as a way of generating more effective solutions to the problems of race and education. "Those entrusted with directing our public schools," he writes, "can bring to bear the creativity of experts, parents, administrators and other concerned citizens to find a way to achieve the compelling interests they face without resorting to widespread governmental allocation of benefits and burdens on the basis of racial classification" (2797). Race-conscious policies that do not employ classifications "present these problems to a lesser degree" (2796).'

Although he does strike the challenged programs in both cases, Kennedy's argument in *Grutter* and *Parents Involved in Community Schools* appears to be a partial rhetorical retreat from his past opinions. In both cases he accepts diversity as a compelling governmental interest in the context of education and rejects the color-blind view. In their larger reasoning and result, however, his more recent opinions remain consistent with his larger conception of equal protection as neutral individualism. Kennedy interprets the Equal Protection Clause to embody an individual right for each citizen not to be classified by government based on factors outside of his or her control. Under such policies, citizens are seen not as individuals, but as markers to be moved by government in a larger game. Kennedy fears the effects on individuals as well as the larger social divisiveness produced when government employs the corrosive practice of classifying citizens by race. Such policies can prevent individuals from developing their own identity.

CONCLUSION: EVALUATING THE EQUALITY OF NEUTRAL INDIVIDUALISM

Kennedy's conception of equality as neutral individualism responds to the position expressed most succinctly by Justice Harry Blackmun in *Bakke:* "In order to get beyond racism, we must first take account of race. There is no other way. And in order to treat some persons equally, we must treat them differently."[60] In response, Kennedy cites Harlan's dissent in *Plessy* that the Constitution "neither knows nor tolerates classes among citizens."[61] Kennedy constructs a larger theory of neutral individualism compelling him to strike any government action that classifies individual citizens on the basis of immutable traits such as race, sex, religion, or sexual orientation.[62] As Kennedy stated in the recent *Seattle* case, "to make race matter now so that it might not matter later may entrench the very prejudices we seek to overcome."[63]

Kennedy's constitutional argument for neutral individualism—like Scalia's and Thomas's arguments for the color-blind Constitution—relies not on text and specific history but on a moral, aspirational reading of equality within the American constitutional tradition.[64] The relevant tradition attributes state-sponsored racism and the denial of individual rights to government acting primarily on the basis of race. Current policies of affirmative action and majority-minority legislative districts, though justified as compensation for that history, may themselves be based on racial stereotypes, harm individuals who benefit as well as those excluded, and produce the same "corrosive" consequences as overt discrimination.

Kennedy's ideal of neutral individualism supports a conception of judicial power that appears restrained but is in fact expansive. It appears restrained because it argues that judges are incapable of determining whether a policy is intended to benefit or to disadvantage a targeted group. Although its expression is clearest in the opinions striking race-based classifications, it is also evident in several other areas of law. For Kennedy, discerning whether a motive is truly benign is a task too difficult for judges to determine and, in the end, irrelevant. The only constitutionally relevant fact is that a group of citizens is classified by law according to ascriptive characteristics. Any such action contradicts the government's obligation to be neutral and to treat individuals equally as individuals.

Kennedy thus attempts to fuse Harlan's *Plessy* dissent to the *Brown* opinion by emphasizing the stigma felt by individual citizens when government classifies people based on ascriptive characteristics. Most charitably understood—and as his later opinions in *Grutter* and the *Seattle* case suggest—Kennedy's ideal of neutral individualism does not require government to be blind to history and the reality of racial discrimination. Rather, it offers a different solution. Neutral individualism derives from an intense sensitivity to the harm that government classifications of citizens can do to the individual and the "corrosive" effects to society they can produce when they are based on characteristics that individuals are powerless to control. Strict judicial scrutiny may even move government to achieve the ends of a discrimination-free society, Kennedy believes, by requiring it to design means that do not reinforce the belief that civic identity and individual personality are determined by group characteristics.[65]

The historical grounds of the argument for neutral individualism do invite challenge. In light of *Dred Scott*[66] and *Plessy,* and even *Brown,* it must be said that American law has never embodied the color-blind principle in theory or in practice.[67] Justices Stevens and Marshall as well as Blackmun forcefully disagree with the equation of current policies to past racial discrimination. As legal scholar David Strauss argues, even the groundbreaking decision in *Brown* "is not rooted in colorblindness at all" but "is deeply race-conscious."[68]

The moral and psychological foundations of neutral individualism require more persuasive justifications and evidence than Kennedy provides. How do we know that individuals who benefit from racial classifications suffer psychological damage and social effects? The *Brown* Court at least offered the "doll test" conducted by Kenneth Clark to show that African American schoolchildren who attended segregated schools suffered from a feeling of inferiority.[69] Kennedy offers no such verifiable evidence about the resentment, alienation, and self-doubt he claims are suffered by those who benefit from preference systems (or those who do not). Although Kennedy may feel that these facts are essential to his ideal of human identity, he could again—as in *Lee v. Weisman*—stand accused of engaging in "psychology practiced by amateurs."[70]

Kennedy's use of judicial power in cases involving equal protection arguments derives from his consistent application of a controversial moral conception of human personality. He looks beyond the stated government motivation and the law's facial neutrality to determine whether the policy embodies stereotypes about individuals in a certain class, produces hostility to members of that group, or leads to individual alienation or social balkanization. He acknowledges a compelling governmental interest and a social obligation to address these problems. Yet Kennedy believes they should be addressed by more general, race-neutral means than simply classifying individuals on the basis of race or other factors they are powerless to control.

Neutral individualism may not be the most specific reading of American political history, and Kennedy's articulation of it may require judges to make empirical and moral determinations beyond their expertise. Nevertheless, rigorous judicial scrutiny of any government classification of citizens based on identifiable factors and perceived stereotypes beyond their control is necessary to assure diversity, liberty, and dignity to all.

5. Splitting the Atom of Sovereignty: Dignity and Divided Power

The federal balance is too essential a part of our constitutional structure and plays too vital a role in securing freedom for us to admit inability to intervene when one or the other level of Government has tipped the scales too far.
—*UNITED STATES V. LOPEZ* (1995)

In cases involving government structure, Justice Kennedy has played a critical role on a sharply divided Court. He has often voted with a majority to limit federal power, but has occasionally upheld federal power and struck state efforts to interfere with the federal sphere.[1] He has also aggressively enforced separation of powers within the federal government. Scholars have called Kennedy's behavior in cases involving government structure enigmatic, unpredictable, and inconsistent.[2]

Kennedy's opinions in these areas reflect his attempt to resolve a constitutional dilemma that he struggled with before coming to the Supreme Court.[3] Since his time on the Ninth Circuit, Kennedy has supported judicial limitations on federal power and preservation of state prerogatives. He considers them so essential to personal liberty that they cannot be left solely to the political process. In light of legal, political, and social developments since the New Deal, however, he despairs whether courts can enforce them. Consistent with his larger jurisprudence, Kennedy recasts questions of government structure to implicate moral dimensions of personal and political liberty in order to defend a judicial role in enforcing boundaries of power. Social, economic, and political changes during the twentieth century make this judicial task difficult, he concedes. But courts still have an obligation to do what they can to restore the dignity of states and prevent the concentration of power in one branch or level of government.

I begin this chapter by examining Kennedy's prenomination commitments to federalism and admitted confusion about how courts are to enforce it. I then survey his application of the "split atom" metaphor to separation-of powers-issues, from his Ninth Circuit decision in *INS v. Chadha* to recent cases involving executive power after 2001. Focusing on the scope and limits of Kennedy's "limited though necessary" concurring opinion in *U.S. v. Lopez,* I next review his behavior in commerce clause cases. Kennedy employs the split atom metaphor to prevent states from interfering in the federal sphere and look at his commitment to state sovereign immunity in a variety of contexts. Kennedy's controlling opinions in two recent cases of statutory construction—*Gonzales v. Oregon* and *Rapanos v. U.S.*—exemplify his conception of the judicial role to enforce federalism and the separation of powers. Finally, I assess the theoretical foundations and practical scope of Kennedy's split atom metaphor. Kennedy portrays federalism as an essential political and moral value. Against the current of larger social, economic, and political changes, however, his attempt to restore federalism through judicial power can have only limited practical impact.

FEDERALISM AS AN "ESSENTIAL VALUE"

Although Kennedy decided no major cases involving federal-state relations on the Ninth Circuit, during the 1980s he made several public addresses calling for a reinvigoration of federalism.[4] Kennedy identified federalism as a moral and uniquely American constitutional value essential to preservation of personal liberty. He stated that it could not be left solely to the political process, but questioned the ability of the courts to protect it. Kennedy's early speeches raise a puzzle: If federalism embodies an essential moral component of constitutional liberty, but there is no political, social, or textual commitment to that value, can courts do anything to restore it?

Kennedy's view of federalism rests within his larger moral approach to constitutional interpretation based on personal liberty and dignity. Kennedy calls federalism "the single unique discovery, the most distinctive contribution to political theory that the Framers made."[5] Federalism must be reinvigorated, but not merely out of "reverence for the Framers" or to preserve "a faint vestige of our once proud diversity." Rather, it preserves an "underlying, essential, ethical, moral value": that "it is wrong, legally wrong, morally wrong, for a person to delegate authority over his or her own life to an entity which is so far removed from his or her ability to control it that he or she parts with the essential freedom that inheres in every human personality" (13).[6]

The original Constitution, to Kennedy, created a novel system to ensure that government would be controlled by the people. As he put it, the Framers "split the atom of sovereignty" to create a system of government that united "a great, disparate territory into a single constitution, using two governments, each with components of republican responsibility" (6). The Framers "dared to challenge" the idea that "there must be an identifiable source, a residuum of power, which by its very definition is indivisible" (3). Each government has "a parallel system of direct responsibilities" and "direct political obligation" to the people. By preventing all power from falling into one set of hands, Kennedy stated, "this dual allocation of authority would be protective of freedom."[7]

Kennedy presents a moral and political defense of state governments. State governments may be superior republican institutions to the federal government, he argues, because they are closer to the people they represent and thus more responsive to their will. "The whole idea of a republic," he stated, is to promote "accountability between office holder and citizen." With "more visible and approachable legislators" as well as "an initiative and referendum process," local and state governments "are likely to be more responsive to the citizen than the federal government." Kennedy's view may well have been influenced by his life and early career in Sacramento as well as his involvement as a lobbyist in California state politics.

Kennedy warns, however, that "there is a very real question whether federalism today is anything more than a legal fiction."[8] "This brilliant idea," he fears, has become a "relic" and is no longer "a viable protection for human freedom." Constitutional changes, such as the Reconstruction Amendments after the Civil War and the Seventeenth Amendment requiring direct election of U.S. senators, have made it "difficult to find effective structural mechanisms to protect the States in the Constitution" (7–8). Although "the idea of preserving the independence, the sovereignty and the existence of states was of course critical to the Constitution and remains critical,"[9] Kennedy admits, the constitutional text "says very little about the power of the states or their place in the federal system" (7). This leaves us, he says, "without any specific institutional balance mechanism to assert the rights of states as autonomous units."[10] "There is no automatic or mechanical check that encourages the holders of federal political office to respect this balance," he concludes. "The states have little or no authority to command it; and the judges have devised no formula for its accomplishment."[11]

Despite this lack of textual support, constitutional protections of state power remain essential to restrain an expanding federal government,

Kennedy believes. He argued for this position most clearly following Justice Blackmun's 1985 majority opinion in *Garcia v. San Antonio Metropolitan Transit Authority*.[12] Garcia, which overruled *National League of Cities v. Usery*,[13] left the protection of state sovereignty solely to the federal political process. Kennedy rejects *Garcia* as inconsistent with the original purpose of federalism. If Blackmun's view were correct, Kennedy states, "the federal government was bound to be the winner, for no other reason than its vast and superior capacity to spend money" (8). The spending power of Congress acts as "a master gear mechanism" for which the Constitution "has no obvious mechanical counterweight," even if its use "causes permanent erosion in state sovereignty."[14] The critical moral and political liberty embodied by state governments, under Blackmun's position in *Garcia*, would always be insecure.

Because neither the Constitution nor the federal political process can be depended upon to preserve federalism, Kennedy states, "the principal protection for the states is that the national government is one of limited power." All constitutional officials must "attempt to devise some principled limits to ensure the political independence of the states,"[15] and all "have a special obligation to ascertain the effects of national policy on the existence of state sovereignty."[16] Kennedy never advocates returning to a pre–New Deal dual federalism, but he does consider the federal balance so vital to individual liberty that courts must intervene to protect it where they can.

Kennedy's defense of the role of states relies just as fundamentally on a fear of federal power. Given Congress's "lack of a principled course of action besides the ethic of re-election," he said in 1984, we cannot assume that members sufficiently consider constitutional concerns when enacting legislation.[17] Congress "must acknowledge its constitutional responsibility and begin to articulate its legislative judgments in constitutional terms." As early as 1982, Kennedy said that if Congress fails to fulfill this responsibility, he "would contend that courts should rescind the rule that legislative act is presumed to be constitutional. A presumption should not exist if it does not mirror reality."[18]

But Kennedy expressed pessimism about the ability of courts to correct imbalances produced by—and perhaps inherent in—the federal political process. He finds an obvious textual limit on federal power in the commerce clause, for example, where "lurking behind every dispute over the definition of commerce was the ultimate question of federal power vis-à-vis the states" (9). The Court attempted in the nineteenth and early twentieth centuries to limit federal power through distinctions between interstate and intrastate commerce and between commerce and agriculture or manufacturing. Nevertheless, Kennedy notes, the Court failed, as "reality shapes the law, and the growth of a national economy made these efforts of the court futile" (10). By the 1980s, he doubted "the likelihood and efficacy of judicial control" in enforcing federalism.[19]

Although Kennedy seeks to preserve an essential role for states to protect individual liberty, by the time he came to the Supreme Court in 1988 there appeared to be no practical way for courts to do so. Facing this dilemma, Kennedy could take one of two paths. He could, like Blackmun, concede defeat and admit that any judicial effort to limit federal power and preserve states would be futile. Or he could devise a novel justification of judicial power to revive the ideals of federalism and separation of powers essential to personal liberty.

Consistent with his general expansion of judicial power across other areas of constitutional law, Kennedy has chosen the latter approach. He recasts questions of constitutional structure in the rhetoric of personal liberty, implicating the same moral considerations as matters of individual rights. Further, he adapts the metaphor of the split atom of sovereignty to limit the reach of the federal government on the basis of an identifiable—if not always precise—functional balance of powers. Kennedy has employed the metaphor to enforce separation of powers within the federal government and to invalidate state violations of the federal sphere under the negative commerce clause. Yet he has primarily used it to strike federal legislation under the interstate commerce clause, to enforce a clear-statement requirement in spending clause cases, to sustain state claims of sovereign immunity against federal legislation, and to protect state interests against federal executive agencies. For Kennedy, preserving the constitutional structure implicates the core moral concerns of political liberty and dignity that courts have an obligation to protect.

SEPARATION OF POWERS

Kennedy has applied his split atom metaphor to cases involving separation of powers since his time on the Ninth Circuit. He considers the duty of the judiciary to police government structure to be as essential as its duty to enforce the individual protections guaranteed by the Bill of Rights. His opinions express a fear that one branch of government (usually Congress, but later the executive) will usurp the power of another (sometimes the executive, usually the courts). He justifies using judicial power to protect individual rights and the effective political liberty of all citizens. Although Kennedy embraced this expansive judicial role during his entire tenure on the Supreme Court, he has asserted it more vigorously—and more controversially—in cases after 2001 involving the extent of executive power to detain suspected enemy combatants.

Separation of Powers before 2001

Kennedy's approach to separation-of-powers issues is evident in his Ninth Circuit opinion in *INS v. Chadha,*[20] where he concludes that the unicameral congressional veto of immigration decisions "is a prohibited legislative intrusion upon the Executive and Judicial branches" (420). In contrast to Chief Justice Warren E. Burger's later majority opinion for the U.S. Supreme Court—a textual argument that the legislative veto violates the presentment clause[21]—Kennedy takes a more functional approach based on the fear of excessive, arbitrary power.[22]

In his opinion Kennedy admits that no federal court had previously found a violation of separation of powers "absent a clause in the Constitution which confers the power upon another branch with great specificity" (420). Yet he cites Montesquieu to support the proposition "that where the whole department is exercised by the same hands which possess the whole power of another department, the fundamental principles of a free constitution are subverted" (421). Separation of powers was designed "to prevent an unnecessary and therefore dangerous concentration of power in one branch" (422, 423).

Kennedy's functional approach differs from Burger's categorical condemnation of the legislative veto. The constitutional principle of separation of powers "is not an inflexible rule." It should be interpreted "pragmatically, in order to preserve the essential design of the Constitution without imposing unworkable limitations." A constitutional violation exists only when there is "an assumption by one branch of powers that are central or essential to the operation of a coordinate branch" in a way that "disrupts the coordinate branch in the performance of its duties" (425).

Turning to the specific veto at issue in this case, Kennedy strikes it as unconstitutional by appealing to the split atom metaphor. Congress, he writes, "has disrupted or severed the Judiciary's relation to the alien in a substantial way." Citing *McCulloch v. Maryland,* among other cases, Kennedy finds that the national government "has a direct relation of power over and protection of the persons it governs." This legislation allowed either house of Congress to set aside rulings made by courts in immigration cases "for any reason, or for no reason at all." It thus "diminishes the strength of the judiciary's structural check on the Executive" (430–431). Legislative exercise of the veto "trespasses upon central functions of the Executive." The veto power allows Congress to reverse an executive decision "in a single case, without an indication of a need to change the standards of general rules to be applied," and it grants Congress power that "detracts from the authority of the second branch, and to that extent undermines its powers" (432).

To Kennedy, the greater sin of this legislative veto is that it detracts from the ability of citizens to hold government officials accountable. The statute challenged in this case—purported to ensure oversight—prevents "efficient administration by the unambiguous assignment of responsibility to specific branches" (432). Despite the "fundamental" constitutional check of bicameralism, under this legislative veto one house of Congress receives unchecked power. In this case, "flexibility is but the structural twin of lawless rule." Although Kennedy concedes "the statute was enacted for the most humanitarian of considerations," courts must "examine enactments from the standpoint of the framers, who were concerned that defects in formal structure be corrected before leading to real or perceived abuses of power at a later date" (436).

Kennedy later publicly disavowed textual and historical explanations for his ruling in *Chadha*. He admits he "was not entirely successful" in arguing as "an interpretivist with a focus on the intent of the framers as set forth in their commentary."[23] Ultimately, he states, "we tried to follow a functional analysis in the balance of the opinion and thus relied on something more than history." That "more" includes the idea that separation of powers, like federalism, contains two axes: one "between the three coordinate branches of the government, protecting each against the aggrandizement of the other," and a second "from the government to the individual" that "preserves the integrity of his relation to it" (5).

Kennedy believes that courts must police questions of constitutional structure to preserve individual liberty from undefined and unaccountable exercises of congressional power. *Chadha*, he hoped, would be "the catalyst for some basic congressional changes." Yet he conceded that his view was "not a sanguine one" because of Congress's "own lack of a principled course of action besides the ethic of ensuring its re-election." Kennedy also acknowledges that his theory of political responsibility may depart from the intentions of the Founders. Although "Madison distrusted the Congress because it would aggrandize the other branches," by the 1980s, he concludes, "the more real concern is its competence within its own legitimate sphere" (8).[24] By abdicating its constitutional responsibility, Kennedy implies, Congress threatens other branches of government and the essential personal and political liberty of all citizens.

Once on the Court, Kennedy reiterates his fear of congressional abdication in his concurring opinion in *Clinton v. New York,* the line-item veto case.[25] Dissenting, Justice Stephen Breyer argues for judicial deference "because the two political branches are adjusting their own powers between themselves." Kennedy disagrees vehemently. "Liberty is always at stake," he argues, "when one or more of the branches seek to transgress the separation of powers" (450). Citing *Federalist* 47, he reiterates that the separation-of-powers doctrine "was designed to implement a fundamental insight: concentration of power in the hands of a single branch is a threat to liberty." Government structure protects individual liberty just as much as—if not more than—the "freedom from intrusive government acts" included in the Bill of Rights. "So convinced were the Framers that liberty of person inheres in structure," he writes, "that at first they did not consider a Bill of Rights necessary." Even today "it would be a grave mistake" to consider "separation of powers of less importance."

To Kennedy, liberty includes a "fundamental political sense" that requires citizens to have the ability to exercise effective control over the actions of their elected representatives by holding them to the powers enumerated in the federal Constitution. "When the people delegate some degree of control to a remote central authority," he writes, "one branch of government ought not to possess the power to shape their destiny without a sufficient check from the other two," he concludes. "Liberty demands limits on the ability of any one branch to influence basic political decisions" (450–451).

The law challenged here—though approved by Congress—has the effect of concentrating excessive power in the president. This change in the balance of power involves not just the two branches, but the power of every individual. Under this act, "a citizen who is taxed has the measure of the tax or the decision to spend determined by the Executive alone, without adequate control by the citizen's Representatives in Congress." When the legislative process "is not subject to traditional constitutional restraints," Kennedy writes, "the individual loses liberty in a real sense." The line-item veto "enhances the President's powers beyond what the Framers would have endorsed" (451). Kennedy reaches this conclusion not from a study of text, history, and original intent, but from his fundamental distrust of Congress. "That a Congressional cession of power is voluntary does not make it innocuous," Kennedy writes. "Abdication of responsibility is not part of the constitutional design" (452). By increasing the power of the president and blurring lines of responsibility for federal spending, the line-item veto "compromises the political liberty of our citizens."

Kennedy thus strikes the line-item veto on functional grounds consistent with his ideal of the split atom of sovereignty. He finds in the Constitution two mechanisms to control federal spending: federalism—"for political accountability is easier to enforce within the States than nationwide"—and "control of the political branches by an informed and responsible electorate." These mechanisms may not assure wise federal fiscal policy. Nonetheless, Kennedy writes, "the Framers of the Constitution could not command statesmanship. They could simply provide structures from which it might emerge."

Kennedy has employed this functional analysis of separation of powers to strike other congressional laws intruding on the executive. For example, his concurring opinion in *Public Citizen v. Department of Justice*[26] struck a congressional act requiring American Bar Association committees advising the president about federal judicial nominees to hold open meetings and to make records of those meetings public. To Kennedy, the act is "a plain violation of the Appointment Clause of the Constitution" (482). Upholding this act "would constitute a direct and real interference with the President's exclusive responsibility to nominate federal judges" (489). Kennedy cites the Constitutional Convention to argue that policing boundaries of government structure "remains one of the most vital functions of this Court." "When structure fails," he writes, "liberty is always in peril" (468).

Separation of Powers after 2001

Since 2001, Kennedy has played a key role on a divided Court to limit claims of executive power. He has written several opinions affirming a judicial role in overseeing executive power concerning habeas corpus during time of war, while claiming—at least rhetorically—to minimize judicial intrusion in the conduct of war. Although his opinions contain some statements of deference, in this area Kennedy defends continuing an independent judicial review over the wartime actions of the executive as needed to enforce individual liberty.

In *Rumsfeld v. Padilla*,[27] Kennedy's concurrence finds federal court jurisdiction for a habeas corpus claim filed by a U.S. citizen, Jose Padilla, held in
military custody as an enemy combatant. But he finds that Padilla's habeas petition was filed against the wrong individual (Defense Secretary Donald H.
Rumsfeld rather than his military custodian) and in the wrong district court
(New York rather than South Carolina where Padilla was held). Kennedy
avoids specific resolutions in this case, stating that "it is difficult to describe
the precise nature of these restrictions on the filing of habeas petitions." To
justify federal jurisdiction, however, such questions "need not be resolved
with finality in this case" (453).[28]

Despite occasional deferential language, Kennedy has written several other
opinions supporting a broad judicial role in adjudicating claims of habeas
corpus. In *Rasul v. Bush*,[29] he voted to affirm federal court jurisdiction to hear
challenges from those held at the permanent U.S. military base in Guantanamo Bay, Cuba. His separate concurring opinion distinguishes this case
from *Johnson v. Eisentrager*,[30] which demonstrated "that there is a realm of
political authority over military affairs where the judicial power may not enter." From *Eisentrager* and *Ex Parte Milligan*,[31] Kennedy deduces "a necessary
corollary" that "there are circumstances in which the courts maintain the
power and the responsibility to protect persons from unlawful detention even
when military affairs are implicated" (487). Guantanamo Bay, he says, "is in
every respect a United States territory, and it is one far removed from any hostilities" (487). Those in Guantanamo "are being held indefinitely, and without
benefit of any legal proceeding to determine their status" (487–488). Because
those held include "friends and foes alike," and many are held indefinitely, he
believes the circumstances suggest "a weaker case of military necessity and
much greater alignment with the traditional function of habeas corpus." This
traditional conception of habeas corpus, of course, requires an expanded role
for courts (489).

One year later, Kennedy provided the key vote in *Hamdan v. Rumsfeld*[32]
striking military tribunals first fashioned by executive order. His concurring
opinion limited the plurality holding about the full application of the Geneva
Conventions, including Common Article 3, to those (like Salim Hamdan)
held at Guantanamo. Instead, Kennedy focuses on "identifying particular de-
ficiencies in the military commission at issue," each of which "raises separation-of-powers concerns of the highest order" (2800).

The concerns that most trouble Kennedy involve the expansive unchecked power granted to the appointing authority—designated by the secretary of defense—both before and during the trial. The appointing authority does not just select the judge for a particular case; it "exercises supervisory powers that continue during the trial"—including any decisions to end a trial without a charge. This process for Salim Hamdan and others held differs from the court-martial procedure outlined by Congress under the Uniform Code of Military Justice (UCMJ). "The concentration of functions, including legal decision making, in a single executive official; the less rigorous standards for composition of the tribunal"; and "the creation of special review procedures in place of institutions created and regulated by Congress," Kennedy finds, serve to "remove safeguards that are important to the fairness of the proceedings and the independence of the court" (2807). To Kennedy, the government provides no explanation for this departure from the UCMJ authorized by Congress (2808).

Kennedy again concludes with some concessions to military necessity. He does not decide whether Common Article 3 "necessarily requires that the accused have the right to be present at all stages of a criminal trial" (2809). As he writes, "the evidentiary proceedings at Hamdan's trial have yet to commence, and it remains to be seen whether he will suffer any prejudicial exclusion." Kennedy also does not address the merits of the charge against Hamdan or the constitutional requirements of any such process. "In light of the conclusion that the military commissions at issue are unauthorized," he writes, "Congress may choose to provide further guidance in this area" (2809).[33]

In these cases, Kennedy exhibits his characteristic embrace of judicial power. He includes language that appears deferential to military necessity and to executive and congressional power, and he refuses to decide every constitutional issue brought before the Court. Fundamentally, however, Kennedy believes that habeas corpus in time of war implicates larger questions concerning the separation of powers and personal liberty that courts have an obligation to address. His reasoning in separation-of-powers cases follows from his belief, expressed in his opinions in *INS v. Chadha* and *Clinton v. New York,* that maintaining limits of government structure is essential to preserving individual liberty. That belief begins with the text of the Constitution, but it rests upon a fear that a concentrated power in one branch will threaten individual liberty and the fundamental political liberty to hold public officials accountable. (Kennedy would continue these patterns of behavior in his opinion for the Court in *Boumediene v. Bush* [2008], discussed in this book's concluding chapter.) Kennedy is just as willing to use judicial power to protect constitutional structure as he is to protect individual rights.

LOPEZ AND "LIMITED THOUGH NECESSARY" LIMITS ON FEDERAL POWER

Although Kennedy joined several opinions limiting federal power during his early years on the Court,[34] his first major statement came in 1995 with his concurring opinion in *United States v. Lopez*.[35] In *Lopez*—the first major battle of the Supreme Court's federalism revolution[36]—Kennedy justifies limiting federal power by appealing to several considerations that he mentioned publicly before coming to the Court. He employs the split atom metaphor, ideals of republican responsibility, and defenses of traditional state authority to strike an act of Congress as beyond its enumerated power to regulate commerce among the several states. For Kennedy, however, *Lopez* previewed no revolution; its holding was "limited though necessary" (574). He clearly intends to use judicial power to police the outer boundaries of federal power, but he does not mean to threaten the political and jurisprudential landscape shaped by the New Deal.[37]

Lopez involves a challenge to the federal Gun Free School Zones Act, which criminalized possession of a weapon within 1,000 feet of any school. Alfonso Lopez, Jr., age eighteen, was arrested for carrying a handgun into his San Antonio, Texas, high school. He challenged the law as beyond the power granted to Congress in Article I to regulate commerce among the several states. For Kennedy, the law challenged in this case "requires us to consider our place in the design of the Government and to appreciate the significance of federalism in the whole structure of the Constitution" (575). Kennedy considers the broad conception of federal commerce power approved in *NLRB v. Jones & Laughlin Steel*[38] and *Wickard v. Filburn*[39] as "within the fair ambit of the Court's practical conception of commercial regulation" (573–574). The New Deal Court, he explains, rightly rejected "rigid formulas" to limit this power. Kennedy accepts the "practical conception" of a national market and does not "call in question the essential principles now in place respecting the congressional power to regulate transactions of a commercial nature" (573).

These essential principles, however, do not compel judicial passivity concerning the federal balance. As in his prenomination speeches, Kennedy praises federalism as "the insight . . . that freedom was enhanced by the creation of two governments, not one," and "the unique contribution of the Framers to political science and political theory." Despite—or because of— this uniqueness, Kennedy notes, there is "much uncertainty respecting the existence, and the content, of standards that allow the judiciary to play a significant role in maintaining the design contemplated by the Framers."

Kennedy defends such a continuing judicial role. He admits Blackmun's position "that the balance between national and state power is entrusted in its entirety to the political process." This balance primarily "rests upon a political judgment," he concedes, as "it is axiomatic that Congress does have substantial discretion and control" (577). Nevertheless, "the federal balance is too essential a part of our constitutional structure and plays too vital a role in securing freedom for us to admit inability to intervene when one or the other level of Government has tipped the scales too far" (578). This judicial intervention cannot be defined by clear rules, Kennedy admits. It involves "a substantial element of political judgment" and represents one of many "questions of constitutional law not susceptible to the mechanical application of bright lines." While Blackmun in *Garcia* and the dissenters in this case argue that this inherently political judgment should be left to the political branches, Kennedy cites *Marbury v. Madison* to defend the Court's "distinctive" duty "to declare 'what the law is'" (579).[40]

In the absence of bright lines to point out the judicial duty to enforce federalism, Kennedy relies on the ideals of political responsibility embodied in his metaphor of the split atom of sovereignty. The Constitution does more than create a system of enumerated powers; it establishes "two distinct and discernible lines of political accountability: one between the citizens and the Federal Government; the second between the citizens and the States." Kennedy moves beyond original intent to consider the purposes of the Constitution. "If, as Madison expected, the federal and state governments are to control each other and hold each other in check by competing for the affections of the people," he writes, "those citizens must have some means of knowing which of the two governments to hold responsible for the failure to perform a given function" (576).

The Court thus has a duty to protect these clear lines of republican responsibility. The Gun Free School Zones Act, however, muddled these relationships by allowing Congress to legislate in areas of crime and education over which states have traditionally exercised control. "Were the Federal

Government to take over regulation of entire areas of traditional state concern, areas having nothing to do with the regulation of commercial activities," he writes, "the boundaries between the spheres of federal and state authority would blur and political responsibility would become illusory."

For Kennedy, blurring lines of responsibility "is more dangerous even than devolving too much authority to the central power" (577). This law "upsets the federal balance to a degree that renders it an unconstitutional assertion of the commerce power" (580). Unlike legislation the Court had affirmed since 1937, here "neither the actors nor their conduct have a commercial character, and neither the purpose nor the design of the statute have an evident commercial nexus" (580). Requiring a commercial nexus is consistent with enforcing the enumerated constitutional text of the commerce clause.

Kennedy goes beyond enforcing enumerated powers, however, when he assesses the effect of this federal legislation on the balance of state power and sovereignty. Education "is a traditional concern of the States"; courts thus "have a particular duty to insure that the federal-state balance is not destroyed" (581). But this federal legislation "forecloses the States from experimenting and exercising their own judgment in an area where States lay claim by right of history and expertise," Kennedy writes, "and it does so by regulating an activity beyond the realm of commerce in the ordinary and usual sense of the term" (582–583). Without "a stronger connection or identification with commercial concerns," Kennedy finds the Gun Free School Zones Act to be an "intrusion on state sovereignty" that "contradicts the federal balance the framers designed and that this Court is obliged to enforce" (583).

Nevertheless, this holding—while "necessary"—is also "limited." Unlike Thomas,[41] Kennedy accepts the substantial effects test of *Wickard*. If an activity is commerce "in the ordinary and usual sense," or if the "purpose or design" of federal action have "an evident commercial nexus," Kennedy would uphold the regulation even if it displaced states from areas they have traditionally regulated. Although Kennedy joined the *Lopez* majority to strike a provision of the Violence Against Women Act in *U.S. v. Morrison*,[42] it should be unsurprising that he later upheld federal authority in *Gonzales v. Raich*.

To be sure, in *Lopez* Kennedy does employ careless language about traditional state activities that the dissenters in *Raich* would toss back at him.[43] The fact that Kennedy did not write separately in *Raich* also raises legitimate confusion. [44] Nevertheless, Kennedy's vote in *Raich* should not be interpreted as a sign of his inconsistent federalism, his general hostility to drug use,[45] or a willingness to recant his vote in *Lopez*, as Blackmun recanted his *Usery* vote in *Garcia*. Rather, it follows from Kennedy's understanding of the limited reach of *Lopez* and his acceptance of the New Deal's substantial effects test. Kennedy later reasserts his judicial boundaries to federal commerce power within the New Deal regime again in *Rapanos*.[46] His concurring opinion in *Lopez* reflects his commitment to judicial enforcement of federalism and his fear that the federal government would be left to determine the extent of its own powers. But, unlike Randy Barnett's application of the presumption of liberty, Kennedy's split atom heralds no revolution.

Kennedy uses judicial power to enforce both separation of powers and federalism in *City of Boerne v. Flores* to strike the application of the federal Religious Freedom Restoration Act (RFRA) to state and local governments.[47] *Boerne* directly implicates the First Amendment's Free Exercise Clause, the Court's decision in *Employment Division v. Smith*,[48] and Congress's enforcement power under Section 5 of the Fourteenth Amendment. In his majority opinion, Kennedy limits the power of Congress to usurp power from the states and from the Court. He describes the RFRA as being "passed in direct response" to *Smith*. To Kennedy, such a response is constitutionally suspect. "Congress does not enforce a constitutional right by changing what the right is," he writes. "It has been given the power 'to enforce,' not the power to determine what constitutes a constitutional violation" (519).

To determine the extent of Congress's remedial enforcement power, courts must find "a congruence and proportionality between the injury to be prevented or remedied and the means adapted to that end" (520). In this analysis, Kennedy seeks to protect state power from federal overreach. RFRA's "sweeping" operation "ensures its intrusion at every level of government, displacing laws and prohibiting official actions of almost every description and regardless of subject matter." Under this federal law, all local regulation and state legislation "is subject to challenge at any time by any individual who alleges a substantial burden on his or her free exercise of religion" (532–533). RFRA "would require searching judicial scrutiny of state law with the attendant likelihood of invalidation." The "stringent" strict scrutiny analysis under RFRA— "the most demanding test known to constitutional law"—would constitute "a considerable congressional limitation into the States' traditional prerogatives and general authority to regulate for the health and welfare of their citizens."

Those consequences belie mere rights protection. To Kennedy, the only justification for such a broad sweep is an attempt by Congress to redefine the extent of free exercise laws contrary to the Court's decision in *Smith* (534). As a result of federal action, local and state decisions would be subject to strict scrutiny "without regard to whether they had the effect of stifling or punishing free exercise." Despite Congress's duty to enforce the Fourteenth Amendment, RFRA—like the Gun Free School Zones Act struck in *Lopez*—"contradicts vital principles necessary to maintain separation of powers and the federal balance" (536).

Kennedy has also voted to limit other federal powers, including the spending power, because they infringe upon the ability of states and citizens to control important political decisions. In *Davis v. Monroe County*,[49] Justice O'Connor's majority opinion rules that states implicitly consented to be sued in federal court for student-on-student sexual harassment when they accepted federal education funds.

Kennedy vigorously dissents. Citing *South Dakota v. Dole*,[50] he concedes that Congress can use the spending power to pursue objectives outside of those enumerated in Article I of the Constitution. Federal actions that pursue these unenumerated ends, however, require the explicit consent of the states and their representatives. Echoing his prenomination description of the spending power as a "master gear," Kennedy writes that, "if wielded without concern for the federal balance," federal authority "has the potential to obliterate distinctions between national and local spheres of influence and power by permitting the federal government to set policy in the most sensitive areas of traditional state concern, areas that otherwise would lie outside its reach" (1677).

To protect areas of traditional state concern, Kennedy states, conditions on federal spending must be "expressed unambiguously." This requirement acts as "a vital safeguard." "Only if the States receive clear notice of the conditions attached to federal funds," he writes, "can they guard against excessive federal intrusion into state affairs and be vigilant in policing the boundaries of federal power." States had no "unambiguous notice" of liability when they accepted federal funds and thus could not have consented to such suits (1677).

Kennedy fears that vindicating the federal government in this case will erode political liberty. Dependence on federal funding will result in local districts "ceding to the federal government power over the day-to-day disciplinary actions of schools" (1678). Citizens will exercise less practical control over education policy, and "the Nation's schoolchildren will earn their first lessons about federalism in classrooms where the federal government is the ever-present regulator." With this decision, Kennedy writes, "the federal government will have insinuated itself . . . into one of the most sensitive areas of human affairs" in a way "contrary to our traditions and inconsistent with the sensible administration of our schools" (1689). Kennedy states that protecting state interests in areas not enumerated in the Constitution "ensures that essential choices can be made by a government more proximate to the people than the vast apparatus of federal power." The "complex and sensitive issues" of education policy, he writes, "are best made by parents and by the teachers and school administrators who can counsel with them."

The majority showed no such restraint. In cases where "the federal balance is at stake," Kennedy wrote, the Court "is duty-bound to exercise that discretion with due regard for federalism and the unique role of the States in our system." Under the language of Title IX of the Education Act, states had no "clear and unambiguous" notice that in accepting federal education funds they would be subject to lawsuits by private citizens seeking monetary damages, and that charges of sexual harassment by one student in its schools against another student constitute gender discrimination. Kennedy asserts that the "watered-down version of the spending clause clear-statement rule" approved by the majority is "intrusive upon the delicate and vital relations between teacher and student, between student and student and between the State and its citizens." Such language provides "no substitute for the real protections of state and local autonomy that our constitutional system requires." The "erosion" of those protections will "impose serious financial burdens on local school districts, the taxpayers who support them, and the children they serve." The majority ignores these injuries to political and individual liberty. "Federalism and our struggling school systems," Kennedy concludes, "deserve better" (1692).

The split atom metaphor guides Kennedy's attempts to outline judicial limits to federal power. He acknowledges that federal powers are enumerated, but he also considers how their exercise affects powers traditionally exercised by states. State power preserves republican responsibility over public policy in areas not enumerated in the federal Constitution. This role must be protected from federal encroachment. When the political branches fail, courts have a duty to provide whatever protection they can.

LIMITS ON STATE POWER
IN THE FEDERAL SPHERE

For Kennedy, the atom of sovereignty splits both ways. In cases involving the negative commerce clause, privileges and immunities of U.S. citizens, and state-enacted term limits on members of Congress, Kennedy breaks with justices who joined him in other federalism decisions to strike state regulations within the sphere of federal power. Just as Kennedy does not defer to Congress's assessments about the scope of its own enumerated powers, he does not defer to states' determinations about the extent of their authority.

In negative commerce clause cases involving state regulations of out-of-state businesses, Kennedy attempts to make "delicate judgments" to distinguish "between regulations that do place an undue burden on interstate commerce and regulations that do not."[51] These judgments demand not deference to state courts, but an independent determination by federal courts. Kennedy considered the extent of limits of the negative commerce clause during his first year on the Court in *Bendix Autolite v. Midwesco Enterprises,* a case involving an Ohio law limiting statutory protection to out-of-state companies that did not hire an agent based in Ohio. When evaluating state economic regulations on out-of-state businesses, Kennedy writes, the Court must "weigh and assess the State's putative interests against the interstate restraints to determine if the burden imposed is an unreasonable one."[52] Commerce clause concerns implicate the sphere of commerce allocated to the federal government. As a result, "state interests that are legitimate for equal protection or due process purposes may be insufficient to withstand commerce clause scrutiny" (893–894). Kennedy finds that the statute in this case "imposes a greater burden on out-of-state companies than it does on Ohio companies." Thus, it constitutes an unreasonable burden on commerce (894–895).[53]

He rejects deference to states and employs this practical conception of commerce in other cases as well. In *Allied Signal v. New Jersey,*[54] Kennedy struck New Jersey's attempt to tax the out-of-state income of a corporation based in another state if that corporation undertakes "integral operational activity" or "acts as a unitary business" in that state. Justice O'Connor in dissent claimed that the Court should, "if reasonably possible, defer to the judgment of state courts in deciding whether a particular set of activities constitutes a unitary business" (794). Kennedy's majority opinion rejects this deference. He engages in a substantive examination of the practical effect of state taxation on interstate commerce, focusing "on the objective characteristics of the asset's use and its relation to the taxpayer and its activities within the taxing State." This inquiry is more difficult and less precise than a categorical rule, he writes, but it is "necessary if the limits of the Due Process and Commerce Clauses are to have substance in a modern economy" (785).

In *Wisconsin Department of Revenue v. Wrigley*,[55] Kennedy dissented from the application of a state franchise tax to a company whose only activity in the state was replacing a small number of packages of stale chewing gum to displays in retail stores. The Wisconsin tax statute in question referred to "business activities," and Kennedy argues that the phrase, "while not unambiguous . . . must be read to accord with the practical realities of interstate sales solicitations." These realities require, again, not deference to state courts but "an objective assessment from the vantage point of a reasonable buyer" (238). Kennedy found that the tax unduly discriminated against out-of-state companies. Even when upholding a state taxation scheme in *Trinova Corp. v. Michigan Department of Treasury*,[56] Kennedy reiterates that the commerce and due process clauses require not merely "facial neutrality" but also a substantively "fair apportionment" (381).

Kennedy has also interpreted the negative commerce clause to limit state power in other contexts. In *Granholm v. Heald*,[57] striking laws that permitted in-state wineries to ship directly to state residents but placed sharp limits on out-of-state wineries, Kennedy's majority opinion found that such regulation "constitutes explicit discrimination against interstate commerce." It acts to "deprive citizens of their right to have access to markets of other states on equal terms," resulting in "an ongoing, low-level trade war" (467, 473). Furthermore, these laws are not authorized under the Twenty-First Amendment. The repeal of Prohibition, Kennedy writes, "does not supersede other provision of the Constitution and, in particular, does not displace the rule that States may not give a discriminatory preference to their own producers" (486). State interests in preventing teen drinking and collecting tax revenue can be accomplished in other nondiscriminatory ways. "If a State chooses to allow direct shipment of wine," he writes, "it must do so on evenhanded terms" (493).

In *Kentucky v. Davis*,[58] Kennedy dissented from a majority upholding state policies exempting interest income from their own municipal bonds—but not those of other states—from its income tax. The majority noted the practices of many states, the long lineage of such practices, and government's need to finance local improvements. Kennedy, joined by Alito, dissented. He finds these "differential" taxation policies constitute "explicit, local discrimination" that violates the dormant commerce clause and the very purpose of the Constitution (1822, 1825). States may support such policies out of self-interest or self-protection, but to Kennedy this is "irrelevant." He fears "further erosion of the Commerce Clause, which must remain as a deterrent to experiments designed to serve local interests at the expense of a national system" (1829).

Kennedy has also secured the privileges and immunities of nonresidents protected under Article IV of the U.S. Constitution. In *Supreme Court of Virginia v. Friedman*,[59] his majority opinion struck Virginia's policy allowing attorneys from other states to gain admission to the bar without taking the exam only if they became permanent residents. Here, Kennedy says, the state is "discriminating among otherwise equally qualified applicants solely on the basis of citizenship or residency" (66–67). Other elements of the Virginia law, such as the requirement that lawyers maintain an office within the state for full-time practice, maintained legitimate state interests in a less discriminatory fashion (68–70).[60]

Kennedy's most dramatic limitation of state power—and his most dramatic break from the four-justice conservative block—came in *U.S. Term Limits v. Thornton*.[61] In *Thornton,* Kennedy provided the fifth vote to strike ballot restrictions imposed by Arkansas that prohibited candidates running for Congress from appearing on the election ballot if they had already served three terms in the U.S House or two terms in the U.S. Senate. Kennedy sidesteps the "intricacy" of the textual debate between Stevens's majority opinion and Thomas's dissent over the meaning of the Qualifications Clause in Article I of the Constitution, which outlines age, citizenship, and residency requirements to serve in Congress. His concurring opinion employs the split atom metaphor to reinforce the discernible lines of responsibility running from citizens to the state and federal governments.

To Kennedy, this case turns on fundamental principles of federalism. "It is well settled," Kennedy states, "that the whole people of the United States asserted their political identity and unity of purpose when they created the federal system." Thomas's dissent "might be construed to disparage the republican character of the National Government," and his discussion of "first principles . . . runs counter to fundamental principles of federalism" (838). According to Kennedy, the Framers "split the atom of sovereignty" so that "our citizens would have two political capacities: one state and one federal, each protected from incursion by the other." The Constitution "created a legal system unprecedented in form and design, establishing two orders of government, each with its own direct relationship, its own privity, its own set of mutual rights and obligations to the people who sustain it and are governed by it" (838–839).

Kennedy uses these principles to reject direct state involvement in "the most basic relation between the National Government and its citizens, the selection of legislative representatives" (841). The federal government, like the states, is "republican in essence and in theory." Kennedy cites Madison's *Federalist* 39 and Marshall's statement in *McCulloch* to demonstrate that "the people of the United States have a political identity as well, one independent of, though consistent with, their identity as citizens of the State of their residence" (840). State restrictions on candidates for federal elections interfere with this essential and direct relationship. Although "limited as to its objects," he writes, "the National Government is and must be controlled by the people without collateral interference from the States."

Even in *Thornton,* Kennedy reiterates his commitment to preserving state powers. "The Framers recognized that state power and identity were essential parts of the federal balance," he admits, and—previewing his sovereign immunity opinions—"the Constitution is solicitous of the prerogatives of the States, even in an otherwise sovereign federal province." But this solicitude extends only so far: "The States have no power, reserved or otherwise, over the exercise of federal authority within its proper sphere" (841). Kennedy connects this opinion to *Lopez,* delivered a month earlier: "That the States may not invade the sphere of federal sovereignty is as uncontestable, in my view, as the corollary proposition that the Federal Government must be held within the boundaries of its own power when it intrudes upon matters reserved to the States" (844).[62]

Kennedy's conception of the split atom of sovereignty compels him to use judicial power to control both state and federal governments. He is no simple advocate of states' rights, and never claimed to be. As he admits in *Thornton,* "there exists a federal right of citizenship, a relationship between the people of the Nation and their National Government, with which the States may not interfere" (845). In neither situation does Kennedy leave the balance of power solely to any political process. He considers the structural protections of federalism to be so vital to individual liberty and responsibility that he will use judicial power to protect that balance—whether the threat comes from the federal government or from the states.

STATE SOVEREIGN IMMUNITY

Although Kennedy has rejected claims of state power involving the negative commerce clause, privileges and immunities, and term limits for members of Congress, he does use judicial power to protect states from the federal sphere in other areas.

Even in *Thornton,* he states that "the Constitution is solicitous of the prerogatives of the States, even in an otherwise sovereign federal province" (841). Kennedy has joined majorities striking federal legislation on grounds that it commandeered state legislative or executive bodies.[63] He has been even more aggressive in protecting state sovereign immunity against federal legislation as a vital protection of political and constitutional liberty. He portrays this immunity not merely as compelled by the text of the Eleventh Amendment,[64] but as inherent within a broader constitutional principle of sovereignty. Using language characteristic of his opinions involving individual rights, Kennedy argues that states retain dignity and respect even when subject to the exercise of enumerated federal powers. He moves beyond text and history to justify state sovereign immunity as necessary to protect state dignity and preserve the proper balance of federal and state power.

During Kennedy's first years on the Court, the main disputes involved how Congress must express its intent to abrogate state sovereign immunity. In *Delmuth v. Muth,*[65] Kennedy wrote for a five-justice majority finding that the Education of the Handicapped Act did not properly do so. He cites the clear-statement rule of *Atascadero Hospital v. Scamlon*[66] to assert that abrogation of sovereign immunity "upsets 'the fundamental constitutional balance between the Federal Government and the States.'" Congress's action, Kennedy writes, strains "the principles of federalism that inform Eleventh Amendment doctrine" and damages "an essential component of our constitutional structure." Adherence to constitutional structure and respect for federalism require "a simple but stringent test": Congress can abrogate the states' immunity "'only by making its intention unmistakably clear in the language of the statute'" (227–228). That intent "must be both unequivocal and textual" (230). Kennedy finds some evidence of intent but deems it neither unequivocal nor textual. The Education of the Handicapped Act "makes no reference whatsoever to either the Eleventh Amendment or the states' sovereign immunity" (232). The text of the statute "lends force to the inference that the States were intended to be subject to damages actions for violations." But, "given the special constitutional concerns in this area," for Kennedy an inference is not enough. (230–231).[67]

Since a majority of the Court reinvigorated constitutional claims of state sovereign immunity under the Eleventh Amendment in *Seminole Tribe v. Florida* in 1996,[68] Kennedy has been among the most aggressive advocates of enforcing and expanding them. In *Idaho v. Coeur d'Alene Tribe*,[69] Kennedy wrote for a majority rejecting an Indian tribe's lawsuit in federal court to assert ownership of land submerged by water. State sovereign immunity is "not limited to the suits described in the text of the Eleventh Amendment," Kennedy writes. It includes "the broader concept of immunity, implicit in the Constitution, which we have regarded the Eleventh Amendment as evidencing and exemplifying" (267–268).

Kennedy also identifies less tangible factors in defense of expanding state sovereign immunity. If such suits such as the Coeur d'Alene Tribe's can proceed in federal court, he writes, "the dignity and respect afforded a State, which the immunity is designed to protect, are placed in jeopardy." Kennedy recognizes "the need to prevent violations of federal law" (268), but this does not authorize Congress to choose any means of redress against the states. State courts must be considered competent to resolve questions of federal law. "It is the right and duty of the States, within their own judiciaries, to interpret and follow the Constitution and all laws enacted pursuant to it," he writes. States can be trusted to accomplish this goal, as the Constitution is "a law to which a State's ties are no less intimate than those of the National Government itself." State and national governments "are bound in the common cause of preserving the whole constitutional order" (275, 276).

The federal government must recognize this cooperative relationship by respecting the sovereignty and status of states. "It would be error coupled with irony," Kennedy writes, "were we to bypass the Eleventh Amendment, which enacts a scheme solicitous of the States, on the sole rationale that state courts were inadequate to enforce and interpret federal rights in every case." Kennedy again expands the Eleventh Amendment to embody "background principles of federalism and comity." The line drawn in *Ex Parte Young*[70] between immunity for states and immunity for state officers is flexible. Kennedy believes "there is no reason why the line cannot be drawn to reflect the real interests of States consistent with the clarity and certainty appropriate to the Eleventh Amendment's jurisdictional inquiry." Allowing Idaho to hear the tribe's lawsuit in its own courts is required, under the Constitution, to recognize the state's "dignity and status" (277–278, 280).

Kennedy has extended state sovereign immunity beyond the text of the Eleventh Amendment to lawsuits in state courts involving a valid federal law. His majority opinion in *Alden v. Maine*[71] struck a congressional act permitting state employees in Maine to sue in state court to enforce valid federal wage laws without the state's consent. In *Alden,* Kennedy lays out at great length his view of the role of the states in the federal system, and he explicitly uses the split atom metaphor and considerations of dignity to defend state sovereign immunity.

Kennedy begins by repeating that "the sovereign immunity of the States neither derives from nor is limited by the terms of the Eleventh Amendment." This immunity is "a fundamental aspect of the sovereignty which the States enjoyed before the ratification of the Constitution" (713). The Constitution "reserves" to the states "a substantial portion of the Nation's primary sovereignty, together with the dignity and essential attributes inhering in that status" (714). Kennedy goes further to protect state dignity and sovereignty. "Even as to matters within the competence of the National Government," the Constitution "secures the founding generation's rejection of the concept of a central government that would act upon and through the States in favor of a system in which the State and Federal Governments would exercise concurrent authority over the people" (714). Strikingly, Kennedy cites James Madison, Alexander Hamilton, and John Marshall to demonstrate that states "retain 'a residuary and inviolable sovereignty.'" Despite *Chisholm v. Georgia,*[72] the 1793 case that rejected state sovereign immunity and resulted in the ratification of the Eleventh Amendment, he finds guarantees of state sovereignty "implicit in the structure of the Constitution" (715).

This sovereignty—though residual—remains strong enough to limit the ways in which the federal government can exercise even its enumerated powers. As he stated in *Coeur d'Alene,* states "are not relegated to the role of mere provinces or political corporations, but retain the dignity, though not the full authority, of sovereignty" (715). Even where Congress is authorized to act under its enumerated powers, state sovereign immunity can trump the Supremacy and Necessary and Proper clauses of the federal Constitution. "The question is not the primacy of federal law," Kennedy writes, "but the implementation of the law in a manner consistent with the constitutional sovereignty of the States." The sovereignty acts as a further limit on the powers enumerated in Article I. Congress thus lacks "the incidental authority to subject the States to private suits as a means of achieving objectives otherwise within the scope of the enumerated powers" (46).

Informed by the split atom metaphor, Kennedy concludes that this immunity prohibits not only suits against unconsenting states in federal courts, but also suits under federal law in its own courts. To determine the extent of immunity, Kennedy says, we must look "to the essential principles of federalism and to the special role of the state courts in the constitutional design." States are more than "residuary sovereigns"; they are "joint participants in the governance of the Nation" (748). And all sovereigns deserve the formality of respect and dignity. "As a logical matter," he writes, "it would be even more indignity to a state if forced by federal law to defend itself in its own court, to face the prospect of being thrust by federal fiat and against its will, into the disfavored status of a debtor" (749). The federal government retains immunity in both state and federal court; states should be entitled to "a reciprocal privilege" (749–750).

Beyond abstract conceptions of state dignity, Kennedy fears the practical political consequences of federal abrogation of state immunity on the "autonomy, decisionmaking ability and the sovereign capacity of states" (750). These suits—like the desegregation order from a federal judge that he struck in *Missouri v. Jenkins*, "would place unwarranted strain on the States' ability to govern in accordance with the will of citizens." Scarce resources should be committed not by "judicial decree mandated by the Federal Government and invoked by the private citizen," but through "balance between competing interests . . . after deliberation by the political process established by the citizens of the States" (751). Again citing the split atom of sovereignty, Kennedy argues that granting private individuals the right to bring suits in state court under federal law "would blur not only the distinct responsibilities of the State and National Governments but also the separate duties of the judicial and political branches of the state governments." If Congress cannot abrogate state immunity in federal court, but could do so in state courts, Kennedy argues, a paradox would exist: "The National Government would wield greater power in the state courts than in its own judicial instrumentalities" (752). Under the Constitution's division of power, "when the Federal Government asserts authority over a State's most fundamental political process, it strikes at the heart of the political accountability so essential to our liberty and republican form of government" (751).

Kennedy does not question the constitutionality of extending of federal wage legislation to state employees, a policy found constitutional in *Garcia*. However, he emphasizes several alternative ways to enforce the law. Congress could use its master lever of the spending power to pry consent from nonconsenting states. Employees could petition the federal government to file a suit on their behalf. The labor regulation was a valid exercise of federal power; enforcement by and through the federal government would express clear responsibility for its action (755–756). Alternative enforcement "strikes the proper balance between the supremacy of federal law and the separate sovereignty of the States" (757). "The people insisted upon a federal structure," Kennedy writes, "for the very purpose of rejecting the idea that the will of the people in all instances is expressed by the central power, the one most remote from their control." The federal government "must accord the States the esteem due them as joint participants in a federal system" (758). Congress has many means to enforce valid federal laws within its sphere, but must admit it is not the ultimate sovereign and must respect the dignity of others.

Kennedy expressed continued support for state sovereign immunity with his dissent in *Nevada Dept. of Human Resources v. Hibbs*.[73] The majority—including Rehnquist and O'Connor—found the federal Family and Medical Leave Act (FMLA) to be a constitutional abrogation of state immunity by Congress under its power to enforce the Equal Protection Clause of the Fourteenth Amendment. Kennedy dissented. He concluded that the legislation was not a proportional and congruent response to a pattern of constitutional violations committed by state governments. Kennedy finds these requirements in the Fourteenth Amendment (see *Boerne*) and in the Eleventh Amendment, "which protects a State's fiscal integrity from federal intrusion by vesting the States with immunity from private actions for damages pursuant to federal laws" (744).

Kennedy, however, finds that the federal government did not provide sufficient justification for its authority to enforce the act against state governments. FMLA documents no pattern of unlawful conduct by states. Although he admits that family leave policies in the private sector demonstrate the existence of sex discrimination in the workplace, "simply noting the problem is not a substitute for evidence which identified some real discrimination the family leave rules are designed to prevent" (746). Congress cited actions of private employers, not state governments; it was based on testimony that occurred seven years before the law was enacted, and it concerned parenting leave, not family leave. Echoing his criticism in the affirmative action case *Richmond v. Croson,* he writes that "the evidence of gender-based stereotypes is too remote to support the required showing" (749). He concludes that Congress did not act to remedy documented discrimination by state governments, but "enacted a substantive benefit program of its own" (754). Congress can do this under its power to regulate interstate commerce, Kennedy writes, but to justify abrogating state sovereign immunity it must show a pattern of unconstitutional actions by states (758).

In voting to strike this lawsuit, Kennedy emphasizes—as in *Alden*—that "individuals whose rights under the Act were violated would not be without recourse." The federal government could bring suit; individuals can sue for injunctive relief. "What is at issue," he writes, "is only whether the States can be subjected, without consent, to suits brought by private persons seeking to collect moneys from the state treasury" (759). The Constitution requires evidence of unconstitutional action and proportionality between violation and remedy, Kennedy writes. In this case "there has been a complete failure by respondents to carry their burden to establish each of these necessary propositions" (759).

In these and other state sovereign immunity cases,[74] Kennedy applies his split atom metaphor most aggressively. He considers states to be essential elements of constitutional structure, and he uses judicial power to maintain their importance as balances against a concentration of control in the federal government, which would erode individual and political liberty. Kennedy considers state and local governments to be positive vehicles of political liberty. They allow citizens to exercise more direct control over policies and over the politicians who make decisions about the issues that most closely and directly affect their lives. It is not enough for the Court to protect states indirectly by enforcing limited and enumerated federal powers; it must also protect them directly by restricting the exercise of enumerated federal powers to ensure the dignity of states and preserve their continued existence as effective republican institutions.[75] By using the same language of dignity that drives his opinions involving individual rights, Kennedy is clearly motivated by the threats that the federal government presents to the states and thus to individual liberty.

FEDERALISM IN STATUTORY INTERPRETATION:
OREGON AND RAPANOS

Kennedy applied his ideals of separation of powers and federalism in two major 2006 cases involving federal statutory interpretation, *Gonzales v. Oregon*[76] and *Rapanos v. U.S.*[77] In these cases, as in *Lopez*, Kennedy tries to reconcile the post–New Deal substantial-effects doctrine of *Wickard v. Filburn* with an active judicial role in policing the boundaries of federal power. Kennedy examines these exercises of executive authority to ensure that actions displacing traditional state authority are justified in express constitutional terms. In practice, however, his opinions do not substantively limit federal authority.

In *Oregon*, Kennedy wrote for a 6–3 majority to overrule a rule issued by the U.S. attorney general interpreting the federal Controlled Substances Act (CSA) to prohibit doctors from prescribing drugs for physician-assisted suicide. Oregon—which allows physician-assisted suicide under state law—challenged this interpretation. Kennedy concluded that the attorney general's interpretation deserved no deference because of the role of state governments and other federal government entities within the larger CSA statutory scheme.

Kennedy did not decide this case on the basis of his own constitutional beliefs about physician-assisted suicide.[78] The attorney general's interpretation that the practice conflicts with the public interest, Kennedy admits, is "at least reasonable" (924). But much of the opinion argues that this judgment is beyond the "limited powers" granted to the attorney general under the CSA (917). Kennedy's analysis of the statute confirms that judgments about whether physician-assisted suicide constitutes a "legitimate medical practice" or is "in the public interest" are not legal interpretations, but "quintessentially medical judgments" (921). Other sections of the CSA explicitly delegate certain medical determinations to the secretary of health and human services. Kennedy asserts that the attorney general's claim to make this policy decision about physician-assisted suicide "is both beyond his expertise and incongruous with statutory purposes and design" (921).

Kennedy's opinion combines separation-of-powers concerns with federalism considerations. With *Wickard* and *Raich* clearly in mind, he admits that "there is no question that the Federal Government can set uniform national standards" in the medical field, even where states traditionally exercise sovereign authority (919). The issue in this case is whether Congress entrusted such broad authority to the attorney general. The CSA "manifests no intent to regulate the practice of medicine generally," Kennedy argues. Its provisions "presume and rely upon a functioning medical profession regulated by the State's police powers" (923). Kennedy, noting the "silence" of CSA on regulating the general practice of medicine, reasons that the statute could not have "impliedly criminalized" physician-assisted suicide (924). Even if the law did intend to federalize medical practice, "the Attorney General is an unlikely recipient of such broad authority" within a statute that in other sections gives the secretary of health and human services "primacy in shaping medical policy" (925).

Kennedy fears the effect of the attorney general's claim on "background principles of federalism." Those principles "belie the notion that Congress would use such an obscure grant of authority to regulate areas traditionally supervised by the States' police power." Kennedy concludes that the attorney general's argument "delegates to a single Executive official the power to effect a radical shift of authority from the States to the Federal Government to define general standards of medical practice in every locality" (925). Congress has the authority to alter the federal balance, but that must be done explicitly and expressly by representatives directly accountable to the people.

In *Rapanos,* Kennedy's separate concurring opinion demonstrates his continued commitment to enforcing limited but necessary boundaries to the federal power under the commerce clause. The federal Clean Water Act prohibits discharge of fill material into "navigable waters" without a permit. The Army Corps of Engineers defines "navigable waters" as including all bodies "adjacent" to such waters, tributaries of such waters, and even some waters physically separated from navigable waters. To build a commercial development, John A. Rapanos filled 54 acres of wetlands without a permit and was subject to civil proceedings. In a companion case, June Carabell and others were denied a permit to fill wetlands by the Corps, and their appeal was denied. Both challenged the Corps' broad definition of "navigable waters" as beyond the statutory definition of the Clean Water Act and beyond the powers of the federal government under the interstate commerce clause.

By a 5–4 vote, the Court struck the lower court rulings upholding the jurisdiction of the Corps, but there was no majority opinion. Kennedy's concurrence held the balance for the Court. The "navigable waters" requirement of the Clean Water Act, Kennedy writes, requires the Army Corps of Engineers to demonstrate a "significant nexus" in each case between the specific bodies of water it seeks to regulate and waters reasonably made navigable.[79] Kennedy's role in *Rapanos* is again pivotal: he provides a fifth vote to overturn the Corps' broad assertion of jurisdiction based on "constitutional and federalism concerns" (2246). The standard he establishes, however, makes it likely that on remand the Corps will prevail. Kennedy's phrasing is clearly connected to the substantial effects test established in *Wickard v. Filburn* to justify federal regulatory authority under the commerce clause and the "evident commercial nexus" standard he articulated in his concurring opinion in *Lopez.*

Kennedy portrays his position as following the Court's majority decision in *Solid Waste Agency of North Cook County [SWANCC] v. Army Corps of Engineers* (2001),[80] but his significant-nexus standard arises primarily not from *stare decisis* or from the text of the statute. The most plausible explanation of Kennedy's concurrence—and the one consistent with his record—is that it arises from his background conception, as expressed in *Lopez,* of constitutional restrictions on federal power under the commerce clause. Kennedy employs judicial power to police the boundaries of federal power under the commerce clause while retaining the expansive federal authority articulated after the New Deal. In light of "constitutional difficulties and federalism concerns," as in past cases Kennedy concludes that any "significant effect" on the integrity of navigable waters must be demonstrated by the government and not merely "speculative or insubstantial" (2245).

Kennedy's language in *Rapanos* echoes some of the confusion of his *Lopez* opinion about traditional state interests. He refers to waters "without a significant nexus" and finds them not "traditionally subject to federal authority." He also expresses concerns about *Wickard*'s aggregation principle, stating that "federal regulation of remote wetlands and non-navigable waterways would raise a difficult Commerce Clause issue notwithstanding those waters' aggregate effects on national water quality" (2246).

Despite voting to limit boundless federal jurisdiction, Kennedy criticizes the "overall tone and approach" of Scalia's plurality opinion as "unduly dismissive of the interests asserted by the United States in these cases" (2246). Requiring the Corps to establish in each case that permanent standing water or flow for some months creates a "significant nexus" to "navigable waters" "makes little practical sense in a statute concerned with downstream water quality." This standard would extend federal jurisdiction to "the merest trickle, if continuous," but deny it to "torrents thundering at irregular intervals through otherwise dry channels." For Kennedy, a "significant nexus" test similar to *Wickard*'s "substantial effects" test would satisfy the Clean Water Act's objective of restoring and maintaining "the chemical, physical and biological integrity of the Nation's waters" while "addressing constitutional and federalism concerns" (2236, 2246).

Kennedy then criticizes the dissenters for finding few, if any, enforceable constitutional limits to the Corps' authority. Stevens "reads a central requirement out—namely, the requirement that the word 'navigable' in 'navigable waters' be given some importance" (2247). The dissenters' broad approach would "permit federal regulation whenever wetlands lie alongside a ditch or drain, however remote and insubstantial," when the waters may "eventually . . . flow into traditional navigable waters." *SWANCC* had rejected federal authority "over isolated ponds and mudflats having no evident connection to navigable-in-fact waters." As in *Gonzales v. Oregon,* for Kennedy deference to determinations made by the executive branch pertaining to the limits of its own power "does not extend so far" (2247).

More significantly, Kennedy requires the significant nexus to be demonstrated by the Corps in every case where it asserts authority to regulate. The Corps has broad jurisdiction, but Kennedy finds a limit to federal authority to be implied by *Wickard:* "When, in contrast, wetlands' effects on water quality are speculative or insubstantial, they fall outside the zone fairly encompassed by the statutory term 'navigable waters.'" The Corps must show evidence of the substantial effect on specific navigable waters. Although "the Corps' conclusive standard for jurisdiction rests upon a reasonable inference of ecological interconnection," for Kennedy reasonable inferences cannot overcome commerce clause and federalism concerns (2248). "Absent more specific regulations" he writes, "the Corps must establish a significant nexus on a case-by-case basis when it seeks to regulate wetlands based on adjacency to nonnavigable tributaries" (2249).

The novel significant-nexus standard, Kennedy admits, "may not align perfectly with the traditional extent of federal authority." But in most circumstances, it "will raise no serious constitutional or federalism difficulty." Applying the test on a case-by-case basis "prevents problematic applications of the statute" (2249). Kennedy's vote may have been motivated by the Corps' refusal to state standards after the Court's decision in *SWANCC.* Nevertheless, his vote to limit federal authority remains consistent with his expansive conception of the judicial role to limit federal power. Federal authority extends broadly under the commerce clause, but it is not unlimited. It must be justified before a court, not merely asserted.

Although Part II of Kennedy's opinion rejects the Corps' assertions of virtually unchecked authority, Part III admits that "the end result in these cases and many others to be considered by the Corps may be the same as that suggested by the dissent; namely, that the Corps' assertion of jurisdiction is valid" (2250). As in *Oregon* and *Lopez*, Kennedy votes to use judicial power to limit federal authority by forcing federal entities to make their arguments for authority in constitutional terms. In *Rapanos*, the district court's finding of a surface-water connection to tributaries of navigable waters would support the Corps' assertion of jurisdiction. That claim would be stronger, he writes, "if supplemented by further evidence about the significance of the tributaries to which the wetlands are connected" (2250). In *U.S. v. Carabell*, a companion case to *Rapanos*, Kennedy would again require more precise evidence supporting the Corps' argument in order to demonstrate jurisdiction. He criticizes "the conditional language" given by the Corps, such as "potential ability" and "possible flooding." This wording "could suggest an undue degree of speculation." To demonstrate the existence of a significant nexus, courts must engage in "a more specific inquiry" and "must identify substantial evidence supporting the Corps' claims" (29).

Kennedy's position was criticized by justices on all sides. Scalia calls the significant-nexus standard a "gimmick" that "appears nowhere in the Act" (2234–2235). Although Stevens admits that Kennedy's "approach is far more faithful to our precedents and to principles of statutory interpretation" than the plurality's, it "fails to defer sufficiently to the Corps" (2252). Breyer fears a problem with applying Kennedy's standard. "In the absence of updated regulations," he writes, "courts will have to make ad hoc determinations that run the risk of transforming scientific questions into matters of law" (2266). For Kennedy, those particular determinations must become matters of law enforced by courts in order to prevent a federal executive agency from serving as the sole judge of its own powers.

Perhaps the most searching criticism of Kennedy's opinion was made in the closing paragraph of the concurring opinion of Chief Justice Roberts. "It is unfortunate," Roberts states, "that no opinion commands a majority of the Court on how precisely to read Congress' limits on the reach of the Clean Water Act." Like Breyer, Roberts fears that "lower courts and regulated entities will now have to feel their way on a case-by-case basis." While such a case-by-case inquiry required by a fractured Court is "not unprecedented," Roberts writes, "what is unusual in this instance, perhaps, is how readily the situation could have been avoided" (2236).

Roberts may be referring to the solution, previewed earlier in his opinion, that after *SWANCC* the Corps could have proposed new rules of jurisdiction. Roberts, like Kennedy, indicates that the Corps of Engineers and the Environmental Protection Agency "would have enjoyed plenty of room to operate in developing *some* notion of an outer bound to the reach of their authority." Instead, however, "the Corps chose to adhere to its essentially boundless view of the scope of its power" (2236). Roberts seems receptive to the substance of Kennedy's argument. Read carefully, however, Roberts's criticism of a fractured Court could also target Kennedy's refusal to join the majority opinion.

Kennedy's opinions in *Gonzales* and *Rapanos* may appear idiosyncratic or muddled. But they are consistent with his long-standing positions regarding the judicial role in enforcing federalism from before his time on the Court and from his concurrence in *Lopez*. Kennedy limits federal power more in theory than in practice. He rejects broad, boundless assertions of authority by the federal government and seeks to maintain a judicial role in policing these boundaries. He uses judicial power to strike broad, unbounded assertions of federal authority, especially when their exercise in practice would shift power away from the states. Yet Kennedy interprets the commerce clause so broadly that he would be receptive to federal regulation as long as officials make a constitutional argument about the extent and limits of their authority based on specific empirical evidence, not mere speculation. Kennedy advocates no revolution in federal-state relations. He only requires the federal government to demonstrate empirical facts in each particular case and a clear constitutional argument so that courts can assess its claim of jurisdiction.

CONCLUSION

Kennedy's jurisprudence involving government structure reflects his effort to establish and enforce principles to limit federal power. He admits several obstacles to this task: the text of the Constitution says little about protections for states, the federal political process provides no specific institutional balancing mechanisms, and larger political and social changes during the twentieth century make such limits on federal power difficult to enforce. Rather than leave such essential and moral safeguards to the political processes, Kennedy employs the structural concept of the split atom of sovereignty, which requires judges to make delicate judgments about whether power has become too concentrated in one branch or level. To Kennedy, employing judicial power to preserve the structural design of the Constitution is just as much a moral imperative as exercising the traditionally accepted duty to protect personal liberties.

Kennedy's split atom metaphor is, most charitably, a partly accurate theory of judicial power under the Constitution. He rejects leaving questions of federal power solely to the political process and properly embraces a judicial role striking federal legislation that surpasses the enumerated powers, concerning both separation of powers and federalism. Furthermore, he rightly strikes state legislation that infringes on federal spheres of commerce and citizenship marked by the Constitution. Kennedy, however, extends his metaphor too far when he examines the effect of the exercise of federal powers on state power. In state sovereign immunity cases he errs in making the residual power, dignity, and sovereignty of the states superior to federal power as enumerated in the Constitution. Kennedy's focus on the balance of power grants the judiciary calculations of wisdom, practicality, and necessity of legislation that rightly belong to the people and their representatives. Although the federal government is a limited one, its limits arise from the enumeration and division of federal powers, not—as the split atom metaphor indicates—by any conception of preexisting state sovereignty, ideals of state dignity, or the need to maintain a balance of power between the state and federal governments.

The difference between Kennedy's split atom of sovereignty and the "residuary and inviolable sovereignty" of the states identified by Madison in *Federalist* 39 ultimately arises from fundamental disagreement about the value of state governments in our constitutional system.[81] In *The Federalist*, Publius focuses on the residuary nature of state power, what remains after federal powers have been properly and expansively interpreted. Kennedy emphasizes the inviolability of state power, requiring the federal government to accord states dignity and respect. This dignity, for Kennedy, is largely procedural: The federal government cannot assert unbounded jurisdiction; it must justify its grant of authority in clear and not speculative terms, and it must not strike at the heart of state power. When state dignity is not respected by the federal government, courts must enforce it.

Although he has given speeches dressed as Madison, Kennedy's emphasis on the dignity and sovereign immunity of states contradicts the ideals expressed by Madison in *Federalist* 45. Answering anti-Federalist arguments, Madison writes, "Is it not preposterous to urge as an objection to a government, without which the objects of the Union cannot be attained, that such a government may derogate from the importance of the governments of the individual states?" He then asks whether the American Revolution was fought "not that the people of America shall enjoy peace, liberty and safety, but that the governments of the individual states, that particular municipal establishments, might enjoy a certain extent of power and be arrayed with certain dignities and attributes of sovereignty?"

Kennedy's expansion of state sovereign immunity directly opposes Madison's answer. "As far as the sovereignty of the States cannot be reconciled to the happiness of the people," Madison writes, "the voice of every good citizen must be, Let the former be sacrificed to the latter."[82] Although Kennedy rightly enforces enumerated limits on federal power, he errs when he justifies those limits based on positive claims of state dignity or sovereignty. Publius feared that the states would threaten liberty and stability by interfering with and encroaching upon the rightful powers of the federal government. Kennedy uses Publius's language to support his fear that the greatest threat to liberty arises not from the states but from congressional and federal overreach.[83] Kennedy's motivations actually invert the assumptions and fears of Madison.

Kennedy's opinions in cases involving federalism and separation of powers rest on an identifiable—but only partly accurate—theory of the Constitution. Although he properly enforces enumerated powers, the protections his split atom metaphor provides for states are largely procedural. These judicial decisions, of limited scope, cannot reverse the larger social, economic, and political trends leading to increased power of the national government. Even if federalism does embody an essential moral element of personal liberty, a Court that actively employs and enforces Kennedy's conception of divided powers would do little in practice to turn back the expansion of federal government or to restore substantial powers to the states.

Conclusion:
Liberty above Democracy

While it is unlikely that we will devise a conclusive formula
for reasoning in constitutional cases, we have the obligation
to confront the consequences of our interpretation, or the
lack of it.
—"UNENUMERATED RIGHTS" SPEECH (1987)

Justice Kennedy has employed an identifiable, coherent, and distinct approach to constitutional interpretation, one with foundations he articulated prior to coming to the U.S. Supreme Court. In method, he rejects the originalism of text and specific tradition advanced by Justice Antonin Scalia and adopts a moral reading of the Constitution similar to that advocated by Ronald Dworkin and former Justice William J. Brennan. The substance of Kennedy's moral conception of liberty, however, departs significantly from Dworkin's focus on equal concern and respect and from Brennan's egalitarian ideal of human dignity.[1] Although Kennedy—like Brennan—believes that the Constitution protects "the essentials of the right to human dignity," Kennedy examines government action to determine whether it causes "injury to the person, the harm to the person, the anguish to the person, the inability of the person to manifest his or her own personality, the inability of a person to obtain his or her own self-fulfillment, the inability of a person to reach his or her own potential."[2] Kennedy's more individualistic conception of human dignity and an expansive ideal of judicial power to enforce it more closely approximates the presumption of liberty advocated by Randy Barnett.[3]

Kennedy's opinions across several areas of constitutional law sketch an ideal of human dignity shaped in rhetoric and substance by post–Vatican II Catholicism. He cites social science research, economic and social developments, and comparative constitutional law as objective referents to justify his conceptions of liberty and dignity. Kennedy examines government actions to determine whether they coerce individual conscience, demean a citizen's standing in the community, or prevent him or her from developing a unique identity and personality. Concerning abortion, he has struggled to reconcile this broad conception of personal liberty with allowing government to enact laws that promote profound moral respect for fetal life. Kennedy takes an expansive ideal of free speech across a broad array of contexts, arguing that each individual has the right to determine which ideas are worthy of consideration, expression, or allegiance.

Kennedy recasts questions in other areas of constitutional law as ones that implicate personal liberty and dignity. Equal protection embodies not a list of suspect classes but a larger principle of neutral individualism that prohibits government from classifying any citizen and treating that individual differently on the basis of characteristics such as race, sex, or sexual orientation that he or she is unable to control. Kennedy considers structural questions of federalism and separation of powers to implicate moral considerations of self-government. To justify judicial intervention in this area, he formulates the metaphor of a split atom of sovereignty and invokes the dignity of state governments.

Kennedy's distinctive approach to constitutional interpretation explains his pivotal position on a divided U.S. Supreme Court. Although his voting behavior moved scholars to group him with Justice O'Connor as a centrist or swing justice,[4] his rhetoric and approach differ fundamentally from hers. O'Connor engaged in strategic accommodation, wrote quasi-legislative, narrow, intensely fact-specific opinions,[5] and acted as a minimalist who disclaimed any "Grand Unified Theory" of constitutional interpretation.[6] In contrast, Kennedy's opinions express a coherent moral vision about the nature of personal liberty and justify expanding judicial power to enforce that vision.[7] On the Court, Kennedy has voted more often than any other justice to strike actions of state and local governments. Such a count actually understates his attempts to expand judicial power; even in areas where he has upheld government actions—including challenges to redistricting for partisan advantage[8] and takings[9] as well as cases involving federalism and political representation—his concurring opinions subject those policies to more searching constitutional review. Because Kennedy's broad theory of liberty justifies judicial intervention in areas favored by both liberal and conservative justices, his assertive judicial role puts him at the center of a divided Court. As Thomas Keck properly notes, Kennedy has "placed no areas of law and policy off limits to judicial action."[10] To Kennedy, liberty in all its dimensions is so essential that its protection can never be left solely to the political process.

TWO EXEMPLARS—AND ONE POSSIBLE
DEPARTURE—FROM KENNEDY'S JURISPRUDENCE

Three majority opinions—two from the 2007–2008 term and one from eight years earlier—exemplify not just Kennedy's critical role in expanding judicial power but his larger interpretive approach. His opinions in *Kennedy v. Louisiana* and *Boumediene v. Bush*, as well as the *per curiam* opinion in *Bush v. Gore*—all decided by a 5–4 vote—demonstrate Kennedy's reliance on the ideal of human dignity, his emphasis on the separation of powers, his rejection of deference to other branches of government, and his defense of independent judicial judgment. Each opinion also produced a dissent expressing political, legal, and constitutional objections that strike at the heart of Kennedy's larger jurisprudential project.

Kennedy v. Louisiana

In *Kennedy v. Louisiana*,[11] which struck the death penalty for those convicted of child rape, Justice Kennedy argues that the "evolving standards of decency" embodied in the Eighth Amendment's prohibition on cruel and unusual punishment "must embrace and express respect for the dignity of the person" (23). His opinion builds upon the ideals of human dignity and independent judgment that he articulated earlier in *Roper v. Simmons*. Although Section III of the opinion in *Kennedy* surveys state laws for "objective indicia of consensus," Kennedy argues that judges must rely on "our own understanding of the Constitution and the rights it secures" (26, 47).[12]

To Kennedy, "decency, in its essence, presumes respect for the individual and thus moderation or restraint in the application of capital punishment" (49). This opinion expresses greater skepticism about capital punishment than any of his previous opinions. "When the law punishes by death," Kennedy writes, "it risks its own sudden descent into brutality, transgressing the constitutional commitment to decency and restraint." Echoing Blackmun's objections in *Callins v. Collins*,[13] Kennedy finds case law regarding the death penalty "still in search of a unifying principle" (26). "Difficulties in administering the penalty," Kennedy writes in his final paragraph, "require adherence to a rule reserving its use, at this stage of evolving standards and in cases of crimes against individuals, for crimes that take the life of the victim" (68). His use of "at this stage" indicates little doubt about the direction in which he believes it is evolving.

Kennedy's concerns echo William Brennan's argument that execution is inherently cruel and unusual punishment because it violates human dignity. Brennan interpreted the Eighth Amendment "as embodying to a unique degree moral principles that substantively restrain the punishments our civilized society may impose on those persons who transgress its laws."[14] Brennan found the death penalty "utterly and irreversibly degrading to the very essence of human dignity," "an absolute denial of the executed person's humanity," and "inconsistent with the fundamental premise of the Clause that even the most base criminal remains a human being possessed of some potential, at least, for common human dignity." Brennan admitted the unpopularity of his position but hoped "to embody a community striving for human dignity for all, although perhaps not yet arrived."

Kennedy does depart from Brennan in several ways. Kennedy focuses on the dignity and potential not just of the accused but of the victim and of the jury that must weigh life and death. Despite these moral objections, Kennedy does not find the death penalty to be inherently unconstitutional.[15] He does, however, argue that the Constitution requires limiting its application. If thousands of eligible child rapists were sentenced to death, Kennedy writes, the expansion in the number of executions "could not be reconciled with our evolving standards of decency and the necessity to constrain the use of the death penalty" (55).

Kennedy makes a moral argument that the taking of life is "unique." Nonhomicide cases "cannot be compared to murder in their 'severity' and 'irrevocability'" (53). As Alito suggests in dissent, states could outline aggravating and mitigating factors in child rape cases similar to those used in the penalty phase for other capital crimes. But, Kennedy reasons, "in this context, which involves a crime that in many cases will overwhelm a decent person's judgment, we have no confidence that the imposition of the death penalty would not be so arbitrary as to be 'freakish'" (55–56). He even concedes that aggravating factors may not be applied consistently in current death penalty deliberations. "The resulting imprecision and tension between evaluating the individual circumstances and consistency of treatment have been tolerated where the victim dies," he writes. "It should not be introduced into our justice system, though, where death has not occurred" (57).

As in other cases, Kennedy employs social scientific research to support his practical fears about the "risks of overpunishment" (59). "It is not at all evident," he finds, "that the child rape victim's hurt is lessened when the law permits the death of the perpetrator" (60). In this section Kennedy focuses on the moral and psychological harms that a prosecution seeking the death penalty can visit upon the victim of the crime. "During the formative years of her adolescence, made all the more daunting for having to come to terms with the brutality of her experience," he writes, the victim becomes "a central figure on the decision to seek the death penalty" (61). Use of the victim by the state to secure the death penalty "forces a moral choice on the child, who is not of mature age to make that choice" (62, 63). This psychological description of the immature child echoes not just his opinion in *Roper* but also his statements in *Hodgson v. Minnesota* about minors who seek abortions.

To Kennedy, prohibiting the death penalty for child rape may even serve a larger moral purpose for the criminal by opening "the possibility that he and the system will find ways to allow him to understand the enormity of the offense" (68). For this Kennedy cites no evidence. Yet this rhetoric resonates with his explanation in *Roper* about why it is cruel and unusual to execute those who commit capital crimes as juveniles. It also (oddly) resonates with his description of flag burner Gregory Johnson, who retains his constitutional rights "whether or not he could appreciate the enormity of the offense he gave."[16] There appears to be no principled reason—other than the fact of continuing popular support for the death penalty—why these same considerations of redemption would not apply to those convicted of taking another's life.

In the final section of his opinion, Kennedy addresses criticism that using "independent judgment" makes the Supreme Court "part judge and part the maker of that which it judges" (67). Such a tension, he finds, is inevitable under an Eighth Amendment that embodies standards of decency "with specific marks in the way to full progress and mature judgment" (67–68). Kennedy's opinion appeals not just to progress but to maturity, with standards of maturity measured not by political consensus but by moral truth. "Standing alone," Kennedy concedes, each of the moral and practical considerations he cites may not suffice to invalidate the Louisiana law that was the subject of the case. "Taken in sum," however, they "lead us to conclude, in our independent judgment, that the death penalty is not a proportional punishment for the rape of a child" (66–67).

Alito's dissent criticizes Kennedy's expansive judicial role. The laws recently passed by Louisiana and other states that make child rape a capital crime may "have been the beginning of a strong new evolutionary line," he writes, but "the Court today snuffs out the line in its incipient stage" and acts to "block the potential emergence" (93). Clearly, however, Kennedy is no mere progressive or historicist; his opinion expresses a desire to prevent some practices before they have the opportunity to develop. Alito criticizes Kennedy's "sweeping holding" of "striking down all capital child-rape laws no matter how carefully and narrowly they are crafted" (97, 95).

More substantively, Alito questions Kennedy's assertion that murder "is unique in its moral depravity and in the severity of the injury it inflicts on the victim and the public" (101). "Is it really true that every person who is convicted of capital murder is more morally depraved than every child rapist?" Alito asks (101–102). "I have little doubt that, in the eyes of ordinary Americans, the very worst child rapists . . . are the epitome of moral depravity." Even assuming that death is unique, "that does not explain why other grievous harms are insufficient to permit a death sentence" (103). An increasing number of states have concluded "that these harms justify the death penalty," Alito writes. The Constitution affords the people this right to come to this conclusion, and Kennedy's "conclusory references to 'decency,' 'moderation,' 'progress' and 'moral judgment' are not enough" to justify invalidating them (106).

Boumediene v. Bush

In *Boumediene v. Bush*,[17] the Court asserted jurisdiction to hear appeals arising from the combat status review tribunal system established for detainees at Guantanamo Bay, Cuba. Lakhdar Boumediene, a foreign national classified as an enemy combatant and held at Guantanamo, argued that he had a constitutional right to habeas corpus, which, under the Detainee Treatment Act (DTA) of 2005, Congress had neither suspended nor replaced with an adequate substitute procedure. Kennedy's opinion for the Court illustrates three aspects of his jurisprudence: the centrality of liberty, the necessity of divided power, and the expansive judicial role in defining and enforcing these limits under the fundamental law of the Constitution.

Kennedy's opinion emphasizes why courts must enforce separation of powers and require Congress to suspend habeas corpus explicitly. Dividing power, he reiterates, "serves not only to make Government accountable but also to secure individual liberty" (35). To Kennedy, habeas corpus is "one of the few safeguards of liberty" explicitly protected under an original constitution that did not contain a Bill of Rights. That gives the guarantee "a centrality that must inform proper interpretation of the Suspension Clause," making it "an essential mechanism in the separation of powers scheme" (30, 36). That mechanism requires "affirming the duty and authority of the Judiciary to call the jailer to account" (40).

Kennedy finds the writ such "an indispensable mechanism" that it "must not be subject to manipulation by those whose power it was designed to restrain" (74). He rejects the government's argument that federal courts lack jurisdiction over Guantanamo, stating that "our basic charter cannot be contracted away like this" (72). He characterizes the issue as whether "the political branches have the power to switch the Constitution on or off at will" (73–74). Accepting this government's argument, to Kennedy, would be tantamount to renouncing the Constitution and *Marbury v. Madison,* "leading to a regime in which Congress and the President, not this Court, say 'what the law is'" (74).

This *Marbury* quote seeks to justify why Kennedy reversed himself and voted to hear the case. He had earlier voted to deny certiorari in this case and authored a statement with Stevens justifying denial, but then the D.C. Circuit gave the case a full hearing and ruling as stated under the Military Commissions Act.[18] In June 2007, Kennedy and Stevens switched their votes to hear the case. For Kennedy, the circumstances of these petitioners differ critically from habeas claims in criminal proceedings. "The gravity of the separation-of-powers issues raised by these cases and the fact that these detainees have been denied meaningful access to a judicial forum for a period of years," he writes, "render these cases exceptional" (85–86). When a person is detained solely by executive order, "the need for habeas corpus is more urgent. The intended duration of the detention and the reasons for it bear upon the precise scope of the inquiry" (103). To make the writ "effective," reviewing courts "must have sufficient authority to conduct a meaningful review of both the cause for detention and the Executive's power to detain" (104).

To Kennedy, meaningful review of habeas corpus requires attention not just to form but also to substance. Ultimately, "what matters is the sum total of protections afforded to the detainee at all stages, direct and collateral" (104–105). Kennedy examines the DTA and finds constraints on the evidence, on assistance of counsel, on cross-examination, and on the issues, facts, and remedies available on appeal from the decision of the Combat Status Review Tribunals (CSRT). This leads to unjustified detentions. "Given that the consequence of error may be the detention of persons for the duration of hostilities that may last a generation or more," he writes, "this is a risk too significant to ignore" (108–109). Collateral review of the record "may not be accurate or complete" (116). Detainees "would still have no opportunity to present evidence discovered after the CSRT proceedings concluded" (112–114). Even those who prevail could not request an order of release but only petition the secretary of defense for a new tribunal. Given his independent judgment of the interests at issue, Kennedy finds this new procedure an "inadequate substitute" for habeas corpus. Congress's stripping of Supreme Court review in the Military Commissions Act is thus unconstitutional.

Kennedy's opinion does attempt to qualify the scope of its ruling. The particular cases "do not involve detainees who have been held a short period of time" (122). He also concedes that "it does not follow that a habeas corpus court may disregard the dangers the detention in these cases was intended to prevent" (124). He emphasizes that the opinion "does not address the content of the law that governs the petitioners' detention" (129). For Boumediene and others held, however, "six years have elapsed without the judicial oversight that habeas corpus or an adequate substitute demands." Thus "the costs of delay can no longer be borne by those who are held in custody" (123).

Kennedy characteristically ends his opinion with sweeping statements about the centrality of liberty, the importance of divided power, and the judicial duty to enforce both under the rule of law. "Security subsists, too, in fidelity to first principles," he writes. "Chief among these are freedom from arbitrary and unlawful restraint and the personal liberty that is secured by adherence to the separation of powers." He does not see this decision limiting the president's constitutional power as commander in chief. "On the contrary," he writes, "the exercise of those powers is vindicated, not eroded, when confirmed by the Judicial Branch" (127). In designing a new system, "the political branches, consistent with their independent obligations to interpret and uphold the Constitution, can engage in a genuine debate about how best to preserve constitutional values while protecting the Nation from terrorism" (128). But the Court must also fulfill its own independent obligation to uphold "the fundamental procedural protections of habeas corpus."

In this final paragraph, Kennedy reiterates his expansive conception of the vital role of courts. As he concludes, "the laws and Constitution are designed to survive, and remain in force, in extraordinary times. Liberty and security can be reconciled; and in our system they are reconciled within the framework of law." In the opinion's final sentence, Kennedy writes that "the Framers decided that habeas corpus, a right of first importance, must be a part of that framework, a part of that law." Kennedy again closes with the most important word, repeated for emphasis.[19] Here the crucial word is not "liberty" (as in *Casey*) or "freedom" (as in *Lawrence* and *Roper*), but "law." Combined with his earlier citation of *Marbury*, this action demonstrates Kennedy's belief in the essential role of courts under our constitutional system.

Although Justice Scalia's emphasis on the terrorist threat attracted more initial attention, the more persuasive objections to Kennedy are raised in the dissent of Chief Justice Roberts. To Roberts, the majority's opinion "makes plain that certiorari in these cases should never have been granted" (137), and any Supreme Court decision on the issue is "grossly premature" (139). "In the absence of any assessment of the DTA's remedies," he writes, "the question whether detainees are entitled to habeas is an entirely speculative one" (141). Although Kennedy mentions the "extraordinary" circumstances of this case, to Roberts "it is, however, precisely when the issues presented are grave that adherence to the ordinary course is most important." Roberts defends procedure and attacks Kennedy. "Charges of judicial activism," he writes, "are most effectively rebutted when courts can fairly argue they are following normal practices" (142). In the Court's "disrespect" for process, it "rushes to decide the fundamental question of the reach of habeas corpus when the functioning of the DTA may make that decision entirely unnecessary, and it does so with scant idea of how DTA judicial review will actually operate" (145). Instead, Roberts writes, the majority steps in to decide the case on "entirely speculative" reasoning based "on abstract and hypothetical concerns" (141, 174–175).

Roberts's ultimate disagreement with Kennedy rests on differing conceptions about the proper constitutional role of the judiciary. The Court does not order a new system to replace the DTA, Roberts observes; it "merely replaces a review system designed by the people's representatives with a set of shapeless procedures to be defined by federal courts at some future date" (134). That remedy, "when all is said and done," may well "end up looking a great deal like the DTA review it rejects" (174). For Roberts, "one cannot help but think . . . that this decision is not really about the detainees at all, but about control of federal policy regarding enemy combatants" (134). The Court is the only winner, Roberts concludes, as the American people "today lose a bit more control over the conduct of this Nation's foreign policy to unelected, politically unaccountable judges" (176–177).

Bush v. Gore

The unsigned *per curiam* opinion for the Court in *Bush v. Gore*[20] that invalidated and ended Florida's recount of the 2000 presidential election exhibits both similarities to and departures from Kennedy's normal rhetoric. It is the rare Kennedy opinion that focuses on equality. The *per curiam* opinion never uses the word "liberty": that only appears in Breyer's dissent, which objects that "the Court is not acting to vindicate a fundamental constitutional principle, such as the need to protect a basic human liberty" (157). The *per curiam* opinion does employ Kennedy's characteristic term "dignity": one source of the "fundamental nature" of the right to vote, he says, "lies in the equal weight accorded to each vote and the equal dignity owed to each voter" (104). That dignity provides the basis for an argument based on equality. "Having once granted the right to vote on equal terms," the opinion states, "the State may not, by later arbitrary and disparate treatment, value one person's vote over that of another" (104–105).

The *per curiam* opinion does contain two hallmarks of Kennedy's reasoning concerning equal protection: appeals to larger notions of fairness and the need to maintain public confidence in government. The statewide recount stated no specific and uniform rules for ballot review, and Kennedy notes that "there must be at least some assurance that the rudimentary requirements of equal treatment and fundamental fairness are satisfied" (109). The "unequal evaluation" (106) and different treatment of ballots in different counties and within counties—including the acceptance of partial counts from some counties and already completed counts from some others as well as a statewide review of undervotes but not overvotes—indicated that the Florida Supreme Court's contest procedure was "not well calculated to sustain the confidence that all citizens must have in the outcome of elections."

Yet this opinion also signals an uncharacteristic defensiveness about judicial power. Rather than explicating a new constitutional principle of general application, the Court emphasizes that its "consideration is limited to the present case, for the problem of equal protection in election processes generally presents many complexities" (109). Most famously, the concluding paragraph claims:

> None are more conscious of the vital limits on judicial authority than are the members of this Court, and none stand more in admiration of the Constitution's design to leave the selection of the President to the people, through their

> legislatures, and to the political sphere. When contending parties invoke the process of the courts, however, it becomes our unsought responsibility to resolve the federal and constitutional issues the judicial system has been forced to confront. (111)

As the dissenters state, the Court could have decided not to hear the case in the first place. Despite some rhetorical unease, the result in *Bush v. Gore* is consistent with Kennedy's expansion of the Supreme Court's power.

The strongest dissenting arguments criticized not the equal protection holding but the Court's previous decisions to accept certiorari and to stay the Florida recount and its remedy of terminating the recount (see Souter at 129; Breyer at 144). As Breyer notes, the Court stops the recount "in the absence of *any* record evidence that the recount could not have been completed in the time allowed by the Florida Supreme Court" (146). By staying and then finally ending the recount, Breyer writes, the majority "harms the very fairness interests the Court is attempting to protect" (147).

Breyer also makes a continuing constitutional and prudential argument for judicial restraint. "However awkward or difficult it may be for Congress to resolve difficult electoral disputes," he writes, "Congress, being a political body, expresses the people's will far more accurately than any court. And the people's will is what elections are all about" (155). He criticizes the Court's involvement, saying that "with one exception, petitioner's claims do not ask us to vindicate a constitutional provision designed to protect a basic human right." For support he cites *Brown v. Board of Education* (152–153). To Breyer, the relevant constitutional provisions and the history of judicial involvement in the disputed 1876 presidential election make the Court's decision to stop the recount "not only legally wrong, but also most unfortunate" (157). From this history, Breyer counsels "judicial restraint." He finds no "fundamental constitutional principle, such as the need to protect a basic human liberty," to justify involvement (157). This opinion reopens the long-running dispute between Breyer and Kennedy—traceable to *Clinton v. New York* and in federalism cases—about the proper judicial role in cases involving governmental structure.

Breyer also addresses Kennedy's argument about sustaining popular confidence in government. Breyer is most concerned that "the appearance of a split decision runs the risk of undermining the public's confidence in the Court itself" (157). Finding that confidence "a public treasure," Breyer fears that with this decision the Court "risk[s] a self-inflicted wound—a wound that may harm not just the Court, but the Nation" (158). Breyer, like Souter, thus concludes that what the Court has done in *Bush v. Gore* it "should have left undone" (158).

KENNEDY'S DEPARTURE FROM POST–NEW DEAL CONSTITUTIONAL THOUGHT

Kennedy's interpretive approach based on the full and necessary meaning of liberty and his justification of expanded judicial power are best understood as a response to jurisprudential developments since the New Deal extolling deference to elected branches. After the Court's rejection of *Lochner v. New York*,[21] constitutional theory and practice moved away from a central focus on liberty—disparaged as substantive due process—and attempted to justify limiting judicial review within a government considered fundamentally democratic. This ideal is epitomized by a statement appearing in footnote 4 in *U.S. v. Carolene Products*. The New Deal Court, in an opinion by Justice Stone, argues that courts should presume that a law is constitutional unless it "appears on its face to be within a specific prohibition of the Constitution, such as those of the first ten amendments, which are deemed equally specific when held to be embraced within the Fourteenth"; "restricts those political processes which can ordinarily be expected to bring about repeal of undesirable legislation"; or is directed at "discrete and insular minorities."[22] Justice Hugo Black's opinion for the Court twenty-five years later in *Ferguson v. Skrupa* seemed a definitive rejection of the "vague contours" of substantive due process.[23] From fear of resurrecting *Lochner*, Justice William O. Douglas's majority opinion in *Griswold v. Connecticut* forcefully disclaimed any judicial duty to strike laws on the basis of Fourteenth Amendment liberty. Douglas instead sought to situate the right of marital privacy within several "specific guarantees in the Bill of Rights."[24]

In constitutional theory, this overriding concern with democratic legitimacy generated Alexander Bickel's characterization of "judicial review as a counter-majoritarian force in our system"[25] as well as John Hart Ely's justification of judicial review to support representation-reinforcement and proper functioning of the democratic process.[26] Over the past decade, scholars such as Cass Sunstein, Mark Tushnet, Larry Kramer, and Jeffrey Rosen have advocated limiting the scope of judicial power.[27] More recently, Justice Stephen

Breyer has sought to promote active liberty within a fundamentally democratic constitution.[28] The motivation of this post–New Deal tradition is the fear that judges will read their own personal economic, political, or social views into the Constitution, thus denying the people their fundamental right to rule themselves.[29]

For all its rhetorical attacks, the originalism of Justice Scalia also adopts this presumption of judicial deference under a fundamentally democratic system. Although Scalia engages in a "vigorous denunciation of post–New Deal liberalism,[30] legal scholars David Schultz and Christopher Smith persuasively argue that his jurisprudence is no "blanket rejection." Rather, Scalia "has rerouted the logic of *Carolene Products* to redefine what rights and values deserve protection, how they will be protected, and what level of protection will be given to each."[31] As political scientist Ralph Rossum concludes, Scalia believes that "the most important right of the people in a democracy" is "the right to govern themselves and not be overruled in their governance unless the clear text or the traditional understanding they have adopted demands it."[32] Despite his opposition to results in particular cases, Scalia fundamentally agrees with the New Deal's conception of the Constitution as essentially majoritarian.

Kennedy's jurisprudence departs from this consensus. It seeks to reorient constitutional interpretation within the legacies of the New Deal and Warren Courts and their originalist critics. Other justices claim to be vindicating versions of democracy. But to Kennedy, the value most central to the Constitution is not democracy, or even equality, but individual liberty. Kennedy's jurisprudence attempts to transcend continuing popular and academic debates between judicial activism and restraint[33] and the derivative debate about how judicial power fits within what is considered the essentially democratic nature of the Constitution. He recognizes social, political, and economic changes as well as legal precedents, and he seeks to modify these multiple jurisprudential traditions within his conception of a broader judicial role to enforce the full and necessary meaning of liberty.[34]

Kennedy's liberty-based constitutionalism rejects the post–New Deal deference to other elected branches of government. As he said in 1982, Congress and all other branches of government "must acknowledge its constitutional responsibility and begin to articulate its legislative judgments in constitutional terms." Should they not do so, he writes, "I would contend that courts should rescind the rule that legislative act is presumed to be constitutional. A presumption should not exist if it does not mirror reality."[35] Barnett optimistically describes Kennedy's liberty-based jurisprudence as heralding a libertarian revolution.[36] Keck more accurately characterizes Kennedy's achievements as having "preserved so much of the Warren Court legacy" and extending that legacy to justify increased judicial enforcement in other areas of constitutional law.[37] During his confirmation hearings Kennedy even cited the Warren Court positively. "It was not the political branches that decided *Brown v. Board of Education,* or that decided the right to counsel case, and it was not the political branches of the government that wrought the revolution of *Baker v. Carr,*" Kennedy stated. "It was the courts."[38]

Before coming to the Court, Kennedy acknowledged the problem of indeterminacy raised by an expansive judicial role. "The judicial branch has the enviable or unenviable position of making up the rules in its own game,"[39] he admitted. But he rejected the "fallacious conclusion" that "judges should be influenced in their interpretation of the law by their own utilitarian view of economics, politics and social theory." Kennedy insisted that results should be "irrelevant" to the process of constitutional interpretation; "the judge must constantly be on guard against letting his or her biases or prejudices or affections enter into the judicial process."[40] Instead, "judges must strive to discover and define neutral juridical categories for decisions, categories neither cast in political terms nor laden with subjective overtones."[41] They "must be bound by some neutral, definable, measurable standard in their interpretation of the Constitution."[42] For Kennedy, the ideal of liberty—which has substantive content in the Western tradition—provides such a standard.

Kennedy's focus on enforcing the full and necessary meaning of liberty minimizes the dilemma of democratic legitimacy that has preoccupied twentieth-century jurisprudence. But his effort predictably raises the accusation of judicial arrogance.[43] This objection arises not merely from his votes, but from the rhetoric and reasoning of his opinions. Many of the considerations that inform Kennedy's conception of liberty are moral, political, and practical rather than historical or legal. His opinions cite social science research, political developments, and comparative law to provide objective referents for potentially subjective conceptions of personality and fulfillment, and his actions rejecting deference to other branches serve to expand judicial power.

Kennedy's decisions and rhetoric expanding judicial power in the name of liberty have led opposing justices from all sides of the current Court to accuse him of resurrecting *Lochner*. This explicit charge has been leveled by Justice Souter[44] and Justice Breyer.[45] Most prominently, these charges have repeatedly come from Justice Scalia's dissents in cases such as *Lee, Romer, Casey, Lawrence,* and *Roper.* For Scalia, Kennedy's method does little more than "rattle off a collection of adjectives that simply decorate a value judgment and conceal a political choice" based only on "personal predilection."[46] Scalia criticizes the judge (like Kennedy) who "assumes that it is up to the judge to find THE correct answer. And I deny that." Many cases before the Court mostly "involve moral sentiments," Scalia says, and thus "you're not going to come up with a right or wrong answer."[47] To Scalia, claims of liberty and dignity are simply value judgments that courts cannot demonstrate as true or false.[48]

For Kennedy, interpreting the Constitution is not a mechanical process that requires only the "essentially lawyer's work" of historical research and the steadfastness provided by life tenure to apply those results of a preferred interpretive approach against the political pressures of the day. Rather, it requires judges as a matter of duty to make difficult and controversial moral and practical judgments. Kennedy self-consciously (if not agonizingly) uses judicial power to apply a conception of the full and necessary meaning of liberty to questions of constitutional structure and to claims of personal liberty not explicitly stated in the Constitution. To do this, it is necessary to make value judgments. As he stated in *Texas v. Johnson,* "The hard fact is that sometimes we must make decisions we do not like. We make them because they are right, right in the sense that the law and the Constitution, as we see them, compel the result." Kennedy believes that legal questions have right answers, that courts can find these answers through legal materials and other objective referents, and that these answers embody a truth not simply reducible to personal preference. Sometimes, in fact, the right answer "exacts a personal toll" and can be "painful . . . to announce."[49] As political scientist Terri Jennings Peretti has written, "the justices are and should be regarded as politicians who share in the difficult but noble task of political leadership, in generating consensual solutions to the often vexing and contentious issues of the day."[50]

Such political leadership requires judges to present the most candid, most reasonable arguments they can to justify their decisions and to accept responsibility for their reasoning and the consequences of their decisions. "While it is unlikely that we will devise a conclusive formula for reasoning in constitutional cases," Kennedy admitted before coming to the Court, "we have the obligation to confront the consequences of our interpretation, or the lack of it."[51] In the end, judicial power is restrained in practice not by consistent application of a particular interpretive theory but by the inherent institutional, social, and political realities that every self-aware judge realizes make courts the least powerful and most dependent branch of government.[52] As Kennedy himself stated, "the imperatives of judicial restraint spring from the Constitution itself, not from any particular judicial theory."[53]

Although the *Lochner* accusation is more name-calling than substance, a continuing tension does exist in Kennedy's jurisprudence between the sweeping rhetoric concerning liberty and judicial power in his opinions and the relatively restrained consequences of his rulings. Many of his decisions striking federal laws, especially in areas of federalism and separation of powers, have attracted much more scholarly attention than popular interest. Others, like *Lawrence*, invalidated laws that were rarely, if ever, enforced.[54] The results of still others of his decisions appear more in line with popular and elite opinion than with the actions of Congress or state legislatures.[55] Kennedy's rhetoric is sweeping and his rulings have expanded the scope of judicial power. But *Bush v. Gore* aside,[56] the limited practical impact of these rulings may disguise the extent of his expansion of the judicial role. So far, Kennedy's (and the Court's) expansion of judicial power in rhetoric and practice has produced no meaningful crisis of popular legitimacy for the institution.

Justice Anthony M. Kennedy began the plurality opinion in *Casey* by stating that "liberty finds no refuge in a jurisprudence of doubt."[57] He does not claim that its content will be uncontroversial or its application unchanging, or that some may not doubt whether the Court's answer in a particular case is the correct one. Rather, he seeks to remove doubt that liberty is America's central constitutional value. Kennedy's interpretive approach stands or falls on whether he is right about the centrality of liberty as a constitutional value, about his conception of the substantive nature of that liberty, and about the proper role of the Court in discovering and enforcing it.

Critics may object that Kennedy's conception of human liberty derives from flawed moral or political foundations or relies more on assumptions or ideals than on empirical reality, that he applies this conception selectively or inconsistently, or that his grand and overwrought rhetoric obscures rather than advances the goal he seeks. The proper response, however, is not to reject Kennedy's project as inevitably personal or as a return to *Lochner,* then continue trying to limit judicial power based on abstract ideals of judicial restraint or democracy, which themselves have little explicit support in the constitutional text. Despite its shortcomings, Kennedy's jurisprudence properly seeks to return constitutional interpretation to the fundamental question of how judges—like all government officials—can fulfill their obligation to discover the meaning of liberty and act most effectively to secure it.

Appendix A

Dear Harry,

After much hesitation, I decided it best for our collegial relation and, I hope, mutual respect to tell you that I harbor deep resentment at your paragraph on page 17 in Ohio v. Akron Center. You say my hyperbole is to incite an inflamed public. To write with that purpose would be a violation of my judicial duty.

I am still struggling with the whole abortion issue and thought it proper to convey this in what I wrote. Though I have not read it, I am told L. Tribe's just issued work, "A Clash of Absolutes," makes the same point, though perhaps at more length.

I do not question the depth of your compassion and understanding, but neither do I yield to the charge that my own is somehow a mask for some improper purpose.

In any event, though it is late in the term, I thought you would want to hear this, and perhaps it will prompt you to reconsider what is a most unfair attribution of motives not consonant with the conscientious discharge of my office.

Yours,

Tony

21 June 1990

Appendix B

Transcription of Blackmun's Notes from
Meeting with Kennedy, May 30, 1992

The 3—
  Roe sound, tho n t trimester sys
AK OR Akron and Thornburgh
  But spousal notif NG
  Otherwise Pa. stat OK
DHS stare decisis
  adopt SOC undue B

  ———————

  can I jam some
  RC agony + harlan
  Electn is urel

CJ-W-T-N [O-K-D] X-S
AMK delegated by O + D?
      AMK 3-30-92 [*sic*]

Notes

INTRODUCTION

[1] According to statistics compiled in the annual September issues of the *Harvard Law Review* from 1994 to 2005, during the natural Rehnquist Court Kennedy cast the fewest dissenting votes in eight of thirteen terms and trailed only O'Connor in four of the other five.

[2] See his recent majority opinions for a 5–4 Court in Boumediene v. Bush, 128 S. Ct. 2229 (2008) (striking the military commissions system for enemy combatants as an inadequate substitute for habeas corpus), and Kennedy v. Louisiana, 2008 U.S. Lexis 5262 (2008) (finding a death sentence for child rape to violate the Eighth Amendment ban on cruel and unusual punishment). I discuss these cases in the conclusion to this book.

[3] For recent examples, see Parents Involved in Community Schools v. Seattle School District No. 1, 127 S. Ct. 2738 (2007); Hamdan v. Rumsfeld, 126 S. Ct. 2749 (2006) (decided 5–3, Roberts not participating); and Rapanos v. Gonzales, 126 S. Ct. 2008 (2006).

[4] See SCOTUS blog, http://www.scotusblog.com/movabletype/archives/Final5-4 visual.pdf.

[5] For recent accounts of Kennedy's influence, see Adam Liptak, "The New 5-to-4 Court," *New York Times*, 22 April 2007, sec. 4, p. 1; Robert Barnes, "Justice Kennedy: The Highly Influential Man in the Middle: Court's 5–4 Decisions Underscore His Power," *Washington Post*, 13 May 2007, p. A1; Jeffrey Rosen, "Supreme Leader: The Arrogance of Justice Anthony Kennedy," *New Republic*, 18 June 2007, p. 16. See also Paul Edelman and Jim Chen, "The Most Dangerous Justice: The Supreme Court at the Bar of Mathematics," 76 *Southern California Law Review* 63, 91 (1997).

[6] For accounts during the last two terms, see Jeffrey Rosen, "Supreme Leader," the issue's cover article; Adam Liptak, "The Fragile Kennedy Court," *New York Times*, 7 July 2006, sec. A, p. 16. For accounts written earlier in his tenure, see Joan Biskupic, "Justices Follow a Mostly Conservative Course: Kennedy Assuming Pivotal Role on a Supreme Court That Continues to Redefine Itself," *Washington Post*, 4 July 1994, p. A1, and—from his first term—"Kennedy Casts Key Vote in Several 5–4 Decisions," *New York Times*, 3 July 1988, sec. 1, p. 14.

[7] See Thomas M. Keck, *The Most Activist Court in History: The Road to Modern Judicial Conservatism* (Chicago: University of Chicago Press, 2004), which groups Kennedy and O'Connor; Earl M. Maltz, "Anthony Kennedy and the Jurisprudence of Respectable Conservatism," in Maltz, ed., *Rehnquist Justice: Understanding the Court Dynamic* (Lawrence: University Press of Kansas, 2004), pp. 140–156.

[8] See, for example, Earl M. Maltz, "Justice Kennedy's Vision of Federalism," 31

Rutgers Law Journal 761 (2000); Christopher E. Smith, "Supreme Court Surprise: Justice Anthony Kennedy's Move Toward Moderation," 45 *Oklahoma Law Review* 459 (1992); Lawrence Friedman, "The Limitations of Labeling: Justice Anthony M. Kennedy and the First Amendment," 20 *Ohio Northern Law Review* 225 (1993); Patrick D. Schmidt and David A. Yalof, "The 'Swing Voter' Revisited: Justice Anthony Kennedy and the First Amendment Right of Free Speech," 57 *Political Research Quarterly* 209 (2004).

[9] See Mark Tushnet, *A Court Divided* (New York: W. W. Norton, 2005), Chap. 6, titled "Anthony Kennedy and Gay Rights"; Stephen E. Gottlieb, "Three Justices in Search of a Character: The Moral Agendas of Justices O'Connor, Scalia and Kennedy," 49 *Rutgers Law Review* 219 (1996); Akhil Reed Amar, "Justice Kennedy and the Idea of Equality," 28 *Pacific Law Journal* 515 (1997); Michael P. Zuckert, "*Casey* at the Bat: Taking Another Swing at *Planned Parenthood v. Casey*," in Christopher Wolfe, ed., *That Eminent Tribunal: Judicial Supremacy and the Constitution* (Princeton, N.J.: Princeton University Press, 2004), pp. 37–57.

[10] See Thomas Hensley, Christopher E. Smith, and Joyce A. Baugh, *The Changing Supreme Court: Constitutional Rights and Liberties* (Minneapolis/St. Paul: Wadsworth, 1997), p. 75.

[11] See Robert Nagel, "Liberals and Balancing," 63 *University of Colorado Law Review* 323, 327 (1992).

[12] See two 1992 articles by Kathleen Sullivan that place Kennedy in opposing interpretive camps. In one, Sullivan describes Kennedy's First Amendment jurisprudence as categorical, embodying a justice of rules. Sullivan, "Post-Liberal Judging: The Roles of Categorization and Balancing," 63 *University of Colorado Law Review* 293, 305–306 (1992). In the other, she praises the balancing approach of the plurality opinion in *Casey* coauthored by Kennedy. Sullivan, "The Justices of Rules and Standards," 106 *Harvard Law Review* 22 (1992).

[13] See Tinsley Yarborough, *The Rehnquist Court and the Constitution* (New York: Oxford University Press, 2000).

[14] David Schultz and Christopher Smith, *The Jurisprudential Vision of Justice Antonin Scalia* (Lanham, Md.: Rowman and Littlefield, 1996), p. 207.

[15] David Yalof, *Pursuit of Justices: Presidential Politics and the Selection of Supreme Court Nominees* (Chicago: University of Chicago Press, 1999), p. 165.

[16] Helen J. Knowles, *The Tie Goes to Freedom: Justice Anthony M. Kennedy on Liberty* (Lanham, Md.: Rowman and Littlefield, 2009).

[17] Terence Moran, "Profiles in Caprice," *New Jersey Law Journal*, 13 July 1992, p. 4 (see also quotes from William Bradford Reynolds); Richard C. Reuben, "Man in the Middle," *California Lawyer* (October 1992), p. 36 (quoting Michael McConnell).

[18] Michael Paulsen, "The Many Faces of 'Judicial Restraint,'" *1993 Public Interest Law Review* 3, p. 17. Garrett Epps and Dahlia Lithwick, "The Sphinx of Sacramento: Will the Real Anthony Kennedy Please Stand Up?" *Slate*, 27 April 2007 (accessible at http://www.slate.com/id/2165133/nav/tap1/).

[19] "While it is true . . . that Justice Kennedy drifted to the left early in his career . . . since the early 1990s his ideal point has remained flat." Lee Epstein et al., "Ideological

Drift among Supreme Court Justices: Who, When and How Important?" 101 *Northwestern Law Review* 1483, 1509 (2007).

[20] Schmidt and Yalof, "The 'Swing Voter' Revisited," p. 210.

[21] U.S. Senate, "Nomination of Anthony M. Kennedy to Be Associate Justice of the Supreme Court of the United States," 14–16 December 1987, p. 154.

[22] Anthony M. Kennedy, "Unenumerated Rights and the Dictates of Judicial Restraint," Palo Alto, California, Canadian Institute for Advanced Legal Studies, 24 July–1 August 1986, p. 20.

[23] Nomination, p. 138.

[24] For descriptions of Scalia's jurisprudence, see Ralph A. Rossum, *Antonin Scalia's Jurisprudence: Text and Tradition* (Lawrence: University Press of Kansas, 2006); Schultz and Smith, *Jurisprudential Vision*; Richard Brisbin, *Justice Antonin Scalia and the Conservative Revival* (Baltimore: Johns Hopkins University Press, 1997). For accounts of Thomas's jurisprudence, see Scott Gerber, *First Principles: The Jurisprudence of Clarence Thomas* (New York: New York University Press, 1999), and Samuel A. Marcosson, *Original Sin: Clarence Thomas and the Failure of the Constitutional Conservatives* (New York: New York University Press, 2002).

[25] Anthony M. Kennedy, "Rotary Speech," Sacramento, Rotary Club, 15 October 1987, p. 6.

[26] Cass Sunstein, *One Case at a Time: Judicial Minimalism on the Supreme Court* (New York: Harvard University Press, 1999), pp. 9, x, xi.

[27] Robert Van Sickel also describes O'Connor as a justice who avoided questions of substantive justice or fundamental rights. Van Sickel, *Not a Particularly Different Voice: The Jurisprudence of Sandra Day O'Connor* (New York: Peter Lang Press, 1998).

[28] Sunstein at one point calls Kennedy a minimalist (p. 9), yet overlooks him in the preface when he categorizes every other then-sitting justice (p. xiii). Sunstein praises Romer v. Evans as minimalist (pp. 137–171), but never mentions Kennedy as author. He considers Kennedy a nonminimalist regarding the First Amendment (p. 58).

[29] Nomination, pp. 122, 231.

[30] Anthony Kennedy, "Comments at Ninth Circuit Judicial Conference," Hawaii, 21 August 1987, pp. 6–7, 87.

[31] "Unenumerated Rights," p. 22.

[32] Nomination, pp. 170–171. The following citations in the text refer to this testimony.

[33] "Unenumerated Rights," p. 7; see also "Rotary Speech," p. 7.

[34] "Unenumerated Rights," p. 4.

[35] Quote is from a speech Kennedy delivered before the American Bar Association in September 1992, cited in Tony Mauro, "Another Solution to the Kennedy Riddle," *Legal Times*, 14 September 1992, p. 6.

[36] These statements did not go unnoticed. See the objections of Republican Senators Charles Grassley and Gordon Humphrey in Nomination, pp. 1458–1459. Grassley and Humphrey nevertheless voted for Kennedy, who was confirmed 98–0.

[37] Randy E. Barnett, *Restoring the Lost Constitution: The Presumption of Liberty*

(Princeton, N.J.: Princeton University Press, 2004), p. 254. I provide a closer comparison of Kennedy and Barnett in chaps. 1 and 5 as well as in the conclusion.

[38] Sue Davis, *Justice Rehnquist and the Constitution* (Princeton, N.J.: Princeton University Press, 1989); Schultz and Smith, *Jurisprudential Vision;* Brisbin, *Scalia and the Conservative Revival;* Christopher Smith, *Justice Antonin Scalia and the Supreme Court's Conservative Moment* (Westport, Conn.: Praeger, 1993); Nancy Maveety, *Justice Sandra Day O'Connor: Strategist on the Supreme Court* (Lanham, Md.: Rowman and Littlefield, 1996), and *Queen's Court* (Lawrence: University Press of Kansas, 2008); Van Sickel, *Not a Particularly Different Voice;* Robert J. Sickles, *John Paul Stevens and the Search for Balance* (State College: Pennsylvania State University Press, 1988); Gerber, *First Principles;* Marcosson, *Original Sin;* Tinsley Yarborough, *David Hackett Souter: Traditional Republican on the Supreme Court* (New York: Oxford University Press, 2005); Rossum, *Antonin Scalia's Jurisprudence.*

[39] Davis, *Justice Rehnquist,* p. vii. For a justification of the division of labor between judicial biography and quantitative behavioral study, see J. Woodford Howard, "Judicial Biography and the Behavioral Persuasion," 65 *American Political Science Review* 704, 714, 706 (1971). See also the reviews of judicial biographies by Robert McCloskey, 77 *Harvard Law Review* 1171, 1172 (1964), and by Walter Murphy, 78 *Yale Law Journal* 725, 728–729 (1969).

[40] Sunstein, *One Case at a Time,* p. 11.

[41] An in-depth study of a justice's prenomination speeches and opinions can provide a more accurate and refined baseline of initial ideology than the attitudinal model's coding of newspaper editorials written about the nominee. See Jeffrey A. Segal and Harold Spaeth, *The Supreme Court and the Attitudinal Model Revisited* (New York: Oxford University Press, 2002), pp. 320–322. Such a methodology has been used before. See the study of Brandeis and Butler conducted by David Danielski, "Values as Variables in Judicial Decision-Making: Notes toward a Theory," 19 *Vanderbilt Law Review* 721 (1966) [cited in Segal and Spaeth, p. 321, n. 37].

[42] For the distinction between judicial biography (a full-life study) and a judicial study (focusing on particular aspects of a justice's tenure seeking "to illuminate the judicial process"), see Richard Posner, "Judicial Biography," 70 *New York University Law Review* 502, 512, 522–523 (1995). See also J. W. Peltason, "Supreme Court Biography and the Study of Public Law," in Gottfried Dietze, ed., *Essays on the American Constitution* (New York: Prentice-Hall, 1964), pp. 217–218; Gerber, *First Principles,* Introduction; Davis, *Justice Rehnquist,* pp. vii–viii. For a classic example of a focused judicial study, see Robert K. Faulkner, *The Jurisprudence of John Marshall* (Princeton, N.J.: Princeton University Press, 1968).

[43] I made no attempt to interview Kennedy, former clerks, or any Court personnel. I follow the prudent advice of Scott Gerber. "It is important to let Justice Thomas's record to speak for itself," Gerber writes, and "interviews are far too vulnerable to manipulation by both the interviewer and subject to be of much use." Gerber, *First Principles,* p. 7. This approach follows Kennedy's own counsel. Testifying before the U.S. House Appropriations subcommittee after Bush v. Gore, he said the Court "will be

judged not by what we say after the fact in order to embellish our opinions or detract from what some of our colleagues say," but "by what we put in our appellate reports. That's the dynamic of the law." "Justices Defend Handling of Florida Election Case," *CNN*, 29 March 2001, http://www.cnn.com/2001/LAW/03/29/scotus.hearing/index .html. Kennedy submitted transcripts of his off-the-bench address to the U.S. Senate Judiciary Committee during his Supreme Court confirmation hearings. I obtained them from the National Archives. I thank Bill Davis at the Archives for his assistance.

[44] I use information acquired from the Thurgood Marshall and Harry A. Blackmun Papers housed at the Manuscript Room of the Library of Congress in Washington, D.C.

[45] As Rogers Smith states: "Interpretive studies can shed light on the inner workings of the beliefs attitudinal models simply count, producing explanations that supplement the predictions those models achieve, and sometimes helping scholars to construct more powerful attitudinal models and to address further questions." Smith, "Symposium: The Supreme Court and the Attitudinal Model," *Law and Courts Newsletter* 7, 9 (Spring 1994). This book thus seeks to "study carefully the role that values . . . have played in the actual judicial decisions that constitute so much of our legal traditions." Rogers Smith, "Political Jurisprudence, The 'New Institutionalism' and the Future of Public Law" 82 *American Political Science Review* 89, 107 (1988).

[46] Anthony M. Kennedy, "Rotary," Sacramento, Rotary Club, February 1984, p. 5.

[47] See Keck, *The Most Activist Court in History*, p. 251.

[48] "Pasadena Dedication," Pasadena California, Special Session of the Judges of the Ninth Circuit, 3 February 1986, p. 8. See also Anthony M. Kennedy, "Federalism: The Theory and Reality," San Francisco, Historical Society for the U.S. District Court for the Northern District of California, 26 October 1987.

[49] Maveety finds that O'Connor engaged in behavioral and jurisprudential accommodationism through strategic voting and careful bargaining over concurring opinions. This book takes a more normative focus. If Kennedy acts strategically, he does so not merely to enhance his personal influence on the Court but to use his position to advance a substantive vision of liberty and conception of judicial power.

CHAPTER ONE. LIBERTY, DIGNITY, AND PERSONALITY

[1] Lee v. Weisman, 505 U.S. 577 (1992).

[2] Lawrence v. Texas, 539 U.S. 558 (2003).

[3] Roper v. Simmons, 125 S. Ct. 1183 (2005).

[4] Roe v. Wade, 410 U.S 113 (1973).

[5] Planned Parenthood of Southeastern Pennsylvania v. Casey, 505 U.S. 833 (1992).

[6] Christopher Smith claims that in *Lee* and *Casey* Kennedy "directly repudiates stated positions from previous cases." Smith, "Supreme Court Surprise: Justice Anthony Kennedy's Move toward Moderation," 45 *Oklahoma Law Review* 459, 475 (1992). See also Lawrence Friedman, "The Limitations of Labeling: Justice Anthony M. Kennedy and the First Amendment," 20 *Ohio Northern Law Review* 225 (1993).

[7] U.S. Senate, "Nomination of Anthony M. Kennedy to Be Associate Justice of the Supreme Court of the United States" 14–16 December 1987, pp. 154, 122. The following citations in the text refer to this testimony.

[8] Although Kennedy testified he had "no fixed view" on abortion, he did state that "it would be highly improper for a judge to allow his, or her, own personal or religious views to enter into a decision respecting a constitutional matter." Nomination, pp. 90–91.

[9] At the time of Kennedy's nomination, Dworkin wrote that Kennedy "appears to accept" a "jurisprudence of principle." Ronald M. Dworkin, "From Bork to Kennedy," *New York Review of Books,* 17 December 1987, p. 42.

[10] In his "Unenumerated Rights" address ("Unenumerated Rights and the Dictates of Judicial Restraint," Palo Alto, California, Canadian Institute for Advanced Legal Studies, 24 July–1 August 1986), Kennedy criticizes Dworkin for attempting "a synthesis between moral principles and the rights and values he finds implicit in the Constitution." Dworkin has fallen victim to "the natural tendency to equate a just regime with the constitutional regime," Kennedy states. Such writings "may be invaluable as critiques of our system," but they are "irrelevant to the judicial authority to reform it under the guise of announcing constitutional rights not justified by the text of the document" (p. 18).

[11] Ronald M. Dworkin, *Taking Rights Seriously* (Cambridge: Harvard University Press, 1977), pp. 134–135. The following citations in the text refer to this work.

[12] Anthony M. Kennedy, "Comments at Ninth Circuit Judicial Conference," Hawaii, 21 August 1987, pp. 6–7.

[13] Ronald M. Dworkin, *Law's Empire* (Cambridge: Harvard University Press, 1986), pp. 229–238.

[14] "Pasadena Dedication," Pasadena, California, Special Session of the Judges of the Ninth Circuit, 3 February 1986, p. 10.

[15] Nomination, p. 17.

[16] Dworkin, *Taking Rights Seriously,* p. 146.

[17] Ibid., p. 185; Dworkin, *Freedom's Law* (Cambridge: Harvard University Press, 1996), Introduction.

[18] Sacramento v. Lewis, 523 U.S. 833, 857 (1998). See also O'Connor's concurring opinion in Michael H. v. Gerald D. 491 U.S. 110, 132 (1989), which Kennedy joined.

[19] Randy E. Barnett, *Restoring the Lost Constitution: The Presumption of Liberty* (Princeton, N.J.: Princeton University Press, 2004). The following citations in the text refer to this book.

[20] "Patent Lawyers," Los Angeles, Patent Lawyers Association, February 1982, p. 9.

[21] Dronenburg v. Zech, 741 F.2d. 1388, 1397–1398 (1984, D.C. Cir.).

[22] Beller v. Middendorf, 632 F.2d. 788 (1980, 9th Cir.). The following citations in the text refer to this case.

[23] See his votes to uphold displays of the Ten Commandments on government grounds in Van Orden v. Perry, 545 U.S. 677 (2005), and McCreary County v. ACLU, 545 U.S. 844 (2005). Kennedy has also supported government funding of religious

groups under neutral government programs. See his opinions in Bowen v. Kendrick, 487 U.S. 589 (1988), and Rosenberger v. Virginia, 515 U.S. 819 (1995), and his vote in Zelman v. Simmons-Harris, 536 U.S. 639 (2002).

[24] Kennedy had little occasion to engage the problems of religion on the Ninth Circuit. The clauses "sometimes point in different directions," he testified, and Supreme Court precedents "are difficult to reconcile." Nomination, pp. 133–134.

[25] Allegheny County v. Greater Pittsburgh ACLU, 492 U.S. 573 (1989). The following citations in the text refer to this case. Blackmun's conference notes indicate that Kennedy, like Scalia, "vacillated." Kennedy believed the display "demeaned by putting the creche in the statehouse," yet did not want to "draw the line at carols." Kennedy found that the Court was "caught in our own rhetoric," and he sought a way out. Blackmun Papers, Box 528, Folder 2.

[26] Westside Community Board of Education v. Mergens, 496 U.S. 226 (1990). The following citations in the text refer to this case.

[27] Blackmun Papers, Box 586, Folder 7.

[28] Blackmun Papers, Box 586, Folder 6.

[29] Blackmun Papers, Box 586, Folder 9. Kennedy says in the initial letter that the barbs were over Lynch v. Donnelly, 465 U.S. 668 (1984), decided four years before he came to the Court. Kennedy corrected himself in a handwritten note sent later that day.

[30] Lee v. Weisman, 505 U.S. 577 (1992). The following citations in the text refer to this case.

[31] Michael Paulsen agrees with Kennedy's articulation of the coercion principle but criticizes his reliance on indirect coercion and peer pressure as a conflation of private and state action. Paulsen, "*Lemon* Is Dead," 43 *Case Western Law Review* 795 (1993).

[32] Scalia likely alludes to Kennedy's vote shift. The meaning of the Constitution, he states, "cannot possibly rest upon the changeable philosophic predilections of the Justices of this Court" (*Lee* at 632).

[33] The Court rejected such a challenge in Elk Grove Unified School District v. Newdow, 542 U.S. 1 (2004), on grounds of prudential standing. Scalia recused himself from the case after making public statements rejecting Newdow's arguments.

[34] See also Kennedy's vote in Good News Club v. Milford, 533 U.S. 98 (2001).

[35] Bowers v. Hardwick, 478 U.S. 186 (1986).

[36] Kennedy, "Unenumerated Rights," The following page citations in the text refer to this address. Regarding *Lawrence,* Thomas Keck writes, "There is no evidence to suggest it can be explained solely as a result of O'Connor's and Kennedy's preexisting political preferences." Keck, *The Most Activist Court in History: The Road to Modern Judicial Conservatism* (Chicago: University of Chicago Press, 2004), p. 272. Kennedy's 1986 speech presents evidence to the contrary.

[37] For an initial version of the argument, see Frank J. Colucci, "From Privacy to Liberty: Justice Kennedy's Interpretive Turn in *Lawrence v. Texas,*" paper delivered at Meetings of the New England Political Science Association, 2004.

[38] Dudgeon v. United Kingdom, 4 ECHR 149 (1981).

[39] Article 8(1): "Everyone has the right to respect for his private and family life, his home and his correspondence."

[40] Nomination, p. 121.

[41] Mèyer v. Nebraska, 262 U.S. 390 (1923).

[42] Pierce v. Society of Sisters, 268 U.S. 510 (1925).

[43] In Troxel v. Granville, 530 U.S. 57 (2000), Kennedy later stated, "*Pierce* and *Meyer*, had they been decided in recent times, may well have been grounded upon First Amendment principles protecting freedom of speech, belief, and religion." Yet "their formulation and subsequent interpretation have been quite different, of course; and they long have been interpreted to have found in Fourteenth Amendment concepts of liberty an independent right of the parent in the 'custody, care and nurture of the child,' free from state intervention" (95).

[44] Kennedy generally seeks to recast constitutional issues of equality into questions implicating individual liberty. I discuss this tendency in my discussion of *Lawrence* below and in the cases mentioned in Chapter 4.

[45] Griswold v. Connecticut, 381 U.S. 479 (1965).

[46] Nomination, pp. 164, 166.

[47] See Randy Barnett, "Justice Kennedy's Libertarian Revolution: *Lawrence v. Texas*," 2003 *Cato Supreme Court Review* 21 (2003).

[48] Kennedy, "Unenumerated Rights," p. 22.

[49] See Scalia's statement in *Casey* that "as long as this Court thought (and the people thought) that we Justices were doing essentially lawyer's work here—reading text and discerning our society's traditional understanding of that text—the public pretty much left us alone. Texts and traditions are facts to study, not convictions to demonstrate about." In contrast, "value judgments . . . should be voted on, not dictated." *Casey* at 1000, 1001.

[50] *Lawrence* at 578. The following citations in the text refer to this case.

[51] Compare this with the plurality opinion in *Casey*, which begins "liberty finds no refuge in a jurisprudence of doubt" (844) and ends "We invoke it [judicial responsibility] once again to define the freedom guaranteed by the Constitution's own promise, the promise of liberty" (901).

[52] Blackmun wrote in *Bowers* that the line of precedents under the right to privacy "has proceeded along two somewhat distinct, albeit complementary, lines. First, it has recognized a privacy interest with reference to certain decisions that are properly for the individual to make. Second, it has recognized a privacy interest with reference to certain places without regard for the particular activities in which the individuals who occupy them are engaged. The case before us implicates both the decisional and the spatial aspects of the right to privacy" (203–204).

[53] Kennedy is the justice most likely to strike government action on grounds of freedom of speech and association. See Chapter 3.

[54] For further investigation of this question, see Vincent Stark, "Public Morality as

Police Power after *Lawrence v. Texas* and *Gonzales v. Carhart*," 10 *Georgetown Journal of Gender and the Law* 165 (2009).

[55] Roe v. Wade, 410 U.S. 113 (1973).

[56] *Casey* at 833; Romer v. Evans, 517 U.S. 620 (1996). I discuss *Romer* in Chapter 4.

[57] PG & JH v. United Kingdom, App. No. 00044787/98 56 (2001); Modinos v. Cyprus, 259 ECHR (1993); Norris v. Ireland, 142 ECHR (1988).

[58] Nomination, p. 153.

[59] *Lawrence* at 578. The following citations in the text refer to this case.

[60] Lochner v. New York, 198 U.S. 45 (1905).

[61] In contrast, Clarence Thomas's short dissent connects the *Lawrence* majority to *Griswold*. Despite his personal opposition to Texas's law, Thomas finds himself "not empowered" to overturn it. He agrees with Justice Potter Stewart's dissent in *Griswold* that he cannot find in the Constitution a "general right of privacy"—"or, as the Court terms it today, the 'liberty of the person both in its spatial and more transcendent dimensions.'" *Lawrence* at 605. To Thomas, Kennedy's liberty-based arguments are in substance no different from the privacy-based argument of *Griswold*.

[62] Internal quote is from Justice Thomas's opinion denying of certiorari in Foster v. Florida, 537 U.S. 990 (2002), 991 fn.* *Foster* challenged whether serving more than twenty years on death row constituted cruel and unusual punishment. In his dissent from the denial of cert., Justice Stephen G. Breyer had cited decisions from several other nations, including Zimbabwe.

[63] Scalia expanded this criticism in a 2005 debate with Breyer at American University. *Lawrence*, he stated, cited European law enacted "not by some democratic ballot but by decree." Further, the Court "did not cite the rest of the world" or countries maintaining criminal prohibitions. U.S. Association of Constitutional Law Discussion, "Constitutional Relevance of Foreign Court Decisions," Washington, D.C., American University, Washington College of Law, 13 January 2005. Transcript available at http://domino.american.edu/AU/media/mediarel.nsf/1D265343BDC2189785256B 810071F238/1F2F7DC4757FD01E85256F890068E6E0?OpenDocument.

[64] See William N. Eskridge, Jr., "United States: *Lawrence v. Texas* and the Imperative of Comparative Constitutionalism," 4 *International Journal of Constitutional Law* 555 (2004).

[65] Stanford v. Kentucky, 492 U.S. 361 (1989).

[66] For an earlier version of the argument in this section, see Frank J. Colucci, "Justice Anthony Kennedy's Comparative Constitutionalism," paper delivered at the Meetings of the Canadian Political Science Association (2005).

[67] Roper v. Simmons, 543 U.S. 551, 125 S. Ct. 1183, 1192 (2005). The following citations in the text refer to this case.

[68] Trop v. Dulles, 356 U.S. 86 (1958).

[69] Controversy arose after Kennedy v. Louisiana, 128 S.Ct. 2641, 2008 U.S. LEXIS 5262 (2008), where Kennedy's survey of political consensus failed to acknowledge recent congressional amendments to the Uniform Code of Military Justice allowing for

the death penalty in cases of child rape. I contend that such "objective indicia" merely provide referents for Kennedy's pre-existing ideal of human dignity. I consider the opinion in *Kennedy* and its aftermath in the conclusion.

[70] See his "Federalism: The Theory and the Reality" address, Sacramento, Historical Society for the United States District Court for the Northern District of California, 17 September 1987, discussed in Chapter 5.

[71] Two months before the decision in *Roper,* Scalia debated Justice Breyer at American University Law School about the appropriate use of comparative law. Scalia's comments in that debate were likely influenced by the opinion-writing process in *Roper.*

[72] Kennedy's Supreme Court Historical Society biography describes him as "a devout adherent to the Roman Catholic faith in which he was raised" (http://www .supremecourthistory.org/justice/kennedy.htm). Kennedy was born in 1936, which means that he would have been old enough at the time of Vatican II to be aware of the changes taking place in the church in general and of *Dignitatis Humanae* in particular.

[73] The pronouncement was given on 7 December 1965. For an English translation, see http://www.vatican.va/archive/hist_councils/ii_vatican_council/documents/vat-ii _decl_19651207_dignitatis-humanae_en.html. The following citations in the text refer to this encyclical.

[74] I offer no deterministic argument. Scalia was born in the same year as Kennedy and is also a devout Catholic. To compare Scalia's interpretation of the relation of Catholicism and constitutional law, see the transcript of his 1996 lecture and question-and-answer session at the Vatican, reprinted in Scalia, "Of Democracy, Morality and the Majority," 22 *Origins* 79 (1996), and his participation in "Religion, Politics and the Death Penalty," on 25 January 2002, University of Chicago. The transcript is available at http://pewforum.org/deathpenalty/resources/transcript3.php3. For an earlier study of religious influence on Scalia, see George Kannar, "The Constitutional Catechism of Antonin Scalia," 99 *Yale Law Journal* 1297 (1990).

[75] Kennedy's more recent opinion in Kennedy v. Louisiana includes more misgivings about the death penalty.

[76] Catechism of the Catholic Church, 2269.

[77] *Roper* at 1196.

[78] See *Persona Humanae (Declaration on Certain Questions concerning Sexual Ethics),* 29 December 1975, 8.3–8.4. English translation available at http://www.vatican .va/roman_curia/congregations/cfaith/documents/rc_con_cfaith_doc_19751229 _persona-humana_en.html.

[79] "Letter to the Bishops of the Catholic Church on the Pastoral Care of Homosexual Persons," 1 October 1986. English translation available at http://www.vatican.va/ roman_curia/congregations/cfaith/documents/rc_con_cfaith_doc_19861001 _homosexual-persons_en.html. The following citations in the text refer to this encyclical.

[80] *Lawrence* at 567, 578.

[81] *Casey* at 983–984, 1000–1001.

[82] Kennedy's use of comparative materials inspired a backlash in Congress, where members of the House and Senate introduced resolutions condemning the use of foreign law by American courts. One House resolution (H.R. 97) was introduced in February 2005, before *Roper* was decided. The resolution specifically mentioned the decision in *Lawrence* and had fifty-four cosponsors. One Senate resolution, S. Res. 92, was introduced on 20 March 2005—less than three weeks after *Roper* was decided. It cited the Court's decisions in *Lawrence* and *Roper*. Neither resolution was moved in committee.

[83] Scalia has not been alone in criticizing Kennedy's habit of citing these nonconventional sources. Pragmatist Richard Posner suggests that use of foreign law is merely "one more form of judicial fig-leafing" that "is probably best understood as an effort, whether or not conscious, to further mystify the adjudicative process and disguise the political decisions that are the core, though not the entirety, of the Supreme Court's output." Richard Posner, "No Thanks, We Already Have Our Own Laws," *Legal Affairs*, August 2004, http://www.legalaffairs.org/issues/July-August-2004/feature_posner_julaug04.msp.

[84] For his classic statement, see Antonin Scalia, "Originalism: The Lesser Evil," 57 *University of Cincinnati Law Review* 849, 863 (1989).

CHAPTER TWO. STILL STRUGGLING:
ANTHONY KENNEDY AND ABORTION

[1] Gonzales v. Carhart, 127 S. Ct. 1610 (2007).

[2] *Gonzales* at 1649.

[3] For a selection of criticism, see Charles Fried, "Supreme Confusion," *New York Times*, 26 April 2007, p. A25; Dahlia Lithwick, "Father Knows Best: Dr. Kennedy's Magic Prescription for Indecisive Women," *Slate*, 18 April 2007 (online at http://www.slate.com/id/2164512/); Ruth Marcus, "Court Knows Best," *Washington Post*, 25 April 2007, p. A17; Garrett Epps and Dahlia Lithwick, "The Sphinx of Sacramento: Will the Real Anthony Kennedy Please Stand Up?" *Slate*, 27 April 2007 (online at http://www.slate.com/id/2165133/). David J. Garrow called Kennedy's opinion "patronizing" and the rhetoric "pure 'Preacher Tony.'" Garrow, "Don't Assume the Worst," *New York Times*, 21 April 2007, p. A15; quoted in Tony Mauro, "Kennedy Reshapes Abortion Conflict as He Refines 'Swing Vote' Role," *Legal Times*, 23 April 2007 (online at http://www.law.com/jsp/article.jsp?id=1177059874125).

[4] Jeffrey Rosen, "Supreme Leader: The Arrogance of Anthony Kennedy," *New Republic* 18 June 2007, p. 18.

[5] Helen J. Knowles, "Clerkish Control of *Carhart*?" Paper presented at the Meetings of the Midwest Political Science Association, 4 April 2008, p. 1.

[6] Geoffrey R. Stone raised the "painfully awkward observation" that "all five justices in the majority in *Gonzales* are Catholic." Stone, "Our Faith-Based Justices," 20 April 2007 (online at http://uchicagolaw.typepad.com/faculty/2007/04/our_faithbased

_.html). When asked about this statement, Stone said he "meant it to be provocative." Quoted in Robert Barnes, "Did Justices' Catholicism Play Part in Abortion Ruling?" *Washington Post*, 30 April 2007, p. A13.

[7] *Gonzales* at 1650. After Stenberg v. Carhart, Laurence Tribe called Kennedy's vote in *Casey* an "optical illusion." Quoted in Joan Biskupic, "Abortion Debate Will Continue to Rage," *USA Today*, 29 June 2000, p. 9A.

[8] Roe v. Wade, 410 U.S. 113 (1973).

[9] Planned Parenthood of Southeastern Pennsylvania v. Casey, 505 U.S. 833 (1992).

[10] See Ginsburg's statement that *Casey* "described more precisely than did *Roe* the impact of abortion restrictions on a woman's liberty." *Gonzales* at 1641, fn. 2.

[11] David A. Strauss wrote that "more than any previous decision . . . *Casey* placed the constitutional right to abortion on a coherent and plausible theoretical basis." Strauss, "Abortion, Toleration and Moral Uncertainty," 1992 *Supreme Court Review* 1 (1993). See also the quotes of Lawrence Tribe and Ronald Dworkin, quoted in David J. Garrow, *Liberty and Sexuality* (Berkeley: University of California, 1994), p. 701. Garrow states in his epilogue that *Casey* "guaranteed that the legacy . . . of *Roe v. Wade* would be enshrined beside *Brown* for all time in America's constitutional pantheon" (705). Stating "what *Roe v. Wade* should have said" in 2005, Jack Balkin uses reasoning and language similar to that of *Casey*. Balkin, "Judgment for the Court," in Balkin, ed., *What* Roe v. Wade *Should Have Said* (New York: New York University, 2005), pp. 31, 35–42. Garrow describes Balkin's effort as "Kennedyesque (Anthony, not John F.)" and "indisputably superior to what the real Justices rendered in 1973." Garrow, "*Roe v. Wade* Revisited," 9 *Green Bag* 2d 71, 72 (2005).

[12] Epps and Lithwick state that Kennedy's "paternalistic rationale was never mentioned in the *Stenberg* dissent." As I show below, such sentiments are evident in opinions he wrote prior to *Stenberg* and in his *Hill* dissent delivered on the same day as *Stenberg*.

[13] Webster v. Reproductive Health Services, 492 U.S. 490 (1989).

[14] Hodgson v. Minnesota, 497 U.S. 417 (1990).

[15] Ohio v. Akron Center for Reproductive Health, 497 U.S. 502 (1990).

[16] Stenberg v. Carhart 530 U.S. 914 (2000).

[17] Hill v. Colorado, 530 U.S. 703 (2000).

[18] *Hill* at 791.

[19] *Casey* at 850; Lawrence v. Texas, 539 U.S. 558, 571 (2003). Ginsburg quotes this passage in her *Gonzales* dissent at 1647. Stone concludes that "it is disconcerting that Roberts, Alito, Antonin Scalia, Anthony Kennedy and Clarence Thomas might not have honored this precept in *Gonzales*." Stone, "Our Faith-Based Justices," *Chicago Tribune*, 30 April 2007, sec. 1, p. 19. None of the other justices Stone names has ever agreed to this statement; Alito and Roberts were not on the Court when it decided *Casey* and *Lawrence*, while Scalia and Thomas explicitly rejected it in both cases. See *Casey* at 979 (dissent of Scalia, which Thomas joined); *Lawrence* at 588 (dissent of Scalia, which Thomas joined), *Lawrence* at 606 (dissent of Thomas). Stone's charge should be directed at Kennedy. For a deeper investigation of the tension between

Kennedy's decisions in these cases, see Vincent Stark, "Public Morality as a Police Power after *Lawrence v. Texas* and *Gonzales v. Carhart,*" 10 *Georgetown Journal of Gender and the Law* 165 (2009).

[20] Ohio v. Akron Center for Reproductive Health, 497 U.S. 502 (1990).

[21] According to the framework established in Roe, the following regulations of abortion are constitutionally permissible: "(a) For the stage prior to approximately the end of the first trimester, the abortion decision and its effectuation must be left to the medical judgment of the pregnant woman's attending physician. (b) For the stage subsequent to approximately the end of the first trimester, the State, in promoting its interest in the health of the mother, may, if it chooses, regulate the abortion procedure in ways that are reasonably related to maternal health. (c) For the stage subsequent to viability, the State in promoting its interest in the potentiality of human life may, if it chooses, regulate, and even proscribe, abortion except where it is necessary, in appropriate medical judgment, for the preservation of the life or health of the mother." *Roe* at 164–165.

[22] Colautti v. Franklin, 439 U.S. 379 (1979). *Colautti* involved a Pennsylvania law requiring doctors—when aborting a viable fetus—to exercise the same care to preserve the fetus's life and health as would be required in the case of a fetus intended to be born alive. Blackmun wrote for a majority striking the law for vagueness.

[23] Harry A. Blackmun Papers, Manuscript Division, Library of Congress, Washington, D.C., Box 536, Folder 7.

[24] According to Blackmun's notes, Kennedy would "use DP, not fundamental rights or [Roman symbol of Venus, representing women and equal protection]" to uphold *Roe*. O'Connor said she would "adhere to what I have written. No reject *Griswold* and *Eisenstadt*. This go no further." Blackmun Papers, Box 536, Folder 7.

[25] *Webster* at 517; see also Marshall Papers, Box 480, Folder 3.

[26] Blackmun Papers, Box 536, Folder 4 (Rehnquist draft, p. 23).

[27] *Webster* at 517. The following citations in the text refer to this opinion.

[28] *Webster* at 521; see also Blackmun Papers, Box 480, Folder 4.

[29] Commentators on both sides believed that Kennedy was merely waiting for the right case to overturn *Roe*. See Susan Estrich and Kathleen Sullivan, "Abortion Politics: Writing for an Audience of One," 138 *University of Pennsylvania Law Review* 119, 121 (1989); James Bopp and Richard E. Coleson, "What Does *Webster* Mean?" 138 *University of Pennsylvania Law Review* 157 (1989); Robert Post, "*Webster*'s Chaotic Aftermath," *Washington Post*, 6 July 1989, Part 2, p. 7.

[30] Farber cited the "liberty interest" and "Dark Ages" passages mentioned above and properly concluded that "*Webster* is actually notable as much for the Court's caution and indecision as for anything else." Daniel A. Farber, "Abortion after *Webster*," 6 *Constitutional Commentary* 225, 229 (1989). To Farber, the plurality-opinion justices "seemed surprisingly gingerly in their handling of the issue," and, "in short, it seems, Rehnquist recognized some sort of constitutional right to abortion" (227). Farber's conclusion seems prophetic if one attributes these statements to Kennedy's influence.

[31] Hodgson v. Minnesota, 497 U.S. 417 (1990).

[32] Ohio v. Akron Center for Reproductive Health, 497 U.S. 502 (1990).

[33] Bellotti v. Baird, 443 U.S. 622, 640 (1979).

[34] *Hodgson* at 480. The following citations in the text refer to this opinion.

[35] According to Blackmun's conference notes, Kennedy upheld requirements that minors obtain parental notice or consent as "consistent with tradition and custom." Blackmun Papers, Box 544, Folder 2.

[36] *Akron Center* at 519–520. The following citations in the text refer to this opinion.

[37] Blackmun Papers, Box 544, Folder 2 (letter from O'Connor to Kennedy dated 19 March 1990).

[38] Nancy Maveety, *Justice Sandra Day O'Connor: Strategist on the Supreme Court* (Lanham, Md.: Rowman and Littlefield, 1993), pp. 4–5, 128. O'Connor's efforts to shape *Webster* are discussed by Maveety on pp. 97–100. O'Connor would continue this strategy in *Stenberg* by writing a concurring opinion emphasizing that laws banning specific abortion procedures must be written narrowly and include a health exception (947).

[39] *Akron Center* at 541. The following citations in the text refer to this opinion.

[40] Blackmun Papers, Box 544, Folder 3 (draft, p. 17).

[41] Blackmun Papers, Box 544, Folder 2 (letter of 21 June 1990). See the Appendix for a complete transcription of this note, where Kennedy mentions Laurence Tribe, *Abortion: A Clash of Absolutes* (New York: W. W. Norton, 1990), published months before. "Though I have not read it," Kennedy writes, he believes Tribe's book "makes the same point, though perhaps at greater length." Michael Dorf—a student of Tribe's— would serve as Kennedy's clerk during the 1991–1992 term when the Court decided *Casey*. See Laurence Tribe and Michael Dorf, *On Reading the Constitution* (Cambridge: Harvard University Press, 1991).

[42] Blackmun Papers, Box 544, Folder 2 (letter of 21 June 1990).

[43] Kennedy note and Blackmun response in Blackmun Papers, Box 544, Folder 2 (letter of 21 June 1990). Blackmun's change is found in *Akron Center* at 541.

[44] Planned Parenthood of Southeastern Pennsylvania v. Casey, 947 F.2d. 682 (1991). Samuel Alito, then a judge on the Second Circuit, voted to uphold the entire statute, including the spousal notification requirement, as consistent with O'Connor's "undue burden" test. *Casey* at 719–727 (Alito concurring and dissenting).

[45] Blackmun Papers, Box 601, Folder 4. Akron v. Akron Center for Reproductive Health, 462 U.S. 416 (1983); Thornburgh v. American College of Obstetricians, 476 U.S. 747 (1986).

[46] Blackmun Papers, Box 602, Folder 1.

[47] Blackmun Papers, Box 602, Folder 5. See Rehnquist draft, pp. 10, 12.

[48] Blackmun Papers, Box 601, Folder 6.

[49] Blackmun Papers, Box 601, Folder 6. Blackmun's note on this meeting is marked 3-30-92, although it is attached to Kennedy's 29 May note requesting the meeting. The date likely should be 5-30-92. See the Appendix for a full transcription of this note.

[50] *Casey* at 849, citing Poe v. Ullman, 367 U.S. 497, 543 (1961) (Harlan, J., dissenting from dismissal on jurisdictional grounds). The larger discussion of Harlan in *Casey* occurs at 848–850.

⁵¹ Blackmun Papers, Box 601, Folder 6. On 17 January 1992, Blackmun prepared a draft dissenting order from an apparent decision to relist the cases for the following Term. "The obvious reason for this is the political repercussions of a decision by this Court in the midst of an election year," Blackmun writes. "I feel that this Court stands less than tall when it defers decision for political reasons." The agenda for the 17 January conference shows that Souter had requested that the case be relisted. He also requested the parties to address the value of stare decisis that should be accorded to *Roe*. At that conference the Court decided to schedule oral argument in *Casey* for April 1992. Blackmun Papers, Box 602, Folder 4–5.

⁵² *Casey* at 923.

⁵³ Blackmun Papers, Box 601, Folder 4 (Kennedy draft, p. 12).

⁵⁴ Ibid.

⁵⁵ "Although I am conscious of the reasons why you have included criticism of the trimester approach early in the opinion," Stevens wrote, "I would like to suggest that the entire opinion would be immeasurably strengthened by placing that discussion in a later section, thereby making it possible for Harry and me to join Parts I and II, and (if you will consider a couple of relatively minor suggestions) Part III as well." Blackmun Papers, Box 601, Folder 6 (18 June 1992 note from Stevens to Kennedy).

⁵⁶ Blackmun Papers, Box 601, Folder 4 (Kennedy first draft, p. 4).

⁵⁷ Ibid., p. 9.

⁵⁸ Ibid., p. 4. For changes in the final opinion, see *Casey* at 883, 885, 887.

⁵⁹ *Casey* at 851, 844, 901, 846. Some commentators noted *Casey*'s shift from privacy to liberty but offered no explanation consistent with the plurality's vote to uphold most of the Pennsylvania statute. See Erin Daly, "Reconsidering Abortion Law: Liberty, Equality and the New Rhetoric of *Planned Parenthood v. Casey*," 45 *American University Law Review* 77 (1995). For a more recent and comprehensive analysis of this change, see Helen J. Knowles, "From a Value to a Right: The Supreme Court's Oh-So-Conscious Move from 'Privacy' to 'Liberty,'" 33 *Ohio Northern Law Review* (2007).

⁶⁰ Blackmun Papers, Box 601, Folder 3. This second draft was circulated around 22 June 1992.

⁶¹ *Casey* at 851.

⁶² *Casey* at 851.

⁶³ I explore Kennedy's free-speech jurisprudence in Chapter 3.

⁶⁴ Turner Broadcasting System v. FCC, 512 U.S. 622 (1994) at 641.

⁶⁵ *Casey* at 850.

⁶⁶ Ibid.

⁶⁷ Kennedy's approach in *Casey* is consistent with the larger ideal of "freedom of the mind" later articulated in Charles Fried, *Saying What the Law Is* (Cambridge: Harvard University Press, 2004), pp. 170–171, 193–200, and with the "hermeneutic Socratism" described in Michael P. Zuckert, "*Casey* at the Bat: Taking Another Swing at *Planned Parenthood v. Casey*," in Christopher Wolfe, ed., *That Eminent Tribunal: Judicial Supremacy and the Constitution* (Princeton, N.J.: Princeton University Press, 2004), pp. 37–58.

[68] *Casey* at 850. The following citations in the text refer to this case.

[69] Strauss, "Abortion, Toleration and Uncertainty," p. 26.

[70] Gerard V. Bradley, "Shall We Ratify the New Constitution? The Judicial Manifesto in *Casey* and *Lee*," *Benchmarks* (1995), pp. 117, 120.

[71] Strauss finds that allowing states to attempt to persuade women not to have abortions is inconsistent with a commitment to tolerance (p. 26).

[72] Bradwell v. Illinois, 16 Wall. 130 (1873).

[73] Hoyt v. Florida, 368 U.S. 57, 62 (1961).

[74] Strauss, "Abortion, Toleration and Uncertainty," pp. 18–27; Zuckert, "*Casey* at the Bat," pp. 52–53.

[75] Terry Carter, "Crossing the Rubicon: Anthony Kennedy Couldn't Have Picked a More Dramatic Moment to Declare His Independence on the Court," 12 *California Lawyer*, October 1992, p. 39.

[76] Lee v. Weisman, 505 U.S. 577 (1992). I discuss this case in Chapter 1.

[77] The opinion mentions how Kennedy and O'Connor disagreed in *Hodgson*, although they claimed to apply the same standard. In *Akron Center*, they agreed on the conclusion but not on the standard.

[78] *Stenberg* at 957. The following citations in the text refer to this case.

[79] *Stenberg* at 957, 958, 959 (three times), 960 (two times), 964, 965, 968, 974, 975, 976.

[80] *Stenberg* at 946–947 (concurring opinion of Stevens), 951–952 (concurring opinion of Ginsburg).

[81] Prior to *Hill*, Kennedy had voted to uphold the claims of abortion protesters in several cases after *Casey*. See Williams and Citizens for Life v. Planned Parenthood Shasta-Diablo, 520 U.S. 1133 (1997), cert. denied (joined Scalia's dissent); Schenck v. Pro-Choice Network of Western New York, 519 .S. 257 (1997) (joining Scalia's opinion concurring in part and dissenting in part); and Madsen v. Women's Health Center, 512 U.S. 753 (1994) (joining Scalia's opinion concurring in part and dissenting in part). See also Bray v. Alexandria Women's Health Clinic, 506 U.S. 263 (1993), where he joined Scalia's opinion for the Court and wrote a short concurring opinion that did not directly address the abortion issue.

[82] Linda Greenhouse, "The Nebraska Case: Court Rules that Governments Can't Outlaw Type of Abortion," *New York Times*, 29 June 2000, p. A1. The article focuses primarily on *Stenberg*. Greenhouse reports that in *Hill* "Justice Scalia and Justice Kennedy read their impassioned dissents in the courtroom this morning for more than half an hour, making clear that this First Amendment debate was in many respects a proxy for the Court's ongoing abortion debate." For audio of Kennedy reading his *Hill* dissent, go to http://www.oyez.org/cases/1990–1999/1999/1999_98_1856/opinion/. Kennedy's reading begins at about the twenty-one-minute mark.

[83] *Hill* at 765.

[84] See Epps and Lithwick, "Sphinx."

[85] *Hill* at 767. The following citations in the text refer to this case.

[86] This desire to enhance dialogue is another recurring theme in Kennedy's overall jurisprudence. See Helen J. Knowles, *A Dialogue on Liberty: The Classical Liberal and Educational Principles of Justice Kennedy's Vision of Judicial Power* (Ph.D. dissertation, Boston University, 2007).

[87] *Hill* at 792.

[88] As Scalia wrote in *Madsen*, "Today the ad hoc nullification machine claims its latest, greatest, and most surprising victim: the First Amendment" (785). The phrase was first used by O'Connor in *Thornburgh* at 814. Kennedy joined Scalia in *Madsen*.

[89] *Hill* at 792.

[90] *Gonzales* at 1619.

[91] In *Gonzales*, Scalia—joined by Thomas—wrote a concurrence stating that the majority "accurately applies current jurisprudence," including *Casey*, but that jurisprudence "has no basis in the Constitution" (1639–1640). Scalia also wrote that "whether the Act constitutes a permissible exercise of Congress' power under the Commerce Clause is not before the Court" (1640). Both had written in *Stenberg* to express the view that *Casey* should be overruled. See *Stenberg* at 956 (dissent by Scalia), *Stenberg* at 982 (dissent by Thomas). Roberts and Alito did not join Scalia and Thomas.

[92] *Gonzales* at 1626. The following citations in the text refer to this case.

[93] In Doe v. Bolton, 410 U.S. 179 (1973), the Supreme Court stated that giving the "attending physician the room he needs to make his best medical judgment . . . operates for the benefit, not the disadvantage, of the pregnant woman (192).

[94] Compare to his suggestions in Grutter v. Bollinger, 539 U.S. 306 (2003) and Parents Involved in Community Schools v. Seattle School District No. 1, 127 S.Ct. 2738 (2007) that striking affirmative policies that classify students by race will inspire development of more race-neutral means of achieving the compelling interest in educational diversity. I discuss Kennedy's affirmative action jurisprudence in Chapter 4.

[95] In Ayotte v. Planned Parenthood, 546 U.S. 320 (2006), the Court stated that "invalidating the statute entirely is not always necessary or justified." "We prefer," wrote Justice O'Connor, "to enjoin only the unconstitutional applications of a statute while leaving other applications in force, for lower courts may be able to render narrower declaratory and injunctive relief." O'Connor drew a distinction with *Stenberg*, stating that "the parties in *Stenberg* did not ask for, and we did not contemplate, relief more finely drawn" (327, 328–329, 330). This was O'Connor's final opinion on the Court.

[96] Ruth Bader Ginsburg, "Some Thoughts on Autonomy and Equality in Relation to *Roe v. Wade*," 63 *North Carolina Law Review* 375 (1985). See also Blackmun's concurrence in *Casey* at 928–929.

[97] Compare Ginsburg's criticism of *Casey*'s broad definition of liberty with Thomas's dissent in *Lawrence*. Thomas "'can find [neither in the Bill of Rights nor any other part of the Constitution a] general right of privacy,' or as the Court terms it today, the 'liberty of the person both in its spatial and more transcendent dimensions.'" *Lawrence* at 606, citing Stewart's dissent in *Griswold* at 530.

[98] Emphasis in original.

[99] Muller v. Oregon, 208 U.S. 412 (1908).

[100] *Webster* at 547, fn. 7.

[101] Knowles, "Clerkish Control?" p. 5.

[102] Kennedy has changed his public position on other issues. In Stanford v. Kentucky, 492 U.S. 361 (1989), Kennedy joined Scalia's opinion upholding the constitutionality of death sentences for those who committed capital crimes when aged sixteen or seventeen. Kennedy changed his view sixteen years later in Roper v. Simmons, 543 U.S. 551 (2005). More generally, however, Kennedy has been one of the most ideologically consistent justices on the current Court. See Lee Epstein et al., "Ideological Drift among Supreme Court Justices: Who, When and How Important," 101 *Northwestern Law Review* 1483, 1507 (2007).

[103] *Mulieris Dignitatem*, 15 August 1988. An English translation is available at http://www.vatican.va/holy_father/john_paul_ii/apost_letters/documents/hf_jp-ii _apl_15081988_mulieris-dignitatem_en.html. The following citations in the text refer to this document.

[104] *Evangelium Vitae* (*On the Value and Inviolability of Human Life*), 25 March 1995. An English translation is available at http://www.vatican.va/holy_father/john_paul_ii/ encyclicals/documents/hf_jp-ii_enc_25031995_evangelium-vitae_en.html. The following citations in the text refer to this document.

[105] Recent developments may force Kennedy to reapply this balance and clarify the extent to which government as moral instructor can legislate to promote profound respect for fetal life. After *Gonzales,* a federal appeals court struck Michigan's partial-birth abortion law. *Northland Family Planning Clinic v. Cox,* 2007 U.S. App. Lexis 12846 (6th Cir), decided 4 June 2007. Kennedy's opinion in *Gonzales* invites applied challenges to the federal ban in discrete cases (1639). Other states have recently passed regulations of abortion that may soon come to the Court. Mississippi requires that a sonogram or audio of fetal heartbeat be offered to women considering abortion. Section 3 of S.B. 2391 (codified as Section 41-41-34, Mississippi Code of 1972). South Dakota requires that women undergoing abortions be informed by their physicians "that the abortion will terminate the life of a whole, separate, unique, living human being; that the pregnant woman has an existing relationship with the unborn human being, and that the relationship enjoys protection under the United States Constitution and under the laws of South Dakota." In addition, doctors are required to give "a description of all known medical risks of the procedure and statistically significant risk factors to which the pregnant woman would be subjected, including: (i) depression and related psychological distress; (ii) increased risk of suicide ideation and suicide." In Planned Parenthood v. Rounds (filed 27 June 2008), the Eighth Circuit by a 7–4 vote upheld South Dakota's requirements and lifted a preliminary judgment against enforcement. Kennedy's record and rhetoric indicate that he would join the other justices in the *Gonzales* majority and uphold the Mississippi and South Dakota laws as "self-evident," facilitating free and informed choice and state promotion of respect for fetal life.

[106] *Casey* at 852.

CHAPTER THREE. KENNEDY'S EXPANSIVE
CONCEPTION OF FREE SPEECH

[1] Eugene Volokh, "How the Justices Voted in Free Speech Cases, 1994–2000," 48 *UCLA Law Review* 1191 (2001), updated at http://www1.1aw.ucla.edu/~volokh/how voted.htm; Thomas M. Keck, "Party, Policy or Duty: Why Does the Supreme Court Invalidate Federal Statutes," 101 *American Political Science Review* 321, 333 (2007).

[2] Cass Sunstein, *One Case at a Time* (Cambridge: Harvard University Press, 1999), p. 58. Sunstein focuses on the *Denver Area* case discussed below.

[3] Lawrence Friedman, "The Limitations of Labeling: Justice Anthony M. Kennedy and the First Amendment," 20 *Ohio Northern Law Review* 225 (1993); Patrick Schmidt and David Yalof, "The 'Swing Voter' Revisited: Justice Anthony Kennedy and the First Amendment Right of Free Speech," 57 *Political Research Quarterly* 209, 216 (2004).

[4] U.S. Senate, "Nomination of Anthony M. Kennedy to Be Associate Justice of the Supreme Court of the United States," 14–16 December 1987, pp. 180, 111.

[5] Ibid. Helen Knowles finds dialogue to be the central focus of Kennedy's jurisprudence generally, and of his free-speech opinions in particular. Helen J. Knowles, *A Dialogue on Liberty: The Classical Liberal and Civic Educational Principles of Justice Kennedy's Vision of Judicial Power* (Ph.D. dissertation, Boston University, 2007), especially Chapter 6.

[6] Turner Broadcasting System v. FCC (*Turner I*), 512 U.S. 622, 641 (1994).

[7] Texas v. Johnson, 491 U.S. 397 (1989). The following citations in the text refer to this case.

[8] Kennedy retreated from this view in Garcetti v. Ceballos, 126 S. Ct. 1951 (2006), and Morse v. Frederick, 127 S. Ct. 2618 (2007). I discuss these cases in the final section of this chapter.

[9] See also Kennedy's dissent from the Court's refusal to issue a stay in Hirsch v. City of Atlanta, 495 U.S. 927 (1990). Joined by Brennan, Marshall, and Scalia, Kennedy writes that a district court injunction preventing a member of the Ku Klux Klan from taking part in public protest is unconstitutional. The Court's decision in National Socialist Party of America v. Skokie, 432 U.S 43 (1977), he writes, "does not distinguish among speakers based on the content of their speech." The four justices voted to overturn the stay, grant certiorari, and vacate the lower court injunction.

[10] Hill v. Colorado, 530 U.S. 703 (2000). The following citations in the text refer to this case. I discussed the elements of Kennedy's *Hill* opinion involving abortion in Chapter 2.

[11] Gentile v. State Bar of Nevada, 501 U.S. 1030 (1991). The following citations in the text refer to this case.

[12] Burdick v. Takushi, 504 U.S. 428 (1992). The following citations in the text refer to this case.

[13] O'Hare Truck Service v. City of Northlake, 518 U.S. 712 (1996).

[14] Legal Services Corp. v. Velasquez, 531 U.S. 533 (2001). The following citations in the text refer to this case.

[15] Simon & Schuster v. Crime Victims Board, 502 U.S. 105 (1991). The following citations in the text refer to this case.

[16] See Kennedy's "continuing concerns" that the existing *Central Hudson* test "gives insufficient protection to truthful, non-misleading commercial speech." Lorillard Tobacco v. Reilly, 533 U.S. 525, 571–572 (2001) (concurring opinion). He also joined Stevens's opinion in 44 Liquormart v. Rhode Island, 517 U.S. 484, 501 (1996).

[17] Edenfield v. Fane, 507 U.S. 761 (1993). The following citations in the text refer to this case.

[18] Florida Bar v. Went For It, Inc., 515 U.S. 618 (1996). The following citations in the text refer to this case.

[19] United States Department of Agriculture v. United Foods, 533 U.S. 405 (2001). The following citations in the text refer to this case.

[20] West Virginia v. Barnette, 319 U.S. 624 (1943).

[21] See Johanns v. Livestock Marketing Association, 544 U.S. 550 (2005), where a majority upheld a head tax on cattle sold or imported in the United States to support generic advertising to urge people to eat beef. Kennedy dissented.

[22] Brown and Hayes v. Legal Foundation of Washington, 538 U.S. 216, 253 (2003).

[23] Buckley v. Valeo, 424 U.S. 1 (1976).

[24] Contrast Kennedy's position with the democracy-enhancing argument for campaign-finance regulation made in Stephen Breyer, *Active Liberty* (New York: Knopf, 2006), esp. pp. 27–36.

[25] On the Ninth Circuit, Kennedy wrote a majority opinion following *Buckley* that upheld limits on contributions to and from political action committees. In California Medical Association v. Federal Elections Commission, 641 F.2d. 619 (1980, 9th Cir.), Kennedy supports these provisions as "designed to uphold the integrity of the political process and to insure that political debate and political speech are effective." Although a contribution is "essentially a proxy," Kennedy writes, "the articulation of ideas by a speaker is more central to political expression" (627).

[26] Austin v. Michigan Chamber of Commerce, 494 U.S. 652 (1990). The following citations in the text refer to this case.

[27] California Democratic Party v. Jones, 530 U.S. 567 (2000). The following citations in the text refer to this case.

[28] See also Kennedy's dissenting opinion in Morse v. Republican Party of Virginia, 517 U.S. 186 (1996), which urges "sensitive consideration of the rights of speech and association" possessed by political parties.

[29] Colorado Republican Federal Campaign Committee v. Federal Election Commission, 518 U.S. 604 (1996). The following citations in the text refer to this case.

[30] Nixon v. Shrink Missouri PAC, 528 U.S. 377 (2000). The following citations in the text refer to this case.

[31] Republican Party of Minnesota v. White, 122 S. Ct. 2528 (2002). The following citations in the text refer to this case.

[32] McConnell v. Federal Elections Commission, 540 U.S. 93 (2003). The following citations in the text refer to this opinion.

[33] Randall v. Sorrell, 126 S. Ct. 2479 (2006).

[34] See Steve Shiffrin, *The First Amendment, Democracy and Romance* (Princeton, N.J.: Princeton University Press, 1990), Chap. 3.

[35] Most recently, Kennedy has voted with Alito and Roberts to constitute 5–4 majorities to strike other provisions of the BCRA. In Wisconsin Right to Life v. FEC, 126 S. Ct. 1016 (2007), the Court struck a provision of BCRA that prohibited corporations from using general funds to broadcast any "issue advertisement" that mentions a candidate for office within thirty days of a primary election or sixty days of a general election. Kennedy joined Scalia's concurring opinion that reiterated the need to overturn much of the decision in *McConnell.* In Davis v. FEC, 2008 U.S. Lexis 5267 (2008), Kennedy joined another 5–4 majority to strike the "Millionaire's Amendment," which eased some contribution and spending limits for those running against "self-financing" candidates who spend more than $350,000 in personal funds.

[36] Ward v. Rock against Racism, 491 U.S. 781 (1989). The following citations in the text refer to this case.

[37] United States v. Kokinda, 497 U.S. 720 (1990). The following citations in the text refer to this case.

[38] International Society for Krishna Consciousness v. Lee, 505 U.S. 672 (1992). The following citations in the text refer to this case.

[39] "If the category of 'traditional public forum' is to be a tool of analysis, rather than a conclusory label," Scalia writes, "it must remain faithful to its name and derive its content from tradition." Burson v. Freeman, 504 U.S. 191, 214 (1992).

[40] Denver Area Educational Telecommunications Consortium v. FCC, 518 U.S. 727 (1996). I discuss this case again below.

[41] *Turner I,* 512 U.S. 622, 641 (1994).

[42] Turner Broadcasting System II v. FCC (*Turner II*), 520 U.S. 180, 194 (1997).

[43] See, for example, his votes in Good News Club v. Milford Central School, 533 U.S. 98 (2001), and Lamb's Chapel v. Center Moriches School District, 508 U.S. 384 (1993).

[44] Rosenberger v. Virginia, 515 U.S. 819 (1995). The following citations in the text refer to this case.

[45] Board of Regents of University of Wisconsin v. Southworth, 529 U.S. 217 (2000). The following citations in the text refer to this case.

[46] Alexander v. United States, 509 U.S. 544 (1993). The following citations in the text refer to this case.

[47] Denver Area Educational Telecommunications Consortium v. FCC, 518 U.S. 727 (1996). The following citations in the text refer to this case.

[48] U.S. v. Playboy Entertainment Group, 529 U.S. 803 (2000). The following citations in the text refer to this case.

[49] Ashcroft v. Free Speech Coalition, 122 S. Ct. 1389 (2002). The following citations in the text refer to this case.

[50] Ashcroft v. ACLU, 122 S. Ct. 1700 (2002). The following citations in the text refer to this case.

[51] U.S. v. American Library Association, 539 U.S. 194 (2003). The following citations in the text refer to this case.

[52] City of Los Angeles v. Alameda Books, 112 S. Ct. 1728 (2002). The following citations in the text refer to this case.

[53] Kennedy joined O'Connor's plurality opinion in City of Erie v. Pap's A.M., 529 U.S. 277 (2000).

[54] Ashcroft v. ACLU, 542 U.S. 656 (2004). The following citations in the text refer to this case.

[55] This development has arisen after Schmidt and Yalof published their study in 2004.

[56] Garcetti v. Ceballos, 126 S. Ct. 1951, 1960–1961 (2006).

[57] Morse v. Frederick, 127 S. Ct. 2618 (2007).

[58] See Tinker v. Des Moines, 393 U.S. 503 (1969).

[59] Grutter v. Bollinger, 539 U.S. 306, 377–378, 395 (2003). I discuss the equal protection aspects of this case in greater detail in Chapter 4.

[60] Vieth v. Jublirer, 541 U.S. 267 (2004). The following citations in the text refer to this opinion.

[61] Kennedy found no such workable standard in LULAC v. Perry, 125 S. Ct. 2594 (2006). He did, however, strike one district under the Voting Rights Act "for its troubling blend of politics and race" (2623).

[62] New York State Board of Elections v. Lopez Torres, 128 S. Ct. 791 (2008). The following citations in the text refer to this case.

[63] Planned Parenthood of Southeastern Pennsylvania v. Casey, 505 U.S. 833, 851 (1992).

[64] *Turner I*, 512 U.S. 622, 641 (1994).

CHAPTER FOUR. KENNEDY'S EQUALITY
OF NEUTRAL INDIVIDUALISM

[1] Parents Involved in Community Schools v. Seattle School District No. 1, 127 S. Ct. 2738 (2007).

[2] I should note my debt to—and departure from—the analysis in Akhil Reed Amar, "Justice Kennedy and the Ideal of Equality," 28 *Pacific Law Journal* 515 (1997). In a brief address at the school where Kennedy taught constitutional law, Amar praised Kennedy's "vision of truly equal citizenship in a diverse, pluralistic, boisterous, participatory democracy" (515). Amar, however, examined only a few of Kennedy's opinions, highlighting where he strikes peremptory challenges of jurors (515). Amar does not address Kennedy's opinions involving majority-minority legislative districts, school desegregation, or affirmative action. In this chapter, I explore Kennedy's ideal of equality across a broader section of cases and situate that ideal within his larger moral reading of the Constitution.

[3] Plessy v. Ferguson, 163 U.S. 537, 559 (1896). Kennedy quotes and cites Harlan's

Plessy dissent in several opinions discussed below. Kennedy, however, never cited (and later explicitly rejected) the opening of Harlan's sentence: "Our Constitution is color-blind."

[4] Brown v. Board of Education, 347 U.S. 483, 493–494 (1954).

[5] Anthony M. Kennedy, "Unenumerated Rights and the Dictates of Judicial Restraint," Palo Alto, California, Canadian Institute for Advanced Legal Studies, 24 July–1 August 1986, p. 14.

[6] See, for example, his opinion in *Lawrence:* "Equality of treatment and the due process right to demand respect for conduct protected by the substantive guarantee of liberty are linked in important respects, and a decision on the latter point advances both interests." Lawrence v. Texas, 539 U.S. 558, 575 (2003).

[7] Grutter v. Bollinger, 539 U.S. 306 (2003); Parents Involved in Community Schools v. Seattle School District No. 1, 127 S. Ct. 2738 (2007).

[8] U.S. Senate, "Nomination of Anthony M. Kennedy to Be Associate Justice of the Supreme Court of the United States" 14–16 December 1987, p. 117. The following citations in the text refer to this testimony.

[9] Flores v. Pierce, 617 F.2d 1386 (1980, 9th Cir.). The following citations in the text refer to this case.

[10] Spangler v. Pasadena, 611 F.2d. 1239 (1979, 9th Cir.). The following citations in the text refer to this case.

[11] Pasadena City Board of Education v. Spangler, 427 U.S. 424 (1976).

[12] Brown v. Board of Education II, 349 U.S. 294 (1955).

[13] Frank J. Colucci, "A Moralist at Heart? Justice Scalia and Affirmative Action," paper delivered at the 1998 Meetings of the Midwest Political Science Association.

[14] Richmond v. J. A. Croson, 488 U.S. 469 (1989). The following citations in the text refer to this case.

[15] Blackmun Papers, Box 517, Folder 4.

[16] Metro Broadcasting v. Federal Communications Commission, 497 U.S. 547 (1990). The following citations in the text refer to this case.

[17] Blackmun Papers, Box 538, Folder 8.

[18] Kennedy joined a later majority in Adarand Construction v. Pena, 515 U.S. 200 (1995), to strike a racial preference in awarding federal contracts as a violation of equal protection. He did not join the separate opinions of Scalia and Thomas, which expressed clear support for a color-blind approach to the Constitution.

[19] See Charles Fried, "*Metro Broadcasting v. FCC:* Two Concepts of Equality," 104 *Harvard Law Review* 107 (1990). Fried contrasts a "liberal" version of equality—which "insists on the primacy of individuals, not groups, in our constitutional scheme and views the individual as the object of fundamental rights"—with the "group rights" perspective of Brennan and Marshall that "creates, and even celebrates, barriers to trade that in the end impoverish the human race" (109). Fried attributes the "liberal, individualistic" version of equality to O'Connor's dissent in *Metro Broadcasting*. I argue that this ideal of equality is more evident in Kennedy's opinions. Fried's article was published while Barack Obama served as president of the *Harvard Law Review*.

[20] Missouri v. Jenkins, 495 U.S. 33 (1990). The following citations in the text refer to this case.

[21] Freeman v. Pitts, 503 U.S. 467 (1992). The following citations in the text refer to this case.

[22] See also Oklahoma City v. Dowell, 498 U.S. 237 (1991).

[23] Shaw v. Reno, 509 U.S. 630 (1993).

[24] Kennedy has announced his willingness to use judicial power to address this political question, although he has not yet struck a district purely on partisan grounds. See Vieth v. Jubelirer, 541 U.S. 267, 306–317 (2004) (concurring in the judgment); LULAC v. Perry, 126 S. Ct. 2594 (2006). I discuss these opinions in Chapter 3 concerning free speech.

[25] Bush v. Vera, 517 U.S. 952 (1996). The following citations in the text refer to this case.

[26] Miller v. Johnson, 575 U.S. 900 (1995).

[27] Abrams v. Johnson, 521 U.S. 74 (1997).

[28] Presley v. Etowah County, 502 U.S. 491 (1992).

[29] Rice v. Cateyano, 528 U.S. 495 (2000) at 517.

[30] Batson v. Kentucky, 476 U.S. 479 (1986).

[31] Holland v. Illinois, 493 U.S. 474 (1990). The following citations in the text refer to this case.

[32] Powers v. Ohio, 499 U.S. 400 (1991). The following citations in the text refer to this case.

[33] Edmonson v. Leesville Concrete, 500 U.S. 614 (1991). The following citations in the text refer to this case.

[34] Campbell v. Louisiana, 523 U.S. 392 (1998). The following citations in the text refer to this case.

[35] J.E.B. v. Alabama, 511 U.S. 127 (1994). The following citations in the text refer to this case.

[36] Church of Lukumi Babalu Aye v. City of Hialeah, 508 U.S. 520 (1993). The following citations in the text refer to this case.

[37] Quote taken from John Harlan's opinion in Walz v. Tax Commission, 397 U.S. 664, 696 (1970).

[38] Kiryas Joel v. Grumet, 512 U.S. 687 (1994). The following citations in the text refer to this case.

[39] Grand Rapids v. Ball, 473 U.S. 373 (1985); Aguilar v. Felton, 473 U.S. 402 (1985).

[40] See Agostini v. Felton, 521 U.S. 203 (1997), as well as Kennedy's majority opinion in Rosenberger v Virginia, 515 U.S. 819 (1995).

[41] Romer v. Evans, 517 U.S. 620 (1996). The following citations in the text refer to this case.

[42] Lynn Baker, "The Missing Pages of the Majority Opinion in *Romer v. Evans*," 68 *Colorado Law Review* 335 (1997).

[43] Bowers v. Hardwick, 478 U.S. 186 (1986); Toni Massero, "Gay Rights Thick and Thin," 49 *Stanford Law Review* 45 (1997). This theory gains some support from

Kennedy's 1987 speech criticizing *Bowers* and his later opinion in Lawrence v. Texas overturning it. Kennedy mentions in *Lawrence* that *Romer* is a decision that undermines the precedent in *Bowers* (*Lawrence* at 574–576). On its own terms, however, Kennedy's opinion in *Romer* is consistent with his theory of neutral individualism.

44 Tobias Barrington Wolff, "Principled Silence," 106 *Yale Law Review* 247 (1997).

45 Steven Smith, *Getting over Equality* (New York: New York University Press, 2001), p. 139.

46 See Cass Sunstein, *One Case at a Time* (New York: Harvard University Press, 1999), pp. 137–150.

47 The text of the amendment reads: "Neither the State of Colorado, through any of its branches or departments, nor any of its agencies, political subdivisions, municipalities or school districts, shall enact, adopt, or enforce any statute, regulation, ordinance or policy whereby homosexual, lesbian or bisexual orientation, conduct, practices or relationships shall constitute or otherwise be the basis of or entitle any person or class to have or claim any minority status, quota preferences, protected status or claim of discrimination."

48 A bill of attainder is a legislative action that declares a person or group of persons guilty of a crime without individual trial and punishes them by depriving them of civil rights. The U.S. Constitution prohibits bills of attainder by Congress (Article I, Section 9) or by the states (Article I, Section 10, Clause 1). For an argument that Colorado's action amounted to a bill of attainder, see Akhil Reed Amar, "Attainder and Amendment 2: *Romer*'s Rightness," 95 *Michigan Law Review* 203 (1996).

49 Compare Kennedy's language in *Romer* to his later discussion in *Lawrence* of the "stigma" and harm to dignity arising from the existence of laws prohibiting sodomy and the demeaning *Bowers* precedent defending their constitutionality.

50 Grutter v. Bollinger, 539 U.S. 306 (2003).

51 Parents Involved in Community Schools v. Seattle School District No. 1, 127 S. Ct. 2738 (2007).

52 In the companion case Gratz v. Bollinger—539 U.S. 244 (2003)—Kennedy joined Rehnquist's majority opinion striking Michigan's undergraduate admissions system, which allotted 20 points to all applicants identifying as an "underrepresented minority." He did not join O'Connor's concurring opinion.

53 Regents of University of California v. Bakke, 438 U.S. 365 (1978).

54 *Grutter* at 387. The following citations in the text refer to this case.

55 See Scalia concurrence in *Grutter* at 347–349, and the Thomas quote at 350.

56 Parents Involved in Community Schools v. Seattle School District No. 1, 127 S. Ct. 2738 (2007). The following citations in the text refer to this case.

57 See Roberts's citation of Harlan's color-blind passage (*Parents* at 2758 n. 14). "The way to stop discrimination on the basis of race," Roberts writes, "is to stop discriminating on the basis of race" (2768). See Thomas's invocation of Harlan's *Plessy* dissent (2783–2786), his equation of Breyer's reasoning to the segregationist argument in *Brown* and to majorities in *Dred Scott* and *Plessy* (2768, 2777), and his closing use of Harlan's color-blind quote (2778).

[58] Parents Involved in Community Schools v. Seattle School District No. 1, 426 F.3d. 1162, 1193 (9th Cir., 2005).

[59] *Bakke* at 407.

[60] *Bakke* at 407.

[61] Mark Tushnet also notes this contrast. Tushnet, *Taking the Constitution Away from the Courts* (Princeton, N.J.: Princeton University Press, 1999), p. 185.

[62] For Kennedy this treatment is limited to the treatment of citizens and does not extend to the prior question of who exactly counts as a citizen. See his majority opinion in Nguyen v. INS, 533 U.S. 53 (2001), upholding a sex classification of parents made by Congress with regard to the citizenship of children born out of wedlock. Kennedy addresses the objection that Congress's classification is based on the same stereotypical thinking that he found in other legislation. "Mechanistic classification of all our differences as stereotypes," he writes, "would operate to obscure those misconceptions and prejudices that are real. The distinction embodied in the statutory scheme here at issue is not marked by misconception and prejudice, nor does it show disrespect for either class. The difference between men and women in relation to the birth process is a real one, and the principle of equal protection does not forbid Congress to address the problem at hand in a manner specific to each gender" (73). Compare Kennedy's description of sex differences in this case to his description of the psychology of women seeking abortions in the cases described in Chapter 2.

[63] *Parents* at 2788.

[64] See, for example, Ronald M. Dworkin, *Taking Rights Seriously* (Cambridge: Harvard University Press, 1977), pp. 134–137; Dworkin, *Freedom's Law* (Cambridge: Harvard University Press, 1996), pp. 7–8. For an argument that appeals to tradition (as opposed to history) are essentially moral, see Sotirios A. Barber, *On What the Constitution Means* (Baltimore: Johns Hopkins University Press, 1984), p. 84.

[65] Early indications may prove Kennedy right. After *Gratz*, the University of Michigan requires all undergraduate applicants to write an essay on diversity. Its 2009 application asks students to "share an experience through which you have gained respect for intellectual, social, or cultural differences" (http://www.admissions.umich.edu/applying/Essay09.pdf). After the Court's 2007 decision striking its plan to classify students as black or nonblack, Jefferson County, Kentucky, shifted to a system that considers socioeconomic class as well as race. See Emily Bazelon, "The Next Kind of Integration," *New York Times Magazine*, 20 July 2008.

[66] Dred Scott v. Sandford, 60 U.S. 393 (1857).

[67] The most direct statement to this effect was the opinion in *Bakke* signed by Justices Marshall, Brennan, and White that stated, "The position that . . . Our Constitution is color-blind has never been adopted by this Court as the proper meaning of the Equal Protection Clause" (*Bakke* at 335). Andrew Kull shows that the Supreme Court in *Brown* and its aftermath rejected Harlan's color-blind argument and calls that interpretation "the road not taken." Kull, *The Color-Blind Constitution* (Cambridge: Harvard University Press, 1992), Introduction, chaps. 9–10.

[68] David Strauss, "The Myth of Colorblindness," 1986 *Supreme Court Review* 99,

100 (1987). See also Tribe, "In What Vision of the Constitution Must the Law Be Color-Blind?" 20 *John Marshall Law Review* 203, 203–206 (1986), and Kull, Chap. 9.

[69] *Brown* at 494, fn. 11.

[70] The quote is from Scalia's dissent in Lee v. Weisman, 505 U.S. 577, 636 (1992).

CHAPTER FIVE. SPLITTING THE ATOM OF
SOVEREIGNTY: DIGNITY AND DIVIDED POWER

[1] Ann Althouse, "Chief Justice Rehnquist and the Search for Judicially Enforceable Federalism," 10 *Texas Review of Law and Politics* 275 (2006); Erwin Chemerinsky, "Reconceptualizing Federalism," 50 *New York Law School Law Review* 729 (2006); Thomas Keck, *The Most Activist Supreme Court in History* (Chicago: University of Chicago Press, 2004), p. 236.

[2] Daniel J. Meltzer, "State Sovereign Immunity: Five Authors in Search of a Theory," 75 *Notre Dame Law Review* 1011, 1042 (2000); Ernest A. Young, "Just Blowing Smoke? Politics, Doctrine, and the Federalist Revival after *Gonzales v. Raich*," 2005 *Supreme Court Review* 1, 49 (2005); Earl Maltz, "Justice Kennedy's Vision of Federalism," 31 *Rutgers Law Journal* 761, 762 (2000).

[3] Kennedy's concern with federalism has been noted but not yet adequately explained. John J. Dinan, "The Rehnquist Court's Federalism Decisions in Perspective," 15 *Journal of Law and Politics* 127, 192, 194 (1999).

[4] In some events—including the Federal Bar Association speech cited below—Kennedy delivered his speech dressed as James Madison. Kennedy, however, stands a foot taller than Madison did.

[5] Anthony M. Kennedy, "Federalism: The Theory and Reality," Sacramento, Historical Society for the United States District Court for the Northern District of California, 17 September 1987, p. 1. The following citations in the text refer to this speech.

[6] See also Anthony M. Kennedy, "Rotary Club," Sacramento, February 1984, p. 7. See also U.S. Senate, "Nomination of Anthony M. Kennedy to Be Associate Justice of the Supreme Court of the United States," 14–16 December 1987, p. 200, where he testified that such delegations of authority are "spiritually wrong."

[7] "Rotary Club," p. 7. See also "Federalism," pp. 3–4.

[8] "Rotary Club," p. 7.

[9] Nomination, p. 93.

[10] Anthony M. Kennedy, "Patent Lawyers," Los Angeles, Patent Lawyers Association, February 1982, p. 6.

[11] Anthony M. Kennedy, "Federal Bar Association," Sacramento, Federal Bar Association for the Eastern District of California, 17 September 1987, pp. 14–15.

[12] Garcia v. San Antonio Metropolitan Transit Authority, 469 U.S. 528 (1985).

[13] National League of Cities v. Usery, 476 U.S. 833 (1976).

[14] "Patent," p. 6.

[15] "Federal Bar Association," p. 14.

[16] Nomination, p. 200.

[17] Anthony M. Kennedy, "Hoover Lecture," Palo Alto, California, Stanford Law Faculty, 17 May 1984, p. 8.

[18] "Patent," p. 9.

[19] "Patent," p. 7.

[20] INS v. Chadha, 634 F.2d. 408 (1980). The following citations in the text refer to this case.

[21] INS v. Chadha, 462 U.S. 919 (1983).

[22] In a later public address, Kennedy stated he "had mentioned the presentment clause" in an earlier version of his opinion in *Chadha* "but struck it from the last draft as superfluous to our holding." "Hoover Lecture," p. 1.

[23] Ibid., p. 4. The following citations in the text refer to this speech.

[24] See also "Patent," p. 9.

[25] Clinton v. New York, 524 U.S. 417 (1998). The following citations in the text refer to this case.

[26] Public Citizen v. Department of Justice, 491 U.S. 440 (1990). The following citations in the text refer to this case.

[27] Rumsfeld v. Padilla, 543 U.S. 426 (2004). The following citations in the text refer to this case.

[28] When Padilla later sued the appropriate commander, Kennedy—joined by Roberts and Stevens—denied certiorari (547 U.S. 1062 [2006]). "Any consideration of what rights he might be able to assert if he were returned to military custody," Kennedy writes, "would be hypothetical, and to no effect, at this stage of the proceedings" (1063). He admits the petitioner "has a continuing concern that his status might be altered again" (1063). Should this occur, the district court "would be in a position to rule quickly." As Kennedy writes, "that Padilla's claims raise fundamental issues respecting the separation of powers, including consideration of the role and function of the courts, also counsels against addressing those claims when the course of legal proceedings has made them, for now, hypothetical" (1064).

[29] Rasul v. Bush, 542 U.S. 466 (2005). The following citations in the text refer to this case.

[30] Johnson v. Eisentrager, 339 U.S. 763 (1950).

[31] Ex Parte Milligan, 71 U.S. 2 (1866).

[32] Hamdan v. Rumsfeld, 126 S. Ct. 2749 (2006). The following citations in the text refer to this case.

[33] Congress soon did so with the Military Commissions Act of 2006 (Public Law 109–366). On 29 June 2007, the Supreme Court reversed itself and decided to hear challenges to this act. See Boumediene v. Bush, 128 S.Ct. 640 (2007). Kennedy switched his vote to grant certiorari. I assess Kennedy's 2008 opinion in *Boumediene* striking Congress's action in the concluding chapter.

[34] See New York v. United States, 505 U.S. 144 (1992); Gregory v. Ashcroft, 501 U.S. 452 (1991); and Missouri v. Jenkins, 495 U.S. 33 (1990).

[35] United States v. Lopez, 514 U.S. 549 (1995). The following citations in the text refer to this opinion.

[36] Compare Erwin Chemerinsky, "The Federalism Revolution," 31 *New Mexico Law Review* 7 (2001), to Steven G. Calabresi, "Federalism and the Rehnquist Court: A Normative Defense," 574 *Annals of the American Academy of Political and Social Science* 24 (2001). See also Larry D. Kramer, "Putting the Politics Back into the Political Safeguards of Federalism," 100 *Columbia Law Review* 215, 218 (2000), n.13.

[37] Much of the following argument borrows from Frank J. Colucci, "The Court's Three Marshalls," 23 *Polity* 127 (2000).

[38] NLRB v. Jones & Laughlin Steel, 301 U.S. 1 (1937).

[39] Wickard v. Filburn, 317 U. S. 111 (1941).

[40] Marbury v. Madison, 1 Cranch 146, 177 (1803).

[41] *Lopez* at 584–602.

[42] U.S. v. Morrison, 529 U.S. 598 (2000).

[43] O'Connor's dissent states that limits on federal power are enforced "not for their own sake, but to protect historic spheres of state sovereignty from excessive federal encroachment." *Gonzales v. Raich*, 125 S. Ct. 2195, 2220 (2005).

[44] See Scalia's opinion in *Raich* at 2215–2221 (concurring in the judgment).

[45] See Lyle Deniston, "Justice Kennedy and the 'War on Drugs,'" *SCOTUSblog*, http://www.scotusblog.com/movabletype/archives/2005/06/commentary_just.html (posted 6 June 2005), and—from the attorney who represented Raich at Supreme Court oral argument—Randy Barnett, "The Ninth Circuit's Revenge," 9 June 2005, *National Review Online*, http://www.nationalreview.com/comment/barnett200506090741.asp.

[46] I discuss *Rapanos* below. Kennedy's "substantial nexus" standard in *Rapanos* seems to parallel the "evident commercial nexus" standard he articulates in *Lopez*.

[47] City of Boerne v. Flores, 521 U.S. 507 (1997). The following citations in the text refer to this case.

[48] Employment Division v. Smith, 494 U.S. 872 (1990).

[49] Davis v. Monroe County, 191 S. Ct. 1661 (1999). The following citations in the text refer to this case.

[50] South Dakota v. Dole, 483 U.S. 203 (1987).

[51] *Lopez* at 580.

[52] Bendix Autolite v. Midwesco Enterprises, 486 U.S. 888, 891 (1988). The following citations in the text refer to this case.

[53] This reasoning drew a sharp rebuke from Justice Scalia. "Weighing the governmental interests of a State against the needs of interstate commerce," he writes, "is . . . a task squarely within the responsibility of Congress and 'ill suited to the judicial function'" (896, 897). Scalia "would therefore abandon the 'balancing' approach" and "leave essentially legislative judgments to Congress" (897).

[54] Allied Signal v. New Jersey, 504 U.S. 768 (1992). The following citations in the text refer to this case.

[55] Wisconsin Department of Revenue v. Wrigley, 505 U.S. 214 (1992). The following citations in the text refer to this case.

[56] Trinova Corp. v. Michigan Department of Treasury, 498 U.S. 38 (1991). The following citations in the text refer to this case.

[57] Granholm v. Heald, 544 U.S. 460 (2005). The following citations in the text refer to this case.

[58] Kentucky v. Davis, 128 S. Ct. 1801 (2008). The following citations in the text refer to this case.

[59] Supreme Court of Virginia v. Friedman, 487 U.S. 59 (1988). The following citations in the text refer to this case.

[60] See also Barnard v. Thornstenn, 489 U.S. 546 (1989), where Kennedy wrote for a majority finding the Virgin Islands's residency requirements for lawyers to violate the privileges and immunities clause. The "blanket exclusion of nonresidents," he writes, is not the most precise solution to the territory's particular circumstances (558).

[61] U.S. Term Limits v. Thornton, 514 U.S. 779 (1995). The following citations in the text refer to this case.

[62] Kennedy reiterates the importance of direct lines of political responsibility in Cook v. Gralike, 531 U.S. 510 (2001). After *Thornton*, Missouri required ballots to indicate whether candidates for federal office agreed with a federal constitutional amendment to enact congressional term limits supported by its state legislature. Kennedy strikes this law because federal officials "are responsible to the people who elect them, not to the states in which they reside" (528). Under our system, "freedom is most secure if the people themselves, not the states as intermediaries, hold their federal legislators to account for the conduct of their office." If ballot instructions such as Missouri's were allowed, he concludes, "accountability would be blurred, with the legislators having the excuse of saying they did not act with the exercise of their best judgment but simply in conformance with a state mandate" (529).

[63] See New York v. United States, 505 U.S. 144 (1992) (involving commandeering of the state legislative process), and Printz v. United States, 521 U.S. 898 (1997) (involving commandeering of the state executive branch).

[64] "The judicial power of the United States shall not be construed to extend to any suit in law or equity, commenced or prosecuted against one of the United States by citizens of another state, or by citizens or subjects of any foreign state."

[65] Delmuth v. Muth, 491 U.S. 223 (1989). The following citations in the text refer to this case.

[66] See Atascadero Hospital v. Scanlon, 473 U.S. 234, 238, 242 (1985).

[67] Scalia's concurrence takes a less rigid position. Kennedy's opinion, Scalia writes, "does not preclude congressional elimination of sovereign immunity in statutory text that clearly subjects States to suit for monetary damages, though without explicit reference to state sovereign immunity or the Eleventh Amendment" (233).

[68] Seminole Tribe v. Florida, 517 U.S. 44 (1996).

[69] Idaho v. Coeur d'Alene Tribe, 521 U.S. 261 (1997). The following citations in the text refer to this case.

[70] Ex Parte Young, 209 U.S. 123 (1908).

[71] Alden v. Maine, 527 U.S. 706 (1999). The following citations in the text refer to this case.

[72] Chisholm v. Georgia, 2 Dall. 419 (1793).

[73] Nevada Dept. of Human Resources v. Hibbs, 538 U.S. 721 (2003). The following citations in the text refer to this case.

[74] Kennedy reiterated the ideals of *Alden* in Board of Trustees of University of Alabama v. Garrett, 531 U.S. 356 (2001), which upheld a state claim of sovereign immunity against a federal suit under the Americans with Disabilities Act (ADA). While conceding that the ADA "will be a milestone on the path to a more decent, tolerant, progressive society," Kennedy found that Congress had presented no "confirming judicial documentation" of "patterns of constitutional violations committed by the State in its official capacity" (375). Because this suit was brought "by private persons seeking to collect money from the state treasury without the consent of the State," and no pattern of constitutional abuses was documented to justify federal enforcement of the Equal Protection Clause, Garrett's lawsuit is prohibited by the Constitution (376).

[75] Kennedy's solicitude for states as "joint participants" within our federal system may explain why in 2007 he joined liberal justices to grant Massachusetts standing to challenge the Environmental Protection Agency's refusal to regulate greenhouse gases. Justice Stevens's majority opinion stated: "It is of considerable relevance that the party seeking review here is a sovereign State and not . . . a private individual." States are "not normal litigants for the purposes of involving federal jurisdiction," Stevens writes. In light of "Massachusetts' stake in protecting its quasi-sovereign interests, the Commonwealth is entitled to special solicitude in our standing analysis." Massachusetts v. EPA, 127 S. Ct. 1438, 1454–1455 (2007). Stevens cites Kennedy's majority opinion *Alden* to support Massachusetts's claim even though he and every other justice in this majority besides Kennedy had dissented in *Alden*.

[76] Gonzales v. Oregon, 126 S. Ct. 904 (2006). The following citations in the text refer to this case.

[77] Rapanos v. U.S., 126 S. Ct. 2208 (2006).

[78] Kennedy joined Justice Rehnquist's opinions rejecting this constitutional claim in Washington v. Glucksberg, 521 U.S. 702 (1997), and Vacco v. Quill, 521 U.S. 793 (1997).

[79] *Rapanos* at 2236. The following citations in the text refer to this case.

[80] Solid Waste Agency of North Cook County [*SWANCC*] v. Army Corps of Engineers, 531 U.S. 159 (2001). Kennedy had joined Rehnquist's opinion for a 5–4 Court.

[81] Alexander Hamilton, James Madison, and John Jay, *The Federalist Papers,* ed. Charles Kesler and Clinton Rossiter (New York: Signet, 2003); *Federalist* 39, p. 213.

[82] *Federalist* 45, pp. 256–257.

[83] Even authors sympathetic to judicial enforcement of limits on federal power find state sovereign immunity ineffective. Ernest Young writes that the doctrine, "to put it plainly, is a poor way to protect state prerogatives in a federal system." Ernest Young, "State Sovereign Immunity and the Future of Federalism," 1999 *Supreme Court*

Review 1, 2 (2000). Charles Fried calls it "awkward and clumsy." Fried, *Saying What the Law Is: The Constitution in the Supreme Court* (Cambridge: Harvard University Press, 2004), p. 37. See also Jesse Choper and John Yoo, "Effective Alternatives to Causes of Action Barred by the Eleventh Amendment," 50 *New York Law School Law Review* 715 (2006). For a qualified defense of *Alden*'s result—though not Kennedy's reasoning—see Ann Althouse, "On Dignity and Deference: The Supreme Court's New Federalism," 68 *University of Cincinnati Law Review* 345 (2000).

CONCLUSION: LIBERTY ABOVE DEMOCRACY

[1] For a concise statement of Dworkin's approach, see his *Freedom's Law* (Cambridge: Harvard University Press, 1996), Introduction. For a classic statement from Brennan, see his "The Constitution of the United States: Contemporary Ratification," speech delivered 12 October 1985 at Georgetown University [reprinted in *The Great Debate: Interpreting Our Written Constitution* (Washington, D.C.: Federalist Society, 1986), p. 11. For scholarly analyses of Brennan's jurisprudence, see David Marion, *The Jurisprudence of Justice William J. Brennan, Jr.: The Law and Politics of Libertarian Dignity* (Lanham, Md.: Rowman and Littlefield, 1997); Frank I. Michelman, *Brennan and Democracy* (Princeton, N.J.: Princeton University Press, 2005).

[2] U.S. Senate, "Nomination of Anthony M. Kennedy to Be Associate Justice of the Supreme Court of the United States," 14–16 December 1987, p. 180.

[3] Randy E. Barnett, *Restoring the Lost Constitution: The Presumption of Liberty* (Princeton, N.J.: Princeton University Press, 2004), p. 254.

[4] Thomas Keck, *The Most Activist Supreme Court in History: The Road to Modern Judicial Conservatism* (Chicago: University of Chicago Press, 2004), pp. 235, 200.

[5] Nancy Maveety, *Justice Sandra Day O'Connor: Strategist on the Supreme Court* (Lanham, Md.: Rowman and Littlefield, 1993), pp. 128–129, and *Queen's Court* (Lawrence: University Press of Kansas, 2008).

[6] Kiryas Joel v. Grumet, 512 U.S. 687, 718 (1994).

[7] Keck, *Most Activist Supreme Court,* p. 281.

[8] Vieth v. Jublirer, 541 U.S. 267, 306 (2004). I discuss *Vieth* in Chapter 3.

[9] For example, in Kelo v. New London, 545 U.S. 469, 491, 493 (2005), Kennedy's concurrence would require judges to determine whether there is a "plausible accusation of impermissible favoritism."

[10] Keck, *Most Activist Supreme Court,* p. 253.

[11] Kennedy v. Louisiana, 128 S. Ct. 2641, 2008 U.S. Lexis 5262 (2008). The following citations in the text refer to the Lexis page numbering of the initial opinion.

[12] Louisiana later petitioned for rehearing because neither party, no amicus brief, and the decision of the Court acknowledged congressional amendments to the Uniform Code of Military Justice in 2006 authorizing the death penalty for child rape and a 2007 Executive Order implementing that provision. Louisiana presented these developments as evidence contrary to the Court's decision finding a "national consensus"

against the practice. "Motion for Reconsideration," filed 21 July 2008, pp. 2–3. On 1 October 2008, the Court refused the motion and clarified one part of its opinion. "The laws of the separate States, which have responsibility for the administration of the criminal law for their civilian populations, are entitled to considerable weight over and above the punishments Congress and the President consider appropriate in the military context," Kennedy wrote. See Kennedy v. Louisiana, 129 S. Ct. 1, 2 (2008). In his own statement, Scalia—joined by Roberts—wrote, "I am voting against the petition for rehearing because the views of the American people on the death penalty for child rape were, to tell the truth, irrelevant to the majority's decision in this case." *Kennedy* at 3.

[13] Callins v. Collins, 510 U.S. 1141, 1143–1159 (1994) (cert. denied).

[14] Brennan, "The Constitution of the United States: Contemporary Ratification," pp. 23–24. The following citations in the text refer to this address. See also Brennan's concurring opinion in Furman v. Georgia, 408 U.S. 238, 257–314 (1972).

[15] Justice Stevens suggested this course of action in his concurring opinion in Baze v. Rees, 128 S. Ct. 1520, 1546–1552 (2008). Kennedy did not join Stevens in *Baze*.

[16] Texas v. Johnson, 491 U.S. 397, 421 (1989).

[17] Boumediene v. Bush, 128 S. Ct. 2229, 2008 U.S. Lexis 4887 (2008). The following citations in the text refer to the initial Lexis pagination of the opinion.

[18] Boumediene v. Bush, 127 S. Ct. 1478 at 1479 (2007).

[19] For example, *Casey* ends this way: "We accept our responsibility not to retreat from interpreting the full meaning of the covenant in light of all of our precedents. We invoke it once again to define the freedom guaranteed by the Constitution's own promise, the promise of liberty." Planned Parenthood of Southeastern Pennsylvania v. Casey, 505 U.S 833, 901 (1992).

[20] Bush v. Gore, 531 U.S. 98 (2000). The following citations in the text refer to this case.

[21] Lochner v. New York, 198 U.S. 45 (1905).

[22] U.S. v. Carolene Products, 304 U.S. 144, 153, fn. 4 (1938).

[23] Ferguson v. Skrupa, 372 U.S. 726, 731 (1963).

[24] Griswold v. Connecticut, 381 U.S. 479, 482, 484 (1965).

[25] Alexander Bickel, *The Least Dangerous Branch: The Supreme Court and the Bar of Politics* (Indianapolis: Bobbs-Merrill, 1962), pp. 16–23.

[26] John Hart Ely, *Democracy and Distrust: A Theory of Judicial Review* (Cambridge: Harvard University Press, 1980).

[27] Mark Tushnet, *Taking the Constitution Away from the Courts* (Princeton, N.J.: Princeton University Press, 1999); Larry D. Kramer, *The People Themselves: Popular Constitutionalism and Judicial Review* (New York: Oxford University Press, 2004); Jeffrey Rosen, *The Most Democratic Branch: How the Courts Serve America* (New York: Oxford University Press, 2006); Cass Sunstein, *One Case at a Time: Judicial Minimalism on the Supreme Court* (Cambridge: Harvard University Press, 1999).

[28] Stephen Breyer, *Active Liberty: Interpreting Our Democratic Constitution* (New York: Knopf, 2005).

[29] For a general overview, see Barry Friedman, "The Counter-Majoritarian

Problem and the Pathology of Constitutional Scholarship," 95 *Northwestern University Law Review* 933 (2001); Friedman, "The Birth of an Academic Obsession: The History of the Countermajoritarian Difficulty (Part Five)," 112 *Yale Law Journal* 153 (2002).

[30] Richard Brisbin, *Justice Antonin Scalia and the Conservative Revival* (Baltimore: Johns Hopkins University Press, 1997), p. 2.

[31] David Schultz and Christopher Smith, *The Jurisprudential Vision of Justice Antonin Scalia* (Lanham. Md.: Rowman and Littlefield, 1993), pp. 207–208.

[32] Ralph A. Rossum, *Antonin Scalia's Jurisprudence: Text and Tradition* (Lawrence: University Press of Kansas, 2006), p. 208.

[33]John Roche aptly stated long ago that "judicial self-restraint and judicial power seem to be opposite sides of the same coin: it has been by judicial application of the former that the latter has been maintained." John Roche, "Judicial Self-Restraint," 49 *American Political Science Review* 762, 772 (1955).

[34] Keck, *Most Activist Supreme Court*, p. 277.

[35] Anthony M. Kennedy, "Patent Lawyers," Los Angeles, Patent Lawyers Association, February 1982, p. 9.

[36] Barnett finds hope in *Lawrence* (see Randy Barnett, "Justice Kennedy's Libertarian Revolution: *Lawrence v. Texas*," 2003 *Cato Supreme Court Review* 21 [2003]), and he praises Kennedy's opinions in several areas of law—U.S. v. Playboy Entertainment Group, 529 U.S. 803 (2000), a case involving free speech; *Casey* and Lawrence v. Texas, 539 U.S 558 (2003), involving liberty; and Romer v. Evans, 517 U.S. 620 (1996), on equal protection—for embodying aspects of the presumption of liberty. Barnett, *Restoring the Lost Constitution*, pp. 233, 339–342, 344 n. 30. Nevertheless, Kennedy's acceptance of the "practical conception" of post–New Deal commerce clause precedents and the substantial effects test conflicts with Barnett's sharper limits on congressional powers (see Chapter 11 of *Restoring the Lost Constitution*). Kennedy—like Barnett—places the burden on government to justify its claim of authority in a particular case. As his votes in Kelo v. New London, 545 U.S. 469 (2005), and Gonzales v. Raich, 545 U.S. 1 (2005), demonstrate, Kennedy is more likely than Barnett is to accept state and federal claims of regulatory authority.

[37] Keck, *Most Activist Supreme Court*, pp. 284–285; Barnett, *Restoring the Lost Constitution*, p. 254.

[38] "Special Session of the Judges of the Ninth Circuit," Phoenix, August 1978, pp. 31–32. As the child of a politically active family in Sacramento during the 1940s and 1950s, Kennedy knew former California governor Earl Warren well.

[39] Anthony M. Kennedy, "Comments at Ninth Circuit Judicial Conference," Hawaii, 21 August 1987, p. 1.

[40] Nomination, p. 139.

[41]Anthony Kennedy, Answers to Senate Judiciary Committee nomination questionnaire, p. 52.

[42] Nomination, p. 139.

[43] See Jeffrey Rosen, "Supreme Leader: The Arrogance of Justice Anthony Kennedy," *The New Republic*, 18 June 2007.

[44] "The resemblance of today's state sovereign immunity doctrine to the *Lochner* era's industrial due process is striking. . . . I expect the Court's late entry into immunity doctrine will prove the equal of its earlier experiment in laissez-faire, the one being as unrealistic as the other, as indefensible, and probably as fleeting." Alden v. Maine, 527 U.S. 706, 813 (1999).

[45] "I do not believe the First Amendment seeks to limit the Government's economic regulatory choices in this way—any more than does the Due Process Clause. Cf. *Lochner.*" U.S. v. United Foods, 533 U.S. 405, 429 (2001).

[46] Planned Parenthood v. Casey, 505 U.S. 833, 983–984 (1992).

[47] U.S. Association of Constitutional Law Discussion, "Constitutional Relevance of Foreign Court Decisions," Washington, D.C., American University, Washington College of Law, 13 January 2005, http://domino.american.edu/AU/media/mediarel.nsf/1D265343BDC2189785256B810071F238/1F2F7DC4757FD01E85256F890068E6E0?OpenDocument.

[48] See Scalia's dissent in *Casey,* which states that the constitutional issue is "not whether the power of a woman to abort her unborn child is a 'liberty' in the absolute sense." By using quotation marks, Scalia derides either the existence or relevance of any true meaning of liberty. In Troxel v. Granville, 530 U.S. 57, 92 (2000), Scalia asserts that the parental direction and raising of children is among the "unalienable rights" endowed by the Creator in the Declaration of Independence and the "other rights retained by the people" mentioned in the Ninth Amendment. Nevertheless, like Bork, Scalia claims, "I do not believe that the power which the Constitution confers upon me as a judge entitles me to deny legal effect to laws that (in my view) infringe upon what is (in my view) that unenumerated right."

[49] Texas v. Johnson, 491 U.S. 397, 420–421 (1989).

[50] Terri Jennings Peretti, *In Defense of a Political Court* (Princeton, N.J.: Princeton University Press, 2001), p. 254.

[51] Anthony M. Kennedy, "Unenumerated Rights and the Dictates of Judicial Restraint," Palo Alto, California, Canadian Institute for Advanced Legal Studies, 24 July–1 August 1986, p. 22.

[52] See Richard Posner, *Law, Pragmatism and Democracy* (Cambridge: Harvard University Press, 2003), pp. 211, 95. Even advocates of the moral reading concede practical constraints on judicial power. Sotirios Barber portrays "the good judge as striving for the interpretation of, say, the equal protection clause that comes as close as politically and institutionally feasible to what her best self-critical effort reveals as the best available version of its true meaning." Barber, *The Constitution of Judicial Power* (Baltimore: Johns Hopkins University Press, 1993), p. 224. Ronald Dworkin argues that moral interpretations of the Constitution "should be resisted in the right way: by pointing out their fallacies or by deploying different principles—more conservative or more liberal—and showing why these principles are better because they are grounded in a superior morality, or are more practicable, or are in some other way wiser or fairer." Dworkin, *Freedom's Law,* p. 38. Terri Peretti writes that "what is distinctive is that each justice does not possess full freedom to rewrite constitutional doctrines *in*

toto from their personal views. Those doctrines evolve—from what has gone before, from what results from compromise within the Court, and from what is politically permissible." Peretti, *In Defense of a Political Court,* p. 253. These practical and political restraints on judicial power reinforce the "simple view of the matter" expressed in *Federalist* 78 that "the judiciary, by the nature of its functions, will always be the least dangerous to the political rights of the Constitution."

[53] "Unenumerated Rights," pp. 4, 20.

[54] Cass Sunstein attempts to read *Lawrence* not as motivated by Kennedy's broad statements of liberty at the beginning and end of the opinion but in light of the fact that sodomy laws have gone unenforced. See Sunstein, "What Did *Lawrence* Hold? Of Autonomy, Desuetude, Sexuality and Marriage," 2003 *Supreme Court Review* 27 (2004). See also Kennedy's reliance in Roper v. Simmons, 125 S. Ct 1183 (2005) on the decreasing number of prisoners executed for crimes committed when they were juveniles. For a similar discussion, see Rosen, *The Most Democratic Branch,* p. 204. At the time of Kennedy v. Louisiana (2008), only two prisoners in the United States had been sentenced to death for child rape.

[55] Rosen, *The Most Democratic Branch,* p. 4.

[56] For a fuller account, see Howard Gillman, *The Votes That Counted: How the Court Decided the 2000 Election* (Chicago: University of Chicago Press, 2001).

[57] *Casey* at 844.

Bibliography

SCHOLARLY SOURCES

Althouse, Ann. "Chief Justice Rehnquist and the Search for Judicially Enforceable Federalism," 10 *Texas Review of Law and Politics* 275 (2006).
———. "On Dignity and Deference: The Supreme Court's New Federalism," 68 *University of Cincinnati Law Review* 345 (2000).
Amar, Akhil Reed. "Attainder and Amendment 2: *Romer's* Rightness," 95 *Michigan Law Review* 203 (1996).
———. "Justice Kennedy and the Idea of Equality," 28 *Pacific Law Journal* 515 (1997).
Baker, Lynn. "The Missing Pages of the Majority Opinion in *Romer v. Evans,*" 68 *Colorado Law Review* 335 (1997).
Balkin, Jack M., ed. *What* Roe v. Wade *Should Have Said.* New York: New York University Press (2005).
Barber, Sotirios A. *The Constitution of Judicial Power.* Baltimore: Johns Hopkins University Press (1993).
———. *On What the Constitution Means.* Baltimore: Johns Hopkins University Press (1984).
Barnett, Randy. "Justice Kennedy's Libertarian Revolution: *Lawrence v. Texas,*" 2003 *Cato Supreme Court Review* 23 (2003).
———. *Restoring the Lost Constitution: The Presumption of Liberty.* Princeton, N.J.: Princeton University Press (2004).
Bickel, Alexander. *The Least Dangerous Branch: The Supreme Court and the Bar of Politics.* Indianapolis: Bobbs-Merrill (1962).
Bopp, James, and Richard E. Coleson. "What Does *Webster* Mean?" 138 *University of Pennsylvania Law Review* 157 (1989).
Bork, Robert. *Slouching toward Gomorrah.* New York: Harper Collins (1996).
———. *Tempting of America: The Political Seduction of the Law.* New York: Simon and Schuster (1990).
Bradley, Gerard V. "Shall We Ratify the New Constitution? The Judicial Manifesto in *Casey* and *Lee,*" *Benchmarks* 117 (1995).
Brennan, William, Jr. "The Constitution of the United States: Contemporary Ratification," Speech delivered 12 October 1985 at Georgetown University. Reprinted in *The Great Debate: Interpreting Our Written Constitution.* Washington D.C.: The Federalist Society (1986).
Brest, Paul. "Affirmative Action and the Constitution: Three Theories," 72 *Iowa Law Review* 283 (1987).
Breyer, Stephen. *Active Liberty: Interpreting Our Democratic Constitution.* New York: Knopf (2005).

———. "Our Democratic Constitution." Cambridge: Harvard University, 17 November 2004. Transcript available at http://www.supremecourtus.gov/publicinfo/speeches/sp_11–17–04.html.

Brisbin, Richard. *Justice Antonin Scalia and the Conservative Revival.* Baltimore: Johns Hopkins University Press (1997).

Calabresi, Steven G. "Federalism and the Rehnquist Court: A Normative Defense," 57 *Annals of the American Academy of Political and Social Science* 24 (2001).

Canon, Bradley. "Review of *The Supreme Court and the Attitudinal Model,*" 3 *Law and Politics Book Review* 98 (September 1993).

Chemerinsky, Erwin. "The Federalism Revolution," 31 *New Mexico Law Review* 7 (2001).

———. "Our Vanishing Constitution," 103 *Harvard Law Review* 43 (1989).

———. "Reconceptualizing Federalism," 50 *New York Law School Law Review* 729 (2006).

Choper, Jesse, and John Yoo. "Effective Alternatives to Causes of Action Barred by the Eleventh Amendment," 50 *New York Law School Law Review* 715 (2006).

Davis, Sue. *Justice Rehnquist and the Constitution.* Princeton N.J.: Princeton University Press (1989).

Dinan, John J. "The Rehnquist Court's Federalism Decisions in Perspective," 15 *Journal of Law and Politics* 127 (1999).

Dworkin, Ronald M. *Freedom's Law: The Moral Reading of the American Constitution.* Cambridge: Harvard University Press (1996).

———. "From Bork to Kennedy," *The New York Review of Books,* 17 December 1987, p. 42.

———. *Law's Empire.* Cambridge: Belknap Press of Harvard University Press (1986).

———. *Taking Rights Seriously.* Cambridge: Harvard University Press (1977).

Edelman, Paul, and Jim Chen. "The Most Dangerous Justice: The Supreme Court at the Bar of Mathematics," 76 *Southern California Law Review* 63 (1997).

Ely, John Hart. *Democracy and Distrust: A Theory of Judicial Review.* Cambridge: Harvard University Press (1980).

Epstein, Lee, Andrew D. Martin, Kevin M. Quinn, and Jeffrey Segal. "Ideological Drift among Supreme Court Justices: Who, When and How Important?" 101 *Northwestern Law Review* 1483 (2007).

Eskridge, William N. "United States: *Lawrence v. Texas* and the Imperative of Comparative Constitutionalism," 4 *International Journal of Constitutional Law* 555 (2004).

Estrich, Susan, and Kathleen Sullivan. "Abortion Politics: Writing for an Audience of One," 138 *University of Pennsylvania Law Review* 119 (1989).

Farber, Daniel A. "Abortion after *Webster,*" 6 *Constitutional Commentary* 225 (1989).

Faulkner, Robert K. *The Jurisprudence of John Marshall.* Princeton. N.J.: Princeton University Press (1968).

Fried, Charles. "*Metro Broadcasting v. FCC:* Two Concepts of Equality," 104 *Harvard Law Review* 107 (1990).

———. *Saying What the Law Is: The Constitution in the Supreme Court.* Cambridge: Harvard University Press (2004).

Friedman, Barry. "The Birth of an Academic Obsession: The History of the Counter-majoritarian Difficulty," 112 *Yale Law Journal* 152 (2002).

———. "The Counter-Majoritarian Problem and the Pathology of Constitutional Scholarship," 95 *Northwestern University Law Review* 933 (2001).

Friedman, Lawrence. "The Limitations of Labeling: Justice Anthony M. Kennedy and the First Amendment," 20 *Ohio Northern Law Review* 225 (1993).

Garrow, David J. *Liberty and Sexuality.* Berkeley: University of California Press (1994).

———. "*Roe v. Wade* Revisited," 9 *Green Bag* 2d 71 (2005).

Gerber, Scott. *First Principles: The Jurisprudence of Clarence Thomas.* New York: New York University Press (1999).

Gillman, Howard. *The Votes That Counted: How the Court Decided the 2000 Election.* Chicago: University of Chicago Press (2001).

Ginsburg, Ruth Bader. "Some Thoughts on Autonomy and Equality in Relation to *Roe v. Wade,*" 63 *North Carolina Law Review* 375 (1985).

Gottlieb, Stephen E. "Three Justices in Search of a Character: The Moral Agendas of Justices O'Connor, Scalia and Kennedy," 49 *Rutgers Law Review* 219 (1996).

Gunther, Gerald. *Constitutional Law,* 12th ed. New York: Foundation Press (1991).

Hamilton, Alexander, James Madison, and John Jay. *The Federalist Papers,* ed. Charles Kesler and Clinton Rossiter. New York: Signet (2003).

Hensley, Thomas, Christopher E. Smith, and Joyce A. Baugh. *The Changing Supreme Court: Constitutional Rights and Liberties.* Minneapolis/St. Paul: Wadsworth, 1997.

Howard, J. Woodford. "Judicial Biography and the Behavioral Persuasion," 65 *American Political Science Review* 704 (1971).

Kannar, George. "The Constitutional Catechism of Antonin Scalia," 99 *Yale Law Journal* 1297 (1990).

Keck, Thomas M. *The Most Activist Court in History: The Road to Modern Judicial Conservatism.* Chicago: University of Chicago Press (2004).

———. "Party, Policy, or Duty? Why Does the Supreme Court Invalidate Federal Statutes?" 101 *American Political Science Review* 321 (2007).

Klarman, Michael J. "*Brown,* Originalism, and Constitutional Theory: A Response to Professor McConnell," 81 *Virginia Law Review* 1881 (1995).

Knowles, Helen J. "Clerkish Control of *Carhart?*" Paper presented at the Meetings of the Midwest Political Science Association (2008).

———. *A Dialogue on Liberty: The Classical Liberal and Educational Principles of Justice Kennedy's Vision of Judicial Power.* Ph.D. dissertation, Boston University (2007).

———. "From a Value to a Right: The Supreme Court's Oh-So-Conscious Move from 'Privacy' to 'Liberty,'" 33 *Ohio Northern Law Review* (2007).

———. *The Tie Goes to Liberty: Justice Anthony M. Kennedy on Liberty.* Lanham, Md.: Rowman and Littlefield (2009).

Kommers, Donald P. "Comparative Constitutional Law: Its Increasing Relevance," in Vicki C. Jackson and Mark Tushnet, eds., *Defining the Field of Comparative Constitutional Law.* Westport, Conn.: Praeger (2002).

Kramer, Larry D. *The People Themselves: Popular Constitutionalism and Judicial Review.* New York: Oxford University Press (2004).

———. "Putting the Politics Back into the Political Safeguards of Federalism," 100 *Columbia Law Review* 215 (2000).

Kull, Andrew. *The Color-Blind Constitution.* Cambridge: Harvard University Press (1992).

Lessig, Lawrence. "Fidelity in Translation," 71 *Texas Law Review* 1165 (1993).

Macedo, Stephen. *The New Right v. the Constitution.* Washington, D.C: Cato Institute (1987).

Maltz, Earl M. "Anthony Kennedy and the Jurisprudence of Respectable Conservatism," in Maltz, ed., *Rehnquist Justice: Understanding the Court Dynamic.* Lawrence: University Press of Kansas (2004).

———. "Justice Kennedy's Vision of Federalism," 31 *Rutgers Law Journal* 761 (2000).

Marcosson, Samuel A. *Original Sin: Clarence Thomas and the Failure of the Constitutional Conservatives.* New York: New York University Press (2002).

Marion, David. *The Jurisprudence of Justice William J. Brennan, Jr.: The Law and Politics of Libertarian Dignity.* Lanham, Md.: Rowman and Littlefield (1997).

Maveety, Nancy. *Justice Sandra Day O'Connor: Strategist on the Supreme Court.* Lanham, Md.: Rowman and Littlefield (1996).

———. *Queen's Court: Judicial Power in the Rehnquist Era.* Lawrence: University Press of Kansas (2008).

McConnell, Michael. "Originalism and the Desegregation Decisions," 81 *Virginia Law Review* 947 (1995).

———. "The Originalist Justification for *Brown:* A Reply to Professor Klarman," 81 *Virginia Law Review* 1937 (1995).

Meltzer, Daniel J. "State Sovereign Immunity: Five Authors in Search of a Theory," 75 *Notre Dame Law Review* 1011 (2000).

Michelman, Frank I. *Brennan and Democracy.* Princeton, N.J.: Princeton University Press (2005).

Nagel, Robert. "Liberals and Balancing," 63 *University of Colorado Law Review* 323 (1992).

Paulsen, Michael. "The Many Faces of 'Judicial Restraint,'" *1993 Public Interest Law Review* 1.

Peltason, J. W. "Supreme Court Biography and the Study of Public Law," in Gottfried Dietze, ed., *Essays on the American Constitution.* New York: Prentice-Hall (1964).

Peretti, Terri Jennings. *In Defense of a Political Court.* Princeton, N.J.: Princeton University Press (2001).

Posner, Richard. "Judicial Biography," 70 *New York University Law Review* 502 (1995).

———. *Law, Pragmatism and Democracy.* Cambridge: Harvard University Press (2003).

———. "No Thanks, We Already Have Our Own Laws," *Legal Affairs,* August 2004.

Reuben, Richard C. "Man in the Middle," *California Lawyer* (October 1992).

Roche, John. "Judicial Self-Restraint," 49 *American Political Science Review* 762 (1955).

Rosen, Jeffrey. *The Most Democratic Branch: How the Courts Serve America.* New York: Oxford University Press (2006).

Rossum, Ralph A. *Antonin Scalia's Jurisprudence: Text and Tradition.* Lawrence: University Press of Kansas (2006).

Scalia, Antonin. "The Disease as Cure," 1979 *Washington University Law Quarterly* 147 (1979).

———. *A Matter of Interpretation: Federal Courts and the Law.* Princeton, N.J.: Princeton University Press (1997).

———. "Originalism: The Lesser Evil," 57 *University of Cincinnati Law Review* 849 (1989).

Schmidt, Patrick D., and David A. Yalof. "The 'Swing Voter' Revisited: Justice Anthony Kennedy and the First Amendment Right of Free Speech," 57 *Political Research Quarterly* 209 (2004).

Schultz, David, and Christopher Smith. *The Jurisprudential Vision of Justice Antonin Scalia.* Lanham, Md.: Rowman and Littlefield (1996).

Segal, Jeffrey A., and Harold Spaeth. *The Supreme Court and the Attitudinal Model.* New York: Cambridge University Press (1993, 2002).

Shiffrin, Steve. *The First Amendment: Democracy and Romance.* Cambridge: Harvard University Press (1990).

Sickles, Robert J. *John Paul Stevens and the Search for Balance.* University Park: Pennsylvania State University Press (1988).

Slaughter, Anne-Marie. "A Global Community of Courts," 44 *Harvard International Law Journal* 191 (2002).

Smith, Christopher. *Justice Antonin Scalia and the Supreme Court's Conservative Moment.* Westport, Conn.: Praeger (1993).

———. "Supreme Court Surprise: Justice Anthony Kennedy's Move toward Moderation," 45 *Oklahoma Law Review* 459 (1992).

Smith, Rogers. "Political Jurisprudence, the 'New Institutionalism' and the Future of Public Law," 82 *American Political Science Review* 89 (1988).

———. "Symposium: The Supreme Court and the Attitudinal Model," *Law and Courts Newsletter* 7 (Spring 1994).

Smith, Steven. *Foreordained Failure.* New York: Oxford University Press (1995).

———. *Getting over Equality: A Critical Diagnosis of Religious Freedom in America.* New York: New York University Press (2001).

Stark, Vincent. "Public Morality as a Police Power after *Lawrence v. Texas* and *Gonzales v. Carhart*," 10 *Georgetown Journal of Gender and the Law* 165 (2009).

Strauss, David A. "Abortion, Toleration and Moral Uncertainty," 1992 *Supreme Court Review* 1 (1993).

———. "The Myth of Colorblindness," 1986 *Supreme Court Review* 99 (1987).

Sullivan, Kathleen. "The Justices of Rules and Standards," 106 *Harvard Law Review* 22 (1992).

———. "Post-Liberal Judging: The Roles of Categorization and Balancing," 63 *University of Colorado Law Review* 293 (1992).

Sunstein, Cass. *One Case at a Time: Judicial Minimalism on the Supreme Court*. Cambridge: Harvard University Press (1999).

———. "What Did *Lawrence* Hold? Of Autonomy, Desuetude, Sexuality and Marriage," 2003 *Supreme Court Review* 27 (2004).

Tribe, Laurence. *Abortion: A Clash of Absolutes*. New York: W. W. Norton (1990).

———. "In What Vision of the Constitution Must the Law Be Color-Blind?" 20 *John Marshall Law Review* 203 (1986).

Tribe, Laurence, and Michael Dorf. *On Reading the Constitution*. Cambridge: Harvard University Press (1991).

Tushnet, Mark. *A Court Divided*. New York: W. W. Norton (2005).

———. *Taking the Constitution Away from the Courts*. Princeton, N.J.: Princeton University Press (1999).

U.S. Association of Constitutional Law Discussion. "Constitutional Relevance of Foreign Court Decisions." Washington, D.C.: American University (Washington College of Law), 13 January 2005. Transcript available at http://domino.american.edu/AU/media/mediarel.nsf/1D265343BDC2189785256B810071F238/1F2F7DC4757FD01E85256F890068E6E0?OpenDocument.

Van Sickel, Robert. *Not a Particularly Different Voice: The Jurisprudence of Sandra Day O'Connor*. New York: Peter Lang (1998).

Volokh, Eugene. "How the Justices Voted in Free Speech Cases, 1994–2000," 48 *UCLA Law Review* 1191 (2001).

Whittington, Keith. "The New Originalism," Paper delivered at the 2002 Meetings of the American Political Science Association.

Yalof, David. *Pursuit of Justices: Presidential Politics and the Selection of Supreme Court Nominees*. Chicago: University of Chicago Press (1999).

Yarbrough, Tinsley. *David Hackett Souter: Traditional Republican on the Supreme Court*. New York: Oxford University Press (2005).

———. *The Rehnquist Court and the Constitution*. New York: Oxford University Press (2000).

Young, Ernest A. "Just Blowing Smoke? Politics, Doctrine, and the Federalist Revival after Gonzales v. Raich," 2005 *Supreme Court Review* 1 (2006).

———. "State Sovereign Immunity and the Future of Federalism," 1999 *Supreme Court Review* 1.

Zuckert, Michael P. "*Casey* at the Bat: Taking Another Swing at *Planned Parenthood v. Casey*," in Christopher Wolfe, ed., *That Eminent Tribunal: Judicial Supremacy and the Constitution*. Princeton, N.J.: Princeton University Press (2004).

ARCHIVAL SOURCES

Harry A. Blackmun Papers. Manuscript Room, Library of Congress, Washington, D.C.
Thurgood Marshall Papers. Manuscript Room, Library of Congress, Washington, D.C.

MAJOR OPINIONS WRITTEN BY
OR INVOLVING KENNEDY

Abrams v. Johnson, 521 U.S. 74 (1997)
Adarand Construction v. Pena, 515 U.S. 200 (1995)
Alabama v. Garrett, 531 U.S. 356 (2001)
Alden v. Maine, 527 U.S. 706 (1999)
Alexander v. United States, 509 U.S. 544 (1993)
Allegheny County v. Greater Pittsburgh ACLU, 492 U.S. 573 (1989)
Allied Signal v. New Jersey, 504 U.S. 768 (1992)
Ashcroft v. ACLU, 535 U.S. 564 (2002)
Ashcroft v. ACLU, 542 U.S. 656 (2004)
Ashcroft v. Free Speech Coalition, 534 U.S. 234, 122 S. Ct. 1389 (2002)
Austin v. Michigan Chamber of Commerce, 494 U.S. 652 (1990)
Barnard v. Thornstenn, 489 U.S. 546 (1989)
Beller v. Middendorf, 632 F.2d. 788 (1980, 9th Cir.)
Bendix Autolite Corp. v. Midwesco Enterprises, 486 U.S. 888 (1988)
Board of Regents of University of Wisconsin v. Southworth, 529 U.S. 217 (2000)
Boumediene v. Bush, 128 S. Ct. 2229 (2008)
Bowen v. Kendrick, 487 U.S. 589 (1988)
Brown and Hayes v. Legal Foundation of Washington, 538 U.S. 216 (2003)
Burdick v. Takushi, 504 U.S. 428 (1992)
Burson v. Freeman, 504 U.S. 191 (1992)
Bush v. Gore, 531 U.S. 98 (2000)
Bush v. Vera, 517 U.S. 952 (1996)
California Democratic Party v. Jones, 530 U.S. 567 (2000)
California Medical Association v. Federal Elections Commission, 641 F.2d. 619 (1980, 9th Cir.)
Campbell v. Louisiana, 523 U.S. 392 (1998)
Church of Lukumi Babalu Aye v. City of Hialeah, 508 U.S. 520 (1993)
City of Boerne v. Flores, 521 U.S. 507 (1997)
City of Los Angeles v. Alameda Books, 112 S. Ct. 1728 (2002)
Clinton v. New York, 524 U.S. 417 (1998)

Colorado Republican Federal Campaign Committee v. Federal Election Commission, 518
　U.S. 604 (1996)
Cook v. Gralike, 531 U.S. 510 (2001)
Davis v. Monroe County, 526 U.S. 629, 191 S. Ct. 1661 (1999)
Delmuth v. Muth, 491 U.S. 223 (1989)
Denver Area Educational Telecommunications Consortium v. FCC, 518 U.S. 727 (1996)
Edenfield v. Fane, 507 U.S. 761 (1993)
Edmonson v. Leesville Concrete, 500 U.S. 614 (1991)
Flores v. Pierce, 617 F.2d 1386 (1980, 9th Cir.)
Frederick v. Morse, 127 S. Ct. 2618 (2007)
Freeman v. Pitts, 503 U.S. 467 (1992)
Garcetti v. Ceballos, 126 S. Ct. 1951 (2006)
Gentile v. State Bar of Nevada, 501 U.S. 1030 (1991)
Gonzales v. Carhart, 127 S. Ct. 1610 (2007)
Gonzales v. Oregon, 126 S. Ct. 904 (2006)
Gonzales v. Raich, 545 U.S. 1 (2005)
Granholm v. Heald, 544 U.S. 460 (2005)
Grutter v. Bollinger, 539 U.S. 306 (2003)
Hamdan v. Rumsfeld, 126 S. Ct. 2749 (2006)
Hill v. Colorado, 530 U.S. 703 (2000)
Hilton v. South Carolina Public Railways Commission, 502 U.S. 197 (1991)
Hirsch v. City of Atlanta, 495 U.S. 927 (1990)
Hodgson v. Minnesota, 497 U.S. 417 (1990)
Holland v. Illinois, 493 U.S. 474 (1990)
Idaho v. Couer d'Alene Tribe, 521 U.S. 261 (1997)
INS v. Chadha, 634 F.2d. 408 (1980, 9th Cir.)
International Society for Krishna Consciousness v. Lee, 505 U.S. 672 (1992)
J.E.B. v. Alabama, 511 U.S. 127 (1994)
Johanns v. Livestock Marketing Association, 544 U.S. 550 (2005)
Kelo v. New London, 545 U.S. 469 (2005)
Kennedy v. Louisiana, 2008 U.S. Lexis 5262 (2008)
Kentucky v. Davis, 128 S. Ct. 2801 (2008)
Kiryas Joel v. Grumet, 512 U.S. 687 (1994)
Lawrence v. Texas, 539 U.S. 558 (2003)
Lee v. Weisman, 505 U.S. 577 (1992)
Legal Services Corp. v. Velasquez, 531 U.S. 533 (2001)
Lorillard Tobacco v. Reilly, 533 U.S. 525 (2001)
LULAC v. Perry, 125 S. Ct. 2594 (2006)
Masson v. New Yorker Magazine, 501 U.S. 496 (1991)
McConnell v. Federal Elections Commission, 540 U.S. 93 (2003)
Metro Broadcasting v. Federal Communications Commission, 497 U.S. 547 (1990)
Miller v. Johnson, 575 U.S. 900 (1995)

Missouri v. Jenkins, 495 U.S. 33 (1990)
Morse v. Republican Party of Virginia, 517 U.S. 186 (1996)
Nevada Department of Human Resources v. Hibbs, 538 U.S. 721 (2003)
New York State Board of Elections v. Lopez Torres, 128 S. Ct. 791 (2008)
Nguyen v. INS, 533 U.S. 53 (2001)
Nixon v. Shrink Missouri PAC, 528 U.S. 377 (2000)
O'Hare Truck Service v. City of Northlake, 518 U.S. 712 (1996)
Ohio v. Akron Center, 492 U.S. 502 (1990)
Parents Involved in Community Schools v. Seattle School District No. 1, 127 S. Ct. 2738
    (2007)
Planned Parenthood v. Casey, 505 U.S. 833 (1992)
Powers v. Ohio, 499 U.S. 400 (1991)
Presley v. Etowah County, 502 U.S. 491 (1992)
Public Citizen v. Department of Justice, 491 U.S. 440 (1989)
Randall v. Sorrell, 126 S. Ct. 2479 (2006)
Rapanos v. Gonzales, 126 S. Ct. 2008 (2006)
Rasul v. Bush, 542 U.S. 466 (2005)
Republican Party of Minnesota v. White, 536 U.S. 765 (2002)
Rice v. Cateyano, 528 U.S. 495 (2000)
Richmond v. J. A. Croson, 488 U.S. 469 (1989)
Romer v. Evans, 517 U.S. 620 (1996)
Roper v. Simmons, 543 U.S. 551, 125 S. Ct. 1183 (2005)
Rosenberger v. University of Virginia, 515 U.S. 819 (1995)
Rumsfeld v. Padilla, 543 U.S. 426 (2004)
Sacramento v. Lewis, 523 U.S. 833 (1998)
Simon and Schuster v. Crime Victims Board, 502 U.S. 105 (1991)
Spangler v. Pasadena, 611 F.2d. 1239 (1979, 9th Cir)
Stenberg v. Carhart, 530 U.S. 914 (2000)
Texas v. Johnson, 491 U.S. 397 (1989)
Trinova Corp. v. Michigan Department of Treasury, 498 U.S. 38 (1991)
Troxel v. Granville, 530 U.S. 57 (2000)
Turner Broadcasting System I v. FCC, 512 U.S. 622 (1994)
Turner Broadcasting System II v. FCC, 520 U.S. 180 (1997)
United States v. American Library Association, 539 U.S. 194 (2003)
United States v. Kokinda, 497 U.S. 720 (1990)
United States v. Lopez, 414 U.S. 549 (1995)
United States v. Playboy Entertainment Group, 529 U.S. 803 (2000)
United States Department of Agriculture v. United Foods, 533 U.S. 405 (2001)
U.S. Term Limits v. Thornton, 514 U.S. 779 (1995)
Vieth v. Jublirer, 541 U.S. 267 (2004)
Ward v. Rock against Racism, 491 U.S. 781 (1989)
Webster v. Reproductive Health Services, 492 U.S. 490 (1989)

Westside Community Board of Education v. Mergens, 496 U.S. 226 (1990)
Wisconsin Department of Corrections v. Schacht, 524 U.S. 381 (1998)
Wisconsin Department of Revenue v. Wrigley, 505 U.S. 214 (1992)

KENNEDY'S MAJOR PRENOMINATION STATEMENTS

"Comments at Ninth Circuit Judicial Conference," Hawaii, 21 August 1987.
"Federal Bar Association," Sacramento, Federal Bar Association for the Eastern District of California, 17 September 1987.
"Federalism: The Theory and Reality," Sacramento, Historical Society for the United States District Court for the Northern District of California, 17 September 1987.
"Hoover Lecture," Palo Alto, California, Stanford Law Faculty, 17 May 1984.
"Judge Kennedy's Comments at the Ninth Circuit Judicial Conference," Hawaii, Ninth Circuit Judicial Conference, 21 August 1987.
"Nomination of Anthony M. Kennedy to Be Associate Justice of the Supreme Court of the United States," Testimony before U.S. Senate Judiciary Committee, 14–16 December 1987.
"Patent Lawyers," Los Angeles, Patent Lawyers Association, February 1982.
"Rotary Club," Sacramento, February 1984.
"Rotary Speech," Sacramento Chapter of the Rotary Club, 15 October 1987.
"Special Session of the Judges of the Ninth Circuit," Phoenix, August 1978.
"Unenumerated Rights and the Dictates of Judicial Restraint," Palo Alto, California, Canadian Institute for Advanced Legal Studies, 24 July–1 August 1986.

PAPAL ENCYCLICALS AND OTHER DOCUMENTS (CITED IN CHAPTERS 1 AND 2)

Dignitatis Humanae (On the Right of the Person and of Communities to Social and Civil Freedom in Matters Religious), 7 December 1965.
Evangelium Vitae (On the Value and Inviolability of Human Life), 25 March 1995.
"Letter to the Bishops of the Catholic Church on the Pastoral Care of Homosexual Persons," 1 October 1986.
Mulieris Dignitatem (On the Dignity and Vocation of Women), 15 August 1988.
Persona Humanae (Declaration on Certain Questions concerning Sexual Ethics), 29 December 1975.

Index